Stepping Away

The American Campus
Founded by Harold S. Wechsler

The books in the American Campus series explore recent developments and public policy issues in higher education in the United States. Topics of interest include access to college and college affordability; college retention, tenure, and academic freedom; campus labor; the expansion and evolution of administrative posts and salaries; the crisis in the humanities and the arts; the corporate university and for-profit colleges; online education; controversy in sport programs; and gender, ethnic, racial, religious, and class dynamics and diversity. Books feature scholarship from a variety of disciplines in the humanities and social sciences.

For a list of all the titles in the series, please see the last page of the book.

Stepping Away

Returning to the Faculty after Senior Academic Leadership

Lisa Jasinski

Foreword by Leo M. Lambert

Rutgers University Press

New Brunswick, Camden, and Newark, New Jersey
London and Oxford

Rutgers University Press is a department of Rutgers, The State University of New Jersey, one of the leading public research universities in the nation. By publishing worldwide, it furthers the University's mission of dedication to excellence in teaching, scholarship, research, and clinical care.

Library of Congress Cataloging-in-Publication Data
Names: Jasinski, Lisa, author.
Title: Stepping away : returning to the faculty after senior academic leadership /
Lisa Jasinski ; foreword by Leo M. Lambert.
Description: New Brunswick : Rutgers University Press, 2023. | Series: The American campus |
Includes bibliographical references and index.
Identifiers: LCCN 2022044945 | ISBN 9781978823846 (paperback) | ISBN 9781978823853 (hardcover) |
ISBN 9781978823860 (epub) | ISBN 9781978823884 (pdf)
Subjects: LCSH: College administrators—Vocational guidance—United States. |
Universities and colleges—United States—Administration. | Universities and colleges—
United States—Faculty. | College teaching—United States. | Mid-career—United States.
Classification: LCC LB2341 .J37 2023 | DDC 378.1/11—dc23/eng/20221109
LC record available at https://lccn.loc.gov/2022044945

A British Cataloging-in-Publication record for this book is available from the British Library.

Copyright © 2023 by Lisa Jasinski
All rights reserved
No part of this book may be reproduced or utilized in any form or by any means, electronic or mechanical, or by any information storage and retrieval system, without written permission from the publisher. Please contact Rutgers University Press, 106 Somerset Street, New Brunswick, NJ 08901. The only exception to this prohibition is "fair use" as defined by U.S. copyright law.

References to internet websites (URLs) were accurate at the time of writing.
Neither the author nor Rutgers University Press is responsible for URLs that
may have expired or changed since the manuscript was prepared.

rutgersuniversitypress.org

For my parents, Pete and Pat, my first teachers

Contents

	List of "Collected Wisdom"	ix
	Foreword by Leo M. Lambert	xi
1	Stepping Away	1
2	Studying Administrative Transitions in the Modern American University	17
3	First Steps: Look as You Leap	50
4	The Messy Middle: Making a Transition Is Making Choices	69
5	"Working for Myself": Life after Administration	99
6	Reimagining Leaders, Reimagining Leadership	128
	Acknowledgments	155
	Appendix: Interview Protocols	159
	Notes	163
	Bibliography	175
	Index	187

List of "Collected Wisdom"

1 Dissecting the Metaphors "Stepping Down" and "Returning to the Faculty" 25

2 Heeding the Whispers: Knowing When It's Time to Step Away 28

3 Sharing Your News 32

4 To Look or Not to Look: Exploring New Job Opportunities 57

5 Helping Others See You Differently 65

6 Identifying, Following, and Breaking the Unwritten Rules 71

7 When Transitions Collide 80

8 Thoughts on Office Space 86

9 You Mean It's *Not* Just about Me? 88

10 It's a Big Change for Them Too: Advice for Spouses and Families 90

11 "Teaching Is Harder than I Remembered" 95

12 Insiders and Outsiders: How Your Past Shapes Your Future 101

13 Sharing Your Skills and Honoring New Boundaries 110

14 Advice for Entering or Reentering an Academic Department 114

15 Finding New Joy 123

16 Advice for Department Chairs Who Supervise Former Senior Leaders 132

17 Advice for Governing Boards That Hire Senior Leaders 142

18 How Governing Boards Normalize and Prepare for Leadership Change 145

19 Rethinking Post-Administrative Salaries 148

Foreword

I completed my presidency of Elon University in March 2018 after more than nineteen years of service in the role. I loved (almost) every minute of the work, cherished the deep sense of community at Elon, and drew energy from working with a marvelously talented senior leadership team, board of trustees, faculty, staff, and generations of students and alumni. I applied for only one presidency in my career and felt quite literally called to Elon because the institution's mission and values fit so perfectly with my own. I had the privilege of guiding the institution through two decade-long strategic plans that raised Elon's academic profile considerably. Our collective ambitions for Elon felt both daunting and exhilarating, but the joyful experience of joining thousands of talented people in building what I liked to call "a new university that has been around since 1889" was the privilege of a lifetime.

To the main point of this book, all presidents know their service will come to an end—all too often abruptly and unceremoniously these days. My hope was that the end of my presidency could be thoughtfully planned and executed and that Elon would avoid the tumultuousness of a failed presidential transition, which often causes a significant loss of institutional momentum, campus morale, and enrollment.

When I was elected Elon's president in 1998, only seven other individuals had held the position in the previous 109 years. Elon's pattern had been to hire young presidents who went on to serve long tenures. My immediate predecessor, J. Fred Young, was thirty-nine years old when he was appointed and served for twenty-five years. Fred's predecessor, James Earl Danieley, was thirty-two years old—the youngest college president in the nation at the time—and went on to serve for sixteen years. I was a comparatively ancient forty-three when I assumed office.

Fred Young and Earl Danieley each blazed quite different post-presidency trails. Earl remained on campus as a professor of chemistry and taught into his nineties. He was a beloved figure on campus, a cherished friend to me, and revered by alumni. Fred Young moved to Pinehurst, North Carolina, and poured his energies into establishing a successful company that recruited international teachers to teach in language-immersion programs in schools in the United States.

Both Fred and Earl were model ex-presidents—supportive, encouraging, and not in the least interested in continuing to be president. When I brought a proposal to the Board of Trustees to change the institution's mascot—the Fighting Christian—during my first six months in office, Earl was lobbied by a small group of alumni to "stop what that new president is trying to do." Earl responded by wearing a shirt emblazoned with our new mascot—the Phoenix—to a golf tournament and communicated volumes without uttering a word. I had long pictured the final chapter of my career as a time of teaching, writing, and service as a professor and president emeritus. Earl Danieley's successful, on-campus, post-presidential service of forty-four years provided a good model of what a president-emeritus career might look like—and that helped me enormously.

Lisa Jasinski asked me to write a personal reflection about my transition out of senior leadership. I want to acknowledge from the outset that every leader's journey in this regard will be unique and vary according to numerous variables, including length of service; the state of relations with the governing board and campus constituencies; the state of affairs on campus, for example, steady or in crisis; whether the leader has "retreat rights" to a faculty role in an academic department; and contract provisions that apply postpresidency. Some former presidents believe the best course of action is to make a clean break, and others leave office under circumstances that make it awkward or impossible to remain on campus. Whatever your path—stay or go—I hope some of the following reflections will assist you in making decisions that are in the best interests of you *and* your institution.

Landing the Plane

Look for a Natural Pause to End Your Administrative Service

Following the signing of my final five-year contract with the Board of Trustees, I quietly signaled to the administrative personnel committee (the board's chair, vice chair, and immediate past chair) that I would likely not extend my service beyond that period. Two primary thoughts guided my thinking. First, as Barbra Streisand sings in "I Stayed Too Long at the Fair," the music does not "play on forever," and I wanted to leave office on a sweet note. Second, the final five-year contract would give me enough time to see our strategic plan largely completed and, hence, allow my successor an ideal juncture to get to know the campus and then begin to chart the next course for Elon.

Be a Thought Partner with Your Board (or Your Boss) about the Transition

A longer transition planning period gave board leaders and me time to do some long-term thinking and ask strategic and tactical questions: Who should be in positions of board leadership during a time of presidential transition? Who might chair a presidential search? Where do we need to direct special energy and resources to accomplish some key goals before I leave? We also determined that my departure date would be flexible in the best interest of the institution in case a presidential search needed to be extended or the president-elect could not begin on the proposed start date. (The latter turned out to be the case.) Reasonable lead times give the governing board leadership (or a boss, such as a provost or president) time to get their heads around a highly consequential change and make thoughtful, well-considered choices about the future.

Help Set Up Your Successor for Success

One critical question you should ask yourself is, "What can I do to facilitate the success of the person who will follow me?" For example, after observing presidencies that have been derailed over controversies regarding the renovation of an official presidential residence (often initiated by a new president with disastrous public relations consequences), Elon's board leadership and I determined that needed renovations to Maynard House, the university's presidential residence, would be completed prior to the hiring of the next president. This plan obviously required that my family and I move out of Maynard House eighteen months ahead of my last day in office, causing my adult daughters to finally reckon with the task of packing their junior high science projects, dolls, trophies, and other assorted treasures of their childhood bedrooms. The task of overseeing the renovation was overseen independently by a special board committee and the university architect and was accomplished without a whiff of controversy.

One of the gifts that I had received as a new president was an exceptionally thoughtful and detailed transition plan, and I wanted to ensure that my successor was the beneficiary of the best thinking of everyone on campus in this same regard. What can the institution do to ensure the new president has the best first day possible? First week? First month? First six months? Who are the key people she or he need to interact with during each of those time frames? While others will be the principal advisers of the new leader on these choices, the outgoing president can be helpful in keeping the institution's focus and attention on planning for the president-elect's success.

Finally, I enjoyed a series of high-level briefings with my predecessor over a period of several months and wanted to extend the same courtesy to my successor. I arrived at Elon with no previous presidential experience, and thus I was grateful that Fred Young instilled in me some valuable lessons from his hard-earned experience. For example, he advised about the importance of working with world-class architects and taking the one-hundred-year view regarding acquiring property bordering the campus. My conversations with my successor, Connie Ledoux Book, focused on a high-level agenda, including working successfully with the governing board and the immediate, major issues that would require her attention. (Connie returned to Elon University after serving as provost of The Citadel. She had risen through the Elon ranks from assistant professor to associate provost and showed exceptional leadership throughout her career, so while she was well-acquainted with the campus culture, she was also striving to see Elon from a fresh vantage point.)

Extend Appreciation Sincerely and Humbly

Ending a long presidency is an emotional experience. You will have established thousands of relationships with people who were instrumental to the success that you achieved and who sustained you during times of trial and failure. The Elon community was gracious in hosting a series of farewell events across the country, including a large gathering of alumni in New York City and an on-campus celebration during Homecoming. Each of these events gave me an opportunity to tell friends, colleagues, and alumni how much they meant to me and to reflect on what we had accomplished together.

One of the institutional achievements of which I am most proud is the establishment of the Odyssey Scholars program, which provides generous need-based financial aid, mentoring, and other key supports for brilliant first-generation students. Odyssey was realized because so many people believed in the vision, made significant philanthropic gifts, and designed a program in which students would truly thrive. College presidents have the immense privilege of envisioning ideas that will improve people's lives and contribute toward creating a better and more just world. But executing that vision is a group project. This reality will come even more sharply into focus when it is time to leave office and you take time to reflect on and thank the people who supported you at every turn, including and especially your family, to help bring your dreams into reality.

Now That You Are No Longer President (or Provost or Dean)

Take a Sabbatical

First off, one of my regrets as president was not taking advantage of the sabbatical opportunities provided to me in my contract. Going more than nineteen years in a very demanding, high-pressure job without a sustained period for reflection and writing was not smart. I would have been wiser to have followed the lead of presidential colleagues who carved out even mid-year opportunities for mini-sabbaticals (e.g., November–February) for creative pursuits.

Once leaving office, I did take a one-year sabbatical with a single hard and fast rule: to stay away from campus unless invited back by my successor for a rare special occasion, such as her inauguration ceremony. Your successor needs space, and you need to respect those boundaries. In fact, at the urging of my wife, Laurie, on my first day out of office, we left the country for a week of rest in the Caribbean. (Becoming anonymous is not like flipping a switch, however. No sooner did we stick our toes in the hotel pool than we encountered alumni who recognized us by shouting, "Elon Phoenix!") My sabbatical project was to complete a book with a colleague for Johns Hopkins University Press, which entailed research travel and long stretches for data analysis and writing. In retrospect, I believe it was healthy to have a big, exciting project to dive into that provided me with new challenges and kept me intellectually stimulated.

While a sabbatical provides you an opportunity to redirect your energies, remember to think through the impact that this life transition will have on your spouse or partner as well. Often our partners have made indispensable contributions to campus life and will be seeking meaning and purpose in their own lives in new ways. It will take both of you time to decompress from life in the pressure cooker and think about how to design a future filled with joy and satisfaction.

Staying out of "the Room Where It Happens"

When it is time to return to campus to resume your new role, much will have changed, and your opinions will not matter like they used to. This is how it should be. My style has been to assume a low profile and focus on teaching, scholarship, and the national and local board service to which I remain committed. My office is in the Martin Alumni Center, a small wood-frame house adjacent to the library and apart from administration or academic departments. I chose not to attend university faculty meetings because I think it would be awkward for all concerned. I make no public comments about the policies or decisions being considered by the university, especially on social media. I attend only special events in which my presence has been specifically requested by the president or university advancement, such as to offer a tribute at a retirement celebration for a dear colleague or to honor a distinguished alum. In sum, my advice is simple: be circumspect and low-key and stay out of the spotlight.

Lend a Hand When Asked

There may be occasions when your successor asks for your assistance, and my practice has been to say yes. For example, when the COVID-19 pandemic struck in the spring of 2020, President Book asked me to chair a large task force to devise a plan for reopening the campus for the fall term. The team worked feverishly to come up with a broad set of recommendations to the president, which were then carried out under the leadership of an implementation team. Elon coordinated COVID-related planning with colleagues at Davidson College, Duke University, and Wake Forest University, and for six months, I served as Elon's representative to that body. I also pitched in with everyone else for weekly shifts to administer weekly COVID tests to our student body in spring 2021, prior to vaccines becoming widely available.

There may be other occasions when your presence—again, by invitation—can add value to an occasion, such as speaking on a panel for the commemoration of the twentieth anniversary of 9/11 or simply being present for a celebration or dedication. Recently, a prominent alumnus and friend to Fred Young, me, and now Connie Book invited all three of us to Montana for a fly-fishing experience. Connie remarked about what a meaningful and historic occasion it was to have fifty years of presidential leadership present to honor our cherished friend. I also try to pay forward what Earl Danieley and Fred Young did for me, which is simply to offer an occasional encouraging word to President Book, because leaders today face challenges that are among the greatest ever faced in the history of US higher education.

You Are Returning to the Most Meaningful Work

I write this foreword as my four-year anniversary of leaving the presidency approaches. I have never thought of my new role as going backward or stepping down—in fact, my mind-set has been quite the opposite. It is the most immense privilege to teach smart, engaging students. It is joyous to have time to write. It is gratifying to serve on national boards and have a hand in shaping the broader conversation about how higher education should advance and evolve. I consider it a privilege when a colleague from another campus calls and asks to talk through a problem. I give thanks for this chapter in my life for creativity, reflection, and more time with my family, while remaining a part of a community I love. I continue to find meaning and fulfillment in life after the presidency, and it is my fervent wish that you will as well.

Leo M. Lambert
President Emeritus, Elon University
Elon, North Carolina

Stepping Away

Stepping Away

CHAPTER 1

Stepping Away

In no other professional field—medicine, law, the military, business, public service, the clergy—do senior leaders habitually return to the rank-and-file workforce in the twilight of their careers. Corporate CEOs rarely conclude their working lives by resuming the duties of a midlevel account executive; on the verge of retirement, four-star generals do not return to the infantry. As a noted exception, former senior leaders in academia, including university presidents, often conclude their careers by reprising the roles and responsibilities of a professor. Beyond the well-worn clichés "stepping down" and "returning to the faculty" that have become the mainstay of university press releases, surprisingly little is known about how senior leaders experience these role changes, what their post-administrative lives look like, and how these changes impact their institutions (for better or for worse).

The cyclical process of senior academic leaders rising from the faculty ranks, only to return years or decades later, is one of higher education's most distinctive traditions. Moments of senior leadership change are commonplace in contemporary higher education.[1] Anecdotally speaking, nary a week goes by that the *Chronicle of Higher Education* or *Inside Higher Ed* does not report on a high-profile leadership exit—either voluntarily or otherwise—at a US college or university. James Martin and James Samels have proclaimed that each year, one-fourth of all institutions "are preparing for presidential change, are in the midst of one, or have just selected a new president."[2] According to data collected by the American Council on Education and other organizations, most postsecondary institutions will experience a change in president, chief academic officer (CAO), or both approximately twice per decade, if not more often; more than 54 percent of sitting presidents expected to leave their posts within five years.[3] Although many of these leaders may retire or seek a position at another university, one in five college presidents will return to the faculty.[4] Historically, the provostship was once seen as a stepping stone to the presidency, but given the increasing demands and complexity of the presidential role, "a significant segment of CAOs is likely to opt to retire or return to a faculty position rather than seek a presidency."[5] The data remain much spottier concerning the career trajectories for deans or other administrators with faculty status. In recent years, the American College President Study tracked a higher percentage of incoming presidents who came directly from deanships, bypassing the provost's office—only time will tell how they will navigate the late stages of their careers.[6]

Many administrative employment contracts incentivize senior academic leaders to return to the faculty—leaving institutions with a hefty bill. James Finkelstein and Judith Wilde have likened the terms of many presidential contracts to "platinum parachutes," having documented the many favorable financial arrangements awaiting individuals who return to the faculty. Their analysis of employment contracts for 116 public university presidents found that at least 48 percent were guaranteed a year's sabbatical at full presidential pay (equivalent to a twelve-month calendar year, not a nine-month academic year). Nearly 70 percent were granted retreat rights as a tenured faculty member, and others had the option of requesting tenure. Compensation structures varied—seventy-seven contracts specified post-administrative salaries—in the following ways: "[The leader would be paid] relative to the highest paid faculty member in the department in which the president will serve (23 percent), as a percentage of the president's most recent salary (17 percent), the same as the average full professor in the president's new department (4 percent) or in some other, undefined manner (23 percent). Regardless of which method is used, not only are past presidents likely to be the most highly paid faculty member in their academic unit, but they are often so by a factor of two or three."[7] Finkelstein and Wilde have called these arrangements a "financial liability" for colleges and universities, noting that under such an arrangement, a former president might be paid as much as $250,000 to teach a single course. They estimated that if an individual were to receive all or most of these benefits and continue to work as a faculty member for a decade, an institution might be obligated to pay that individual $4.5 million in base salary and up to another $1 million in fringe benefits.[8] Of course, this analysis tells us little about the contracts and terms awaiting the leaders of private universities. When senior academic leaders step away, there can be serious, long-term financial consequences for their universities.

The year 2020 proved to be an especially tumultuous one for senior academic leadership worldwide.[9] In Australia, more than half of the country's forty institutions found themselves searching for or on-boarding a new vice chancellor.[10] While the pandemic might have contributed to the mass exodus, presidents cited a variety of related reasons for their exits—be it years of service, declining health, advanced age, a desire to live closer to family, or ideal timing (e.g., completion of a strategic plan). It remains too soon to say how the pandemic—and the related stresses and demands it brought for higher education's senior stewards—will impact university leadership in the future. One recent survey of academic deans suggests that the pandemic has little influence on their thinking about how long they might stay in their role.[11]

In a book about life transitions, the theorist Kathryn Ecclestone argues that it is possible to distinguish among factors that result in success or failure. She contends, "effective transitions require a better understanding of how people progress cognitively, emotionally and socially between different subjects at different stages of their learning, and how they navigate the complex demands of different contexts."[12] Despite the value that such studies might bring, few empirical research studies have investigated the late-career experiences of senior academic leaders who return to the faculty.[13] Much of what we know about how leaders experience these leadership transitions has been passed down through personal reflection and informal advice.[14] Every few years, an academic journal, the *Chronicle of Higher Education*, or *Inside Higher Ed* will publish an essay on the topic. The titles alone suggest that the journey is not for the faint of heart: "Back to the Faculty: Not as Easy as It Sounds," "Leaving the Dark Side for the Light," and my personal favorite, "Going Back to the Faculty Can Be an Ordeal for All."[15] Often written with brutal candor, these contributions explore what the journalist Courtney Leatherman has called the "uncomfortable" personal, psychological, and institutional dimensions associated with this type of role change.[16] These perspectives provide a rich point of departure for a more sustained investigation of the phenomenon across individuals and institutions.

The underlying premise of this book is that those of us who work in colleges and universities share the responsibility to make these inevitable changing-of-the-guard moments feel beneficial—both for institutions and for leaders. Examining senior leadership transitions from the inside out provides opportunities to imagine change on transactional and transformational levels. Transactional changes might engineer more successful leadership transitions with informal and formal structures. Transformational changes, on the order of new habits and paradigms, might make it possible to assign new meanings to what we have always called, rather reductively, "going back to the faculty." Savvy institutions that invest thought and care in shepherding a smooth leadership transition may be rewarded with the full

4 STEPPING AWAY

richness of a former leader's talents and gifts. In losing a president or a provost, a college might gain a mentor, an enthusiastic teacher, an accomplished researcher, a public intellectual, a capable fund-raiser, a sage mediator, or a wise department chair. Less attentive institutions that leave things to chance may end up with an expensive, disgruntled colleague.

The professional journeys of fifty-two former senior academic leaders (running the gamut from chancellors to provosts to assistant deans) contained in this book reveal dramatic emotional arcs, friction points, complex decisions, and most importantly, the joy that is associated with returning to the faculty. For the participants who contributed to this study, changing jobs entailed significant shifts in their daily duties and more: many former leaders reported getting fewer emails but grading more student papers. The deeper changes associated with role change prompted former leaders to reformulate their identities. Without discounting their challenges, most former senior leaders characterized their transitions as positive, affirming, liberating, and rewarding—few lamented the loss of authority, status, salary, or other benefits (though a handful mourned the loss of their courtside basketball seats). Upon resuming a faculty role, former administrators described regaining autonomy over their time, strengthening relationships with friends and family, and engaging in a host of rewarding professional pursuits. Their examples encourage us to abandon the use of derogatory language that likens "stepping down" to a demotion. The leaders who generously shared their stories with me would surely applaud the *Chronicle of Higher Education* for recently retitling its long-running column "Appointments, Resignations, Retirements, Awards, and Deaths" to the more neutral "Transitions." I take this as a sign that things might be moving in the right direction.

Who Should Read This Book?

Stepping Away is primarily written for senior academic leaders—including those who are preparing for or already amid a professional transition. I hope that these readers, learning from the examples of their peers, are better positioned to navigate the opportunities and challenges that lie ahead. I have tried to channel the advice of Ronald Ehrenberg, former academic vice president at Cornell University, who warned, "when you go back [to the faculty] remember that your administrative experience has fundamentally changed you; you are a different person and you have to do different things."[17] *Stepping Away* is designed to help former academic leaders become more attuned to these differences and to leverage this knowledge effectively. The book aims to address a long-standing imbalance: while there is a plethora of resources available to aspiring campus leaders, there is remarkably little available to those who aspire to move on. As Carol J. Pardun told the *Chronicle of Higher Education* of leaving her deanship to return to the faculty, "people are on their own to sort this through."[18]

While the book strives to guide former academic leaders on their professional journeys, lessons from their transitions can help us create stronger and better-functioning colleges. As Judith Shapiro, former president of Barnard College, has written, "presidents come and go; the colleges and universities they serve are what endure."[19] I envision that the book might inform the work of central administrators and staffers who strive to provide continuity after a leader steps away. Understanding what former administrators want and need from a transition is also useful information for members of governing boards who negotiate contracts for new presidents. Board members might benefit from more explicit guidance on when to interact with a former president (if at all) in their faculty capacity. The answer of course is, "it depends."

I have written this book to give professional associations, including the American Council on Education, the Association of Governing Boards, the Annapolis Group, the Association of Academic Deans, the Council of Independent Colleges, and the Association of American Colleges and Universities, executive search firms, and leadership coaches insights and recommendations that will help them be more attentive to the needs of their members and clients at pivotal moments. Despite the abundance of resources available to aspiring and new leaders, returning to the faculty is often a solitary journey.

As a secondary market, beyond practitioner audiences, this book could be adopted in graduate courses devoted to the study of leadership, higher education administration, shared governance, workplace culture, and qualitative research methods. Scholars interested in the structural and symbolic changes to the offices of president, provost, and dean in contemporary US higher education might learn from the firsthand accounts of current and former leaders. When former leaders talk about stepping away, their stories demonstrate how power narratives and interpersonal politics shape the decisions made by postsecondary institutions; unexpected intersections concerning gender, race, and academic leadership; and what trustees and regents *really* value behind closed doors. While the book is primarily concerned with better understanding and managing administrative traditions, the implications for this research are broader.

The Changing Nature and Pay of College Administrations

This book is situated within a larger conversation about the changing nature, character, and size of college administrations.[20] It accepts the premise that "inevitably, a certain tension will exist between faculty members and their administrative leadership."[21] These tensions, both real and perceived, between administrators and faculty members have only escalated with the rise of what Sheila Slaughter, Larry Leslie, and Gary Rhoades have termed "academic capitalism," the enhanced market-like competition for resources and prestige among postsecondary institutions.[22] In practice, academic capitalism has been linked with several contemporary trends: the marginalization of faculty in university governance; declining state support; adjunctification; threats to tenure and academic freedom; and the acute influence of market forces on university operations.[23] Tracing an increase of simmering hostility, Benjamin Ginsberg offers, "During my five decades in the academic world, the character of the university has changed, and not entirely for the better. . . . Today, institutions of higher education are mainly controlled by administrators and staffers who make the rules and set more and more of the priorities of academic life. . . . Administrators and staffers actually outnumber full-time faculty members at America's colleges and universities."[24] For Ginsberg, the proliferation of "managers and deanlets" has undermined the research and teaching mission of the modern university, exchanging the pursuit of knowledge for the betterment of society in the name of managerial control, operational efficiency, and profit maximization. At the same time that universities are more focused on the bottom line, salaries for top campus administrators have soared, while, in contrast, wages for faculty have stagnated.[25] A study by the American Council of Trustees and Alumni (ACTA) examined the administrative-to-instructional cost ratio at a variety of institution types, finding a broad range. On the high end, small, private baccalaureate colleges spent an average of $0.64 of every dollar on administrative costs, while the average large, public research institutions spent only $0.17. While larger institutions benefit from some economies of scale, administrative costs remain significant in an operating budget that exceeds $1 billion. ACTA warned that current and growing administrative expenditures "risk signaling misplaced priorities."[26]

This context creates added urgency to explore the processes by which individuals traverse an ever-widening gulf between faculty and administrative roles. Moving between the two camps, former leaders help us learn more about misperceptions and assumptions that groups harbor for one another. Indeed, in losing a president or provost, the campus might be positioned to gain a dual citizen fluent in the languages and customs of the board room and the department meeting. If we ever want to lessen the ever-widening gulf between faculty culture and the administrative culture—to call an end to the us-versus-them rhetoric pervasive on too many US college campuses—we need more people who can effectively code-switch and bridge the divide.

Former administrators who fully embrace their faculty credentials might prove to be our best hope to heal decades of growing internal strife and pernicious mistrust, one hallway conversation at a time.

Not One Transition but Many

Rather than see stepping away as a strictly linear process with a distinct beginning, middle, and end, it is better characterized as a series of interrelated and co-occurring processes. Over a period of two or more years, administrators in this study encountered a series of transitions of varying difficulty, frequency, magnitude, and length. These include (a) *imagining parallel futures*, (b) *experiencing role and status confusion*, (c) *experiencing and using time differently*, (d) *reinventing the self*, (e) *becoming reacquainted*, (f) *adding value*, and (g) *negotiating autonomy*.

Borrowing a term from computing, I have taken to thinking of these smaller negotiations as *microprocesses*; a microprocessor is a single electrical component the size of a postage stamp that enables a computer to perform its critical functions. Within the microprocessor, an army of microscopic circuits and transistors perform varied functions quickly and simultaneously, thus allowing the computer to execute sophisticated operations with apparent ease. What appears to the user as a single function is really the sum of countless discrete commands.

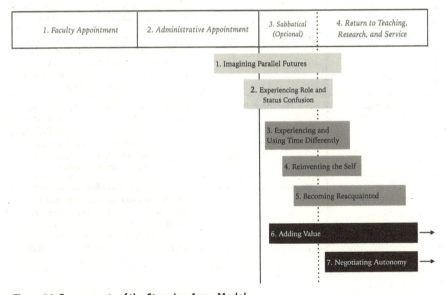

Figure 1.1. Components of the Stepping Away Model

Table 1.1. Components of the Stepping Away Model

Phase	Microprocess	Description
First Steps	Imagining parallel futures	Returning to the faculty often includes contemplation and quiet plan making; leaders formulate the personal and professional goals that will guide the late stages of their careers.
First Steps	Experiencing role and status confusion	Former leaders—and members of their university communities—often struggle to make sense of what it means to "return to the faculty." Former leaders find themselves inhabiting an uncertain social status in the relational hierarchy of the university, uneasily on the continuum between senior administrator and faculty peer.
The Messy Middle	Experiencing and using time differently	One of the largest adjustments of stepping away is exchanging a highly scheduled, demanding calendar for a relatively flexible and self-determined daily schedule. While the change is often welcomed, for many, it brings challenges.
The Messy Middle	Reinventing the self	Change in professional responsibilities and a new daily schedule can entail adjustments to other parts of one's identity, which may extend to scholarly interests and activities, dressing differently, and taking on new roles at home.
The Messy Middle	Becoming reacquainted	It often takes time for a former senior leader to gain comfort with their faculty status and for other faculty members to see (and accept) their former administrative leader as a peer.
Life after Administration	Adding value	Former leaders contribute to their campuses, disciplines, and local communities through service and mentorship. Former leaders leverage their professional experiences, networks, and institutional memory to "give back."
Life after Administration	Negotiating autonomy	Many former leaders find closure to the stepping away process by balancing their own goals and causes greater than themselves. When balance is achieved, a former leader spends less energy on adjusting and more time enjoying their (faculty) lives.

While a former senior academic leader need not complete one micro-process to go onto the next, there is a general chronological pattern; some microprocesses will predate a leader's actual departure from office, others will surface during a sabbatical leave (assuming that the leader takes one), and a few may not present themselves until the former leader resumes full-time teaching, research, and service. Not all microprocesses have clear endpoints, especially *adding value* and *negotiating autonomy*. An aspect of returning to the faculty that is easy for one participant may be debilitating for another—therefore, the relative amount of energy or consternation expended on any microprocess varies greatly from one leader to another.

The microprocesses embedded throughout administrator-to-faculty transitions have four defining characteristics: they can be *recurring, iterative, concurrent,* and *interrelated*. Microprocesses are *recurring* in that they can happen more than once. For example, individuals may engage in many acts of *self-reinvention* across the domains of life—a former dean might cease serving as an arbiter of personnel issues and instead return to the archive as a researcher, or he might (gladly) swap out wool suits for professorial corduroy. Both are acts of becoming something else. Microprocesses can be *iterative* in that when they repeat, a former leader applies what they learned from the past to inform future actions. For instance, when it comes to *experiencing and using time differently*, many of my study participants discussed their initial challenges adjusting from a full administrative calendar set by others to the comparatively sparse demands of sabbatical; for many, this felt abrupt, like braking hard to avoid an imminent collision. Later, because of what they learned about managing their time during leave, leaders reported that they felt better prepared to overcome the disorientation of returning to full-time teaching and self-managing their daily commitments. A third characteristic of microprocesses is that they can be *concurrent*; an individual might find themselves juggling more than one at the same time. For example, while adjusting to having fewer scheduled commitments at work, the individual might be experiencing additional growing pains at home, facing the looks of disappointment when they come home from the grocery store with the wrong cereal. At last, microprocesses can be *interlinked* and mutually informing in complex ways. Demonstrating the full scope of one's reinvention, a former dean, casually dressed in jeans, might teach a seminar in the morning to have the afternoons free to spend with their children (or grandchildren), resulting in a day that feels almost entirely unrecognizable to their former administrative life. A close examination of each microprocess enables us to appreciate the larger trajectories of stepping away—every decision, shift, or adjustment might be relatively minor on its own, but they can add up to truly transformational differences.

Forging Your Own Path, Guided by Well-Worn Trails

A major theme that runs through this book is that each pathway to and from an administrative office is made distinct by personal factors and made familiar through common patterns. All careers are shaped to some degree by personal preference, timing, institutional context, and a smidgen (or more) of good luck. While many who return to the faculty will grapple with common questions—whether to reengage in research and, if so, what kind?—similarly situated individuals will arrive justifiably at different outcomes. One person might set to work on a book within a familiar area of disciplinary specialization, while another will use their administrative know-how to write about higher education policy, and a third might invest their full energy in teaching and service, opting out of research entirely. In my analysis, I found no discernable pattern between these individual choices (e.g., publishing in a discipline, opting out of research) and personal demographics (e.g., gender, age, race), disciplinary affiliation (e.g., humanities, STEM), institutional characteristics (e.g., public/private, large/small), or past administrative roles (e.g., dean, provost, or president). Even when the circumstances surrounding a leader's departure differ (e.g., voluntary/involuntary), the sequence of events that come after leaving office might be remarkably similar. For the fifty-two participants in my study, I could discern no correlation between these predictor variables and the choices leaders made.

While individual choices impact how and why a leader returns to the faculty, much can be learned from the overlapping elements of their stories. As administrators explained their experiences stepping away, four loosely structured narratives emerged: (a) out on top; (b) burned out; (c) irreconcilable differences; and (d) a temporary stint. These roughly drawn schematics are not intended to be mutually exclusive; we know that administrators return to the faculty for a combination of reasons and individuals might identify with more than one set of experiences.

Out on Top

Senior leaders who went "out on top" self-initiated their departure from office upon completing a significant project for the university, and the timing proved convenient in their own life (e.g., the retirement of a spouse). The planned departure allowed the university sufficient time to conduct a national search for a replacement, to fête them with lavish celebrations, and to facilitate a smooth handoff between an outgoing and incoming leader. When on sabbatical, these leaders visited campus infrequently, both to grant their successor the space to establish their authority and to gift themselves the time and headspace to concentrate on a scholarly project and disconnect from the campus. Facing only minor obstacles, these "out on top" leaders completed their paid leave and settled into a comfortable routine of teaching, research, and service.

Burned Out

Leaders who exhibited "burnout" typically had long administrative appointments, often a decade or more. The leader might have stepped away sooner, but external factors led to their extended service, such as a provost agreeing to stay on in the wake of an unexpected presidential departure. The compounding and cumulative strain of their jobs took a toll on these leaders' physical and mental well-being, leaving them to feel disengaged and to perform tasks on "autopilot." "Burned out" leaders would approach their sabbatical leave as a vacation, focusing on personal restoration and giving little thought to university matters. Eventually, "burned out" leaders returned to campus as an agreeable but disengaged faculty colleague, meeting the minimum professional expectations and doing little university service or traditional scholarship.

Irreconcilable Differences

Some leaders rose progressively through the administrative ranks only to find themselves in a strained and ultimately untenable working relationship, with a superior, a board, or a faculty they serve. Sometimes the tension started with the arrival of a new leader; a seasoned provost might clash with a new president, or a new provost seeks to replace all the deans with their own people. Due to "irreconcilable differences," a leader's administrative appointment could end abruptly, even midsemester—often in response to a triggering incident, such as a pivotal disagreement or no-confidence vote. Since the timing of their exit was unexpected and not always wanted, the leader used their sabbatical as a time to recover emotionally from the shock and weigh their options. These leaders often think seriously about leaving the institution. When a leader steps away because of "irreconcilable differences," their faculty career can go a few different ways. A leader might experience continued friction with their foe, but the same leader might find that they have faculty allies in their home department who welcome them back with open arms. Or a leader might be the subject of frequent rumors and criticism. Finding few sympathies, they accept their status as persona non grata and direct their faculty energies outside the university, busying themselves with off-campus research collaborations and speaking engagements.

Open a New Door

Some stepping away trajectories begin with the premise that serving on the faculty will be a brief sojourn. It does not matter whether an individual returned to the faculty of their own accord or felt pressured to resign, but it will only be a matter of until they "open a new door." Either as a result of applying extensively for other positions, having a too-good-to-be-true opportunity fall into their lap, or choosing to accelerate their retirement, the former leader will soon leave the university. Knowing that the arrangement will be temporary, individuals who "open a new door" are unlikely to engage in the same level of self-reinvention as their peers who permanently embrace faculty work.

Much like familiar Hollywood genres, these basic plots give way to endless permutations specific to individuals and their contexts. As lived experiences, these trajectories share many central paradoxes: continuity and disruption, becoming and undoing, visibility and invisibility, action and inaction, doubt and certainty, and anxiety and resolution. In negotiating these and other dualities, participants expressed emotions: relief, happiness, anger, loneliness, angst, nostalgia, curiosity, and even hope.

Organization of the Book

This book is organized into six chapters to answer two central questions. How do the senior academic leaders (e.g., presidents, chief academic officers, and deans) at four-year colleges and universities in the United States in this study describe the process of returning to the faculty after administrative service? Second, how do they describe their experiences as faculty members after serving as a senior administrator? In addition to producing interesting accounts of how individuals traverse periods of personal and professional change, the answers point toward practical recommendations to guide the actions of individuals and institutions.

The chapters are punctuated by nineteen nuggets of "Collected Wisdom," each examining a specific moment or aspect of the transition. This book-within-a-book forms a primer of just-in-time, practical guidance on matters ranging from selecting an office location to deciding to apply for a new position and how to ease the return to the classroom after an extended absence. These sections can be read on their own—or reread at pivotal junctures—if and when an ex-leader seeks another perspective on a specific challenge. Each chapter ends with a brief synopsis of strategies that senior leaders used to overcome the many challenges associated with this aspect of returning to the faculty.

Chapter 2 situates my research within the broader scholarly literature about leadership transitions in the academy, including what we know about what motivates administrators to return to the faculty, what we know about those transitions, and how those transitions are informed by personal characteristics like gender and race. The chapter also includes a description of how I developed a constructivist grounded theory methodological approach to guide data collection and analysis. The chapter concludes with a description of the demographic characteristics and institutional affiliations of the more than fifty leaders who participated in the study.

In chapters 3, 4, and 5, I explain the key features of the "Stepping Away Model" (figure 1.1). This model is an abstract depiction of how former administrators understand and perform their roles as returning faculty members—including how they see themselves, how they spend their time, the tasks they perform, and how they interact with others. Chapter 3 focuses on the two microprocesses that most frequently occur earliest in the sequence: *imagining parallel futures* and *experiencing role and status confusion*. Facing the prospect of no longer serving in an administrative role—or being abruptly removed from a position of leadership—prompts individuals to formulate new expectations for their professional and personal lives. Whether having a passing daydream about standing before a classroom, responding to an inquiry from a headhunter, or purchasing a new home, leaders engage in considerable and often unseen planning about their futures. The first half of the chapter examines the complex calculus that leaders use to balance comfort, possibility, uncertainty, and the many trade-offs of a midlife job change. The second half of the chapter considers the social dimensions of stepping away—identifying the ways in which leaders (and others) make sense of role change. Upon ceasing to be a dean or president, many individuals come to occupy a new role—one that can feel unfixed and fluid in their own minds as well as in the minds of others. Former administrators describe what it feels like to exchange one status for another and share proven strategies to address misconceptions about *who* they are and *what* they do, to help alleviate confusion.

Stepping away at its core is a process shaped by making choices and living with the consequences. Chapter 4 explores three decisions that have serious ramifications for leaders who return to the faculty—how to use their time, which opportunities to pursue (inside and outside the workplace), and how (and when) to make themselves seen and heard. One of the most impactful changes that individuals described upon leaving an administrative position is that their calendars opened up immediately and abruptly (*experiencing and using time differently*). Leaders responded to this change in many ways—some luxuriated in newfound freedom to do as they pleased, some struggled to stay focused, a few worried about frittering away their days, and others maintained a more or less full-time, "8:00 a.m. to 5:00 p.m." schedule consumed by scholarly projects, writing, reading, and thinking. A second common set of choices awaiting leaders who step away from administrative duties is how to become different versions of themselves (*reinventing the self*). Participants blended aspects of their pasts, emergent interests, and social identities into inventive combinations bridging their old and new lives. Finally, for many leaders, returning to the faculty was a chance to refresh their disciplinary knowledge and allow others to get to know them outside of their formal leadership role (*becoming reacquainted*). Each of these choices hinges on learning to balance strategic visibility and strategic absence and signaling a former leader's newfound status in the social architecture of campus.

Chapter 5, the final of the three chapters dedicated to the components of the Stepping Away Model, describes the late-career experiences of senior academic leaders. At the conclusion of Barbara's appointment as a senior leader at a small private institution, she said, "It feels more like I'm working for myself, even though I'm still working for the same institution." Upon resuming full-time teaching, research, and service duties, individuals often wrestled with two competing impulses—some more external and other-orientated (*adding value*) and others more inward and self-focused (*negotiating autonomy*). The chapter concludes by highlighting some ways that former leaders satisfied their individual desires while also addressing the demonstrated needs of communities, proving that it is indeed possible for these transitions to be a win-win for all parties.

Chapter 6 explores the practical implications of returning to the faculty. I end by proposing recommendations to guide the actions of leaders, the policies and practices of their institutions, and the services that professional organizations might provide to better support their members to address persistent voids. The experiences of the more than fifty study participants invite us to reshape our understanding of leadership to incorporate an understanding of late-career work and to enact the structural changes needed to ease the strain of future leadership transitions.

Returning to the Faculty May Not Be the Path for All

While the focus of this book is to understand the process of returning to the faculty, to be clear, this path is not recommended or preferred by all. Some administrators will consider their work done, having satisfied the terms of their administrative contracts, crafted legacies worthy of pride, and achieved a level of financial stability to engage in more leisurely pursuits. Retirement might offer desirable freedom—to travel, to rest, to move to a new city, to attend to caregiver commitments, or to engage in as much (or as little) scholarship or consulting as one chooses. For those not as easily convinced by the merits of retirement, William G. Bowen concluded his memoir, *Lessons Learned: Reflections of a University President*, with strong words informed by his more than sixteen years of service leading Princeton: "When you leave, leave!"[27] His directive was not reserved for senior leaders whose exits came in response to scandal, moral indiscretion, maleficence, or fiscal mismanagement, though I suspect that Bowen would have endorsed recent actions by the University of Michigan and Cal State System to include a proviso in the contracts for any future administrators to revoke retreat rights for leaders fired for cause.[28] Bowen's rationale for a clean break was rooted in the potential benefits to the university. He explained, "Genuinely fresh thinking, including a reexamination of established policies and procedures, is healthy, and much easier to achieve in the absence of the person responsible for putting in place many of the policies and procedures in question. . . . Finding other ways of making sure that there is some real distance between the retired president and the institution is in everyone's interest—and certainly in the interest of the institution itself."[29] For Bowen, what a former leader chooses to do upon stepping away is immaterial—be it moving onto a new position elsewhere, professional service beyond the university, or doting over grandchildren full-time.

For leaders who are seriously contemplating their options, this book can be a companion to guide their thinking. Rather than endorse or condemn the practice outright, this book will enable leaders to feel better informed and equipped to make good choices. While it may prove elusive to structure administrative transitions that are a win-win for former leaders and their institutions, it remains my sincere belief that it is possible: the anonymous leaders profiled in this book have given us some excellent models from which to learn.

Language and Terminology

Throughout this book, the terms "senior academic leaders" and "administrators" are used interchangeably in reference to a myriad of postsecondary leadership positions that are traditionally held by tenured faculty members, including chancellor/president, provost / chief academic officer (CAO) / vice chancellor / vice president, or dean. I used the umbrella term "other senior leaders" to describe leadership positions in central administration that require or award tenure as a condition of hire, including associate vice president, assistant or associate dean, vice provost, special assistant, or registrar. To preserve the confidentiality of participants, I refrained from using any nonstandard titles that are unique to a person or institution.

I add the prefix "ex-" or the terms "former," "exiting," or "departing" to refer to leaders who plan to leave or have already left their administrative position but remain employed in a faculty capacity. The word "retired" is reserved for those who have formally separated from their institutions and are no longer employed full-time (though many participants retained emeriti affiliations and privileges). I use the terms "college" and "university" interchangeably to refer to four-year, accredited, not-for-profit postsecondary institutions; occasional references to community colleges are noted explicitly.

CHAPTER 2

Studying Administrative Transitions in the Modern American University

To understand the process by which senior academic leaders step away from their administrative positions and resume faculty roles, it is helpful first to understand how people experience transitions in general. Existing research on transitions provides transferrable insights to explain why some individuals move through periods of change and instability with relative ease while others experience considerable stress or get stuck along the way. These models provide a context to understand how former senior leaders approach the task of returning to the faculty.

What do we know, in general, about how people experience and adapt to life transitions?

Transition Theory

The developmental psychologist Nancy Schlossberg developed one of the first—and most enduring—theories of how humans adapt to life transitions. Characterizing transitions as a normal part of life, she offered this definition: "An event or nonevent that results in changes in relationships, routines, assumptions, and/or roles within the settings of the self, family, health, and economics."[1] Her description is, at once, broad enough to include events, such as getting married, earning a degree, or becoming a parent, and nonevents, such as having an anticipated job promotion not materialize. By including the many and varied forms of transition, Schlossberg's theory provides a way to understand how individuals make sense of events and nonevents, respond

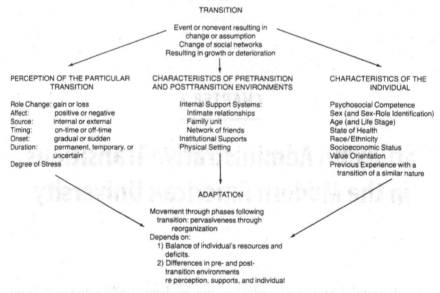

Figure 2.1. Schlossberg's transition theory

to them, and move forward. Her theory explains why one person might emerge stronger or wiser in the wake of a transition, while another person encountering a similar travail might fall to pieces. Schlossberg attributes an individual's ability to adapt to transition to three interconnected factors: perception, environment, and personal characteristics (figure 2.1).

1 An individual's perception of the transition impacts the likelihood of successful adaptation. Some factors that result in successful adaptation include perceiving the event (or nonevent) positively ("this is a good thing"), initiating the transition by choice ("I made this happen"), and having time to prepare in advance ("I'm taking steps to be ready when the change comes"). Conversely, factors that make adaptation more challenging include perceiving the event (or nonevent) negatively ("This isn't a good thing"), having the transition come about due to factors beyond one's control ("This is someone else's doing"), and having the transition come about suddenly ("I did not see this coming").

2 The pre- and post-transition environments influence an individual's ability to move to and through a period of change. For Schlossberg, "supportiveness" is determined by the presence (or absence) of relationships and the degree to which the environment is hospitable to change. She rea-

soned that an individual with a strong support network, the availability of resources, and a stable environment is better equipped to come out on the other side of a transition than someone who lacks these assets.

3   Schlossberg pointed toward individual characteristics, broadly defined, that make adaptation easier or harder. Her taxonomy includes inborn traits (e.g., race, sex, or sex identification), socially salient identities (e.g., socioeconomic class), and acquired wisdom (e.g., psychosocial competence that comes from having lived through and learned from a transferrable situation). She reasoned that an individual who possesses more privileged traits and identities is better positioned to adapt to a transition.

The longevity of Schlossberg's model is evident in the many subfields it has inspired. Scholars have expanded on her model by further nuancing her definition, identifying the conditions that enable individuals and organizations to learn from transitions, and proposing new ways to measure successful transitions. Much of this subsequent research has emerged from the discipline of nursing research: given that nurses are so often present and interact with patients during moments of instability and change (be it developmental, situational, or health related), the field has advanced many of the concepts present in Schlossberg's model. For example, the nursing researchers Norma Chick and Afaf Ibrahim Meleis expanded Schlossberg's definition of transition beyond events and nonevents to a "passage or movement from one state, condition, or place to another," adding that the "defining characteristics of transition include process, disconnectedness, perception, and patterns of response."[2] Whereas Schlossberg's model emphasizes the relationship between an individual's perception and resources and the outcome of a transition, Chick and Meleis encourage us to think about transitions as processes. They propose that attending to transitions as a series of actions allows us to better understand how individuals adapt to a "before" and "after."

Adding to these scholarly foundations, a broader community of researchers and journalists have offered practical advice to guide how individuals and organizations respond to transitions. Much of this writing concerns the workplace, as our professional lives are sites of near-constant change: individuals initiate and respond to career shifts, and organizations respond to leadership transitions and industry-wide disruptions (e.g., automation, economic fluctuations, global pandemics). In this vein, the business writer Herminia Ibarra draws an important distinction between the preemptive mental work of preparing for a workplace or career transition and the labor of enacting it. She explains that when it comes to making a major life change, "*thinking* on its own is far from sufficient. We rarely think our way into a new way of acting. Rather, we act our way into new modes of thinking and being." Ibarra enhances our conceptual understanding by reminding us that transitions are fundamentally active and reactive processes, not imagined ones. Ibarra proposed that workplace transitions follow a three-part cycle: *separation*, *liminality*, and *reintegration*. Separation, which can mean physically distancing oneself from an environment or mentally disconnecting, is often a necessary precursor for what Ibarra calls "habit discontinuity." Being away from familiar people, places, and rituals is vital for reinvention because detachment makes it easier to break patterns. When the familiar is no longer readily at hand, an individual has no choice but to start over. After separation, an individual enters a liminal state, a proverbial "betwixt and between zone," in which they are free to experiment, gather new knowledge, and make informed choices about alternative ways of being. This period of temporary experimentation affords individuals the "rare opportunities to learn about ourselves and to cultivate new knowledge, skills, resources, and relationships." In reintegration, the third and final stage, an individual incorporates newly acquired insights and habits into their routines. Ibarra found that the period for incorporating new habits and behaviors is remarkably brief. As proof, she references the "goal-oriented motivation" that many workers feel upon returning to work after a vacation. Many of us know how quickly that motivation can dissipate when we resume our established routines. By contrast, she reasons that it is easier to make more substantial changes after a more significant separation; whereas a New Year's resolver might struggle to exercise more, a person who moves to a new city might find it comparatively easier to create a weekly schedule that incorporates attending regular fitness classes. Ibarra warns that the window for making lasting changes is a short one: individuals must act with urgency when the conditions for reintegration present themselves. If the person who moves to a new city falls into a familiar routine of not attending fitness classes, it will be much harder to disrupt the new pattern once established.[3]

Transition theory yields several practical insights that illuminate the process by which senior academic leaders step away from their administrative positions and rejoin the faculty. If we reason that returning to the faculty is a process, it is easy to imagine how an individual's perception of their transition, the characteristics of their environment, and their personal characteristics and past experiences play a role in determining how that process will unfold. And then, we can reason that an individual who separates (physically and mentally) from their previous role is better positioned to adapt to change and adopt new habits and behaviors moving forward. For example, a burned-out college president who views his return to the faculty as something that is unwelcome and imposed by external forces and, as a result, tries to hold onto his habits and administrative identity is likely to have a bumpy transition. On the other extreme, a provost who has initiated her own departure, having achieved her goals, has enjoyed the full support of an accommodating department chair, and has taken full advantage of new opportunities afforded by her role change is likely to characterize her transition as generative. We can also expect that leaders will move progressively through a transition over time and that during that time, they will try out a variety of new habits and identities before settling into something more permanent.

Expectation States and Social Interaction Theories

While transition theory yields valuable insights about how individuals experience and respond to life changes, it is equally important to think about how others (and systems) respond to transition. Social interaction theory maps the effect of an individual's transition on others. In a landmark paper, Joseph Berger et al. described how unconscious and unspoken judgments about power, status, and credibility influence group dynamics. The authors presumed that all people hold implicit assumptions and expectations about others that are shaped by prevailing social and cultural stereotypes; these factors influence the unspoken "power-prestige hierarchy" within a group. Characteristics such as race, gender, wealth, age, and occupation "determine the observable power and prestige within the group, whether or not the external status characteristic is related to the group's tasks."[4] Subsequent generations of sociologists have examined how these statuses affect perceptions of credibility, documenting how people modulate their behavior when they encounter a person who possesses traits that are associated with greater social-cultural clout.[5] With the knowledge that group dynamics are shaped by unspoken hierarchies and perceptions of presumed competence, it stands to reason that possessing an administrative identity will have consequences for how a former leader is viewed within faculty circles.

Building on Berger et al., the sociologists Theodore D. Kemper and Randall Collins measured how power and status are gained or lost throughout social interactions. Within organizational settings, they determined that "there are divisions between order givers and order takers."[6] Socially relevant roles and identities impact the balance of power (both between individuals and within groups). Since administrators often find themselves, by virtue of their positions, as order *givers* and decision-*makers*, and many also possess high-status characteristics (e.g., affluence), they occupy a privileged status on campus. Kemper and Collins contend that once an individual is recognized as an "order giver," that association may continue even after a loss of positional authority. This helps explain why in the context of a department meeting, faculty members might show greater deference to a former dean (even if that dean is now ostensibly a peer) compared to an untenured faculty member.

Expectation states theories reveal that all human interactions hinge on fluctuating dynamics structured by power and identity. Some of our identities are a function of outward appearance, while others might extend from the roles we play in families, organizations, politics, culture, or broader society. Relative positions of superiority and inferiority are continually negotiated among individuals in changing contexts. For example, a cis-gender woman of color in her forties from a working-class background might comfortably command a classroom of traditional-age undergraduates. The same woman might feel marginalized in a trustees' meeting surrounded by a dozen affluent White men in their sixties. The latter exchange need not contain overtly discriminatory acts, but insofar as Western societies afford implicit unearned advantages to some individuals while depriving others of them, it stands to reason that those with more social capital can move more easily through the world than those with less.

These models prompt us to expect that the processes of stepping away from an administrative role and returning to the faculty will be complicated by the interplay of identities. Individuals who possess more social capital may slip in and out of different contexts facilely, while those with less need to work harder to establish credibility. Expectation states theory supposes that a person's having once possessed an administrative identity will influence their future interactions with individuals and groups.

What do we know, more specifically, about how senior academic leaders experience and adapt to professional role transitions?

Role Changes in Academia

There are numerous methodological challenges associated with mapping the career trajectories of college administrators. Limited centralized data sources make it nearly impossible to trace an individual's career across multiple institutions.[7] In the 1970s, Michael Cohen and James March posited that the careers of college presidents followed a normative, five-rung ladder, beginning with a faculty appointment, proceeding hierarchically from department chair to dean to provost, and culminating in a presidency.[8] More than a generation later, their model retains some value while being subject to some limitations. The most recent administration of the American College President Study (ACPS)—the most robust and comprehensive data source about the leaders of postsecondary institutions—found that more than 80 percent of sitting presidents were hired from within higher education.[9]

While the overall number of presidents hired from outside academia remains small, some high-profile, nontraditional hires have garnered increased attention.[10] These presidents and chancellors are often hired based on their records in elected or appointed government office, the nonprofit sector, K–12 education, or the military.[11] Historically, religiously affiliated institutions and colleges with fewer than one thousand students were most likely to have hired presidents without faculty or higher-ed experience. Presidents with nontraditional backgrounds tend to encounter steep learning curves acclimating to internal campus politics and the norms of an unfamiliar industry.[12] The practice continues to be met with skepticism by higher-ed insiders; Iowa State faculty expressed low confidence in a business executive who was named as a president.[13] Critics attributed the ten-month tenure of businessman Timothy Wolfe, former president of the University of Missouri system, to an inability to work within a shared governance model and his "authoritarianism and autocratic decision-making."[14]

While most current administrators began their careers on the first step of Cohen and March's ladder (a faculty appointment), they are increasingly taking a variety of intervening rungs to the top.[15] College presidents' career trajectories are increasingly "complex, fragmented, and overlapping."[16] Only one in four new presidents served previously as a provost or chief academic officer, with a greater number of deans bypassing the provostship and moving directly to the presidency.[17] While the provostship was once seen as a stepping-stone to the presidency, "a significant segment of CAOs is likely to opt to retire or return to a faculty position rather than seek a presidency."[18] Rather than ascending to the presidency from the provost's office or a deanship, top leaders are increasingly likely to enact lateral moves; almost a quarter of all ACPS respondents served previously as a president, up from 19.5 percent in 2011.[19] We might interpret this trend as one of inputs or outputs. It might reveal a desire on the part of sitting presidents to seek lateral roles that afford either a stronger individual-institutional fit or greater prestige. We could also read this as a growing skepticism on the part of governing boards to hire an untested executive. Or both might be true.

Leadership pathways differ considerably across gender and racial lines. Given that Cohen and March's ladder model was developed in the 1970s—a time when there was little gender and racial diversity among college presidents—the model may be showing its limitations in an increasingly diverse workplace. A higher percentage of provosts of color have reported intending to seek a presidency compared to their White counterparts.[20] At historically Black colleges and universities, most presidents have embarked on a linear, traditional career path.[21]

Across industries, the administrative careers of women are more likely to be nonlinear, containing both lateral and upwardly mobile moves; a higher percentage of women have reported altering their career progression to accommodate their spouse's or partner's career or to care for a dependent, spouse, or parent.[22] A report in the *Harvard Business Review* concludes that nearly four in ten women "step off the career track" at some point, often to raise children, care for elderly parents, or attend to their health or simply because they no longer find their jobs meaningful. By comparison, only 24 percent of men report having ever taken a voluntary leave of absence from corporate work.[23] The gender gap persists in the college presidency; only about 30 percent of universities have a woman president.[24] Still, far more women lead universities than Fortune 500 companies (only about 2 percent of CEOs are female).[25] Marjorie Hass, current president of the Council of Independent Colleges and veteran of two college presidencies, sketched some differences between how male and female leaders approach their career trajectories: "As I got to know my male counterparts, I learned that their discernment process about career advancement was very different than mine. They weren't as racked about shifting identities. They weren't conflicted about their ambition or worried that they might lose a friend. They were confident about their talents and usually felt that they deserved the job. And while most (but not all) were sensitive to the impact of a potential move on their families, they seemingly gave no thought at all to the ways that money, power, and identity could change their relationships."[26] Hass's book *A Leadership Guide for Women in Higher Education* describes many of the barriers that women face in the academy—intersecting forms of resistance further compounded by sexism, racism, and ageism; she frames her own career as a "personal and spiritual journey."[27] Her insights align with other empirical research findings. A study of twelve women who served in positions of academic leadership found that nearly all had initiated their return to the faculty to improve work-life balance.[28] A qualitative study of three women who served as mid-level administrators in Ivy League institutions determined that all chose to leave their roles due to poor advancement opportunities, conflicts with their supervisors, and a work schedule that left little personal time.[29] Future studies might build on these findings to identify ways to overcome the systemic factors that lead women to either shy away or step away from senior leadership roles, both in the Ivory Tower and the C-suite.

COLLECTED WISDOM 1

Dissecting the Metaphors "Stepping Down" and "Returning to the Faculty"

The linguists George Lakoff and Mark Johnson have argued, "Metaphor is pervasive in everyday life, not just in language, but in thought and action. Our ordinary conceptual system, in terms of which we both think and act, is fundamentally metaphorical in nature."* Accepting that conceptual metaphors reveal consciously and unconsciously held cultural values, we can learn a great deal from how leaders make sense of the familiar idioms "stepping down" and "returning to the faculty." In short, many senior leaders in this study believed that these images failed to capture their lived experiences and prompted higher education to adopt better terminology.

Deconstructing Stepping Down

Allie, who previously worked as an other senior leader at a private college, argued that "stepping down" overemphasized hierarchy: "Personally, and I think for the other faculty around me, it certainly wasn't a demotion. Although I did get less pay, . . . I didn't feel like I was being demoted. I don't feel like others thought that. I think in my case it's almost a physical stepping down because the office I was in was on the third floor of a building." Mack, a former college president, explained his choice of words: "I will always say '[stepping] aside' because there are inevitable hierarchies in any organization. If you're at the top of the hierarchy, then there's only one way you can go. But in fact, you're stepping aside so that someone else can occupy that position."

Pelotons

Sid, a former chief academic officer at a small private institution, provided a new way of thinking about administrators who return to the faculty:

> I use the analogy of the peloton. If you follow the Tour de France or any other kind of professional cycling, you'll know what I'm talking about. The peloton is the rider in front, he who is bracing the wind for everybody else. He can only do that for a short period of time and has to peel back in a way and return to the group. And so that was the case for me. The other reason [I'm going back to the faculty] is that I've never lost my commitment to in-the-classroom teaching and engaging the students and my scholarship. And so, the return to the faculty was really a step *back* into the life of the academy that first attracted me to teaching back in the beginning. It was really a cyclical move back to where I began.

---

* Lakoff and Johnson, "Conceptual Metaphor in Everyday Language," 454.

26 STEPPING AWAY

From the Center to the Margin

When Ralph left his presidency, he was both proud and sad; completing his term marked the end of an enjoyable and defining period of his life. He characterized his impending change laterally: "to go from being the center of everything to being marginal is going to be an adjustment." Rather than going from the top to the middle, Ralph helps us see returning to the faculty as stepping away from the action.

When and Why Do Senior Leaders Leave Their Roles?

It is unlikely that any current or future university president will surpass Eliphalet Nott's astonishing sixty-two-year stint at the helm of Union College or Nicholas Murray Butler's four-decade tenure leading Columbia University.[30] Over the past thirty years, the tenure of a college president has been on a steady decline.[31] In the 1970s, it was assumed that a college president would serve a minimum of two terms (ten to twelve years), but contemporary presidents rarely serve half as long.[32] Institution type has the greatest influence on the length of service. Presidents of private institutions, on average, serve longer than their public university counterparts. Presidents of private, doctoral-granting institutions served an average of 7.4 years, compared to just 6.2 years at comparable publics.[33] The private-public divide also holds for master's institutions (7.8 years for privates, 5.7 for publics) and bachelor's colleges (6.0 years for privates, 4.9 for publics). Between 2001 and 2006, a president of a public institution was 52 percent more likely to serve less than five years compared to a president at a comparable private institution.[34] Compared to presidents, data concerning the average tenure of provosts, deans, and other senior leaders (roles such as assistant deans or center directors) are spottier. Across institution types, chief academic officers serve on average for five years and deans just over six.[35]

Presidents of public institutions are often subject to greater scrutiny and lower salaries. James Duderstadt, who led the University of Michigan for nearly a decade, observed that presidents at private universities "are usually allowed to step down with honor, grace, and dignity," while at public universities, many a career has ended abruptly by "stepping on a political landmine."[36] Presidents, deans, and provosts in public institutions increasingly find themselves the targets of politically motivated attacks.[37] A recent wave of presidential exits at public institutions has been attributed to mishandled pandemic operations, increasingly partisan divides with governing boards, and heightened financial insecurity stemming from the pandemic.[38]

An analysis performed a decade ago determined that public university presidents earned, on average, 50 percent less than their peers at equivalent private institutions, amounting to a $215,183 mean salary difference.[39] The changing nature of the administrative roles, especially the presidency, may be fueling the expedited rate of turnover, especially in public universities.[40] When surveyed, half of the presidents of private universities said they were "extremely satisfied" with their jobs, compared to just a third at publics.[41] The cumulative and compounding effects of high stress and low job satisfaction has led many administrators to vacate their roles.[42] While presidents of private universities might be more satisfied in the aggregate, presidents at small, private Christian colleges have attributed financial hardship to accelerating the pace of leadership turnover.[43]

What factors prompt a leader to stay in their role or depart? The Academic Leadership Longevity Survey, administered in partnership between the American Council of Academic Deans (ACAD) and the Council of College of Arts and Sciences (CCAS), identified that job satisfaction—measured by the level of support the dean felt from the faculty and senior administrators, as well as the perceived ability to make a difference—had the strongest impact on a dean's decision to continue to serve.[44] Deciding how, when, and why to leave a leadership role is rarely a light undertaking; even voluntary exits "come after conflicted feelings and self-searching."[45] While stories of failed administrators loom large in our collective consciousness, instances of gross misappropriation of funds or moral indiscretions remain quite rare. Factors such as a lack of privacy, having limited time for rest and exercise, and the all-consuming nature of academic leadership drive most voluntary exits.[46] Press releases announcing administrative transitions often name the motivating factor as a desire: to spend more time with loved ones, to do less demanding work, to focus on research or other academic pursuits, to attend to a personal illness or an ailing parent/spouse, or to return to teaching.[47] Administrators report that their job demands negatively impact their home lives, noting that the "wear and tear" of the office often extends to their families.[48]

COLLECTED WISDOM 2

Heeding the Whispers: Knowing When It's Time to Step Away

Deciding to resign as president of Rollins College after more than a decade of service, Rita Bornstein explained that the "the exploratory period lasted several years; it began with anxiety and concluded with acceptance, even peace."*

A single cause rarely prompts a leader to step away from an administrative role. Surely, some leaders might be motivated by a compelling personal reason (e.g., a serious illness) or because the time is "right" for the university (e.g., the completion of a capital campaign), but for most people, the choice to step away is the result of multiple factors.

Here are some questions to guide your thinking about this consequential choice:

- Are we approaching a milestone that will allow me to leave on a high note? Have we finished a fund-raising campaign or a strategic plan? Where am I in my contract?
- Is my staff in a good place? Am I leaving my successor with a capable, experienced, and functional team?
- What else is happening with the senior leaders at my institution? Would a new president/VP/dean be better served by selecting their own cabinet? Can my staying on—for another year or more—provide stability? If there is a lot of other change happening, do I have the stamina and commitment to onboard a new colleague?
- Is this job still interesting? Do I feel challenged and rewarded by this work? What am I learning? Am I still having fun?
- Will my mental and physical health suffer I keep going at this rate?
- Am I the right person to be in this office at this point in my institution's history? Are my skills the right ones to move us ahead?
- Can I put off writing that book another year?
- Do I feel called back to the classroom?
- What opportunities am I passing up by continuing to be an administrator?
- What does continuing to work mean as my spouse or partner retires? Does this role come at the cost of spending quality time with my children or grandchildren? Do I need more flexibility in my schedule to care for my aging parents?
- Am I staying in this role because deciding what to do next is scary? Am I staying because it feels easier to stay than to go?
- If not now, when?†

---

* Bornstein, *Legitimacy in the Academic Presidency*, 198.

† Some of this text appeared as "Adding Value and Embracing New Joy: Returning to the Faculty after the Deanship," in *Resource Handbook for Academic Deans: The Essential Guide for College and University Leaders*, 4th ed., edited by A. Adams (Baltimore: Johns Hopkins University Press, in press).

What Do We Know about Successful Individual and Institutional Leadership Transitions?

Much of what has been written about leadership change in higher education does not distinguish between leaders who retire outright or those who return to the faculty. Both researchers and practitioners have shared first-hand experiences and general advice to make these transitions smoother.

Guidance for Individuals

Broader societal conversations about the impending retirement of the baby-boom generation provides some insight into how current workers think about their retirement.[49] An article in the *Harvard Business Review* describes a business executive approaching the end of his career: "Simon had really been looking forward to retirement. The constant pressure that came with his job had really been getting to him. Too many meetings, too much travel, too much of everything. Unfortunately, retirement didn't quite pan out the way he'd hoped. Grocery shopping was giving him only a limited sense of fulfillment, and he missed the daily streams of emails and phone calls. He missed talking to his colleagues. He missed being in the middle of things. Basically, he felt lost."[50] Insofar as a job is inextricably tied to a sense of self and identity, it is hardly surprising that executives like Simon struggle to fill the void marked by the "end" of work. One long-retired president observed, "presidents and spouses who have the most difficult time leaving and letting go are those whose personal identity and sense of self are confined to the presidency—those who have no identity separate from the role."[51]

Across industries, the number of retirees who continue to work is rising.[52] While some retirees might continue to work to make ends meet, others might turn to consulting or part-time work as a strategy to blur the disorientation between working and not working. Unlike Simon, for college administrators, it need not be an all-or-nothing prospect—returning to the faculty might offer the perfect balance between "too much of everything" and the "lost" feeling that comes when there is suddenly not enough.

What can academic leaders do to prepare themselves for the eventuality that, one day, their roles will end? One former college president advised, "the day you begin the presidency of a university, you had better begin thinking about how you are going to get out of it with your health, sense of humor, and reputation intact."[53] But as much as anyone might try to orchestrate desired outcomes, the business writer Margaret Heffernan has documented the limitations of even our most sophisticated forecasting tools to overcome the "ineradicable uncertainty" of human life.[54] Heffernan advises that in the absence of certainty, we are left to rely on creativity, resilience, and the wisdom to avoid the false sense of security that the job transition will manage itself.

The psychologist Michael Firmin further cautions senior leaders to recognize that some aspects of a job transition cannot be foreseen and must be managed in real time. His research found that former administrators displayed signs of withdrawal from addiction when dealing with the loss of job perks, power, discretionary spending, and control. Extending the addiction metaphor, Firmin argues that "the longer the individual serves in administration—the more deeply embedded the elements become." He found that when these job-related benefits "are taken away, psychological withdrawal systems can occur," resulting in depression, anxiety, and reduced motivation. He advised, "Physical addictions can be broken via both gradual and cold turkey means. The psychological addictions that administrators must break will occur in the latter method."[55] Withdrawing from a psychological addiction often impairs cognitive and emotional functioning. To counteract these effects, Firmin recommends that former administrators reframe their thinking about their situations to emphasize the positive, try to enjoy the benefits of a faculty role, enlist the support of friends and family, and let go of any lingering negative feelings about leaving their role.

In one of the few empirical studies about senior leaders who returned to the faculty, Frederick R. Cyphert and David L. Boggs interviewed twenty-four former presidents, deans, vice presidents, and directors who stepped away; nearly all were men who worked at public, doctoral-granting institutions. Their analysis showed that the transition from academic leader to professor consisted of two phases: *pre-transition* and *transition-in-progress*. In the *pre-transition* phase, leaders express anticipation and anxiety about several things, including reconnecting with their academic disciplines, returning to the classroom, and being accepted as an equal by faculty peers. In the subsequent *transition-in-progress*, former leaders align their expectations with their new reality, gain confidence in teaching and scholarship, and develop new routines. The study's findings are largely encouraging. With time and effort, participants resumed research activities, felt accepted by their faculty peers, enjoyed having greater control over their schedules, and grew accustomed to being less visible on campus. While most participants experienced positive transitional arcs and enjoyed their return to the classroom, a few found aspects of their faculty roles to be tiresome.[56]

Gaye Luna and Catherine Medina's study of twelve women who returned to the faculty at two large public universities found that many departing leaders reported feeling underprepared for the psychological and professional adjustments associated with role change. Nearly all study participants experienced unanticipated emotional challenges, feeling "sad, depressed, underappreciated, powerless, used, disillusioned, alone, and ashamed." One woman in the study acknowledged how sexism magnified these challenges: "men are looked at as seasoned professionals, women are looked at as old horses."[57] Like the participants in Cyphert and Boggs's study, many of the leaders interviewed by Luna and Medina eventually overcame these obstacles. In the end, the women in the study achieved emotional stability, readjusted to their faculty roles, redefined their relationships, prioritized work-life balance, and (re)affirmed their self-worth.

Despite the generally positive findings in the research literature about returning to the faculty, advice columns in the *Chronicle of Higher Education* paint a very different picture. Courtney Leatherman describes the "mixed feelings" that many former presidents had about their "uncomfortable" transitions, in "Returning to the Faculty Can Be an Ordeal for All." A former dean recounted the challenges of "resurrect[ing] a dormant research program, engaging personal critics, and interacting with their successor."[58] Other articles inventory the daily struggles associated with returning to the faculty: returning to the classroom after an extended absence, making positive service contributions, and juggling a post-administrative workload that is "unexpectedly weighty."[59]

Beyond reacclimating to professional responsibilities, former leaders detail the psycho-emotional toll of the transition and resulting job change. In the essay "Back to the Faculty: Not as Easy as It Sounds," Fred Schwarzbach recounts some of the trials he experienced after leaving his position as dean of liberal studies at New York University. Much like the fictional "Simon" described in the pages of the *Harvard Business Review*, stepping away from the limelight left Schwarzbach feeling depressed: "You will miss the way in which everyone paid attention when you entered a meeting. Or how, as if by magic, the room grew quiet when you spoke. And as much as we all decry gossip, you might miss being 'in the loop,' knowing all the inside scoops about who in the central administration was up and who was down. I felt all of that." For some others, anxiety stems from the fear of being forgotten; as one former provost put it, "I still have emotional reactions at times when the university passes by and I'm not in parade."[60]

Especially in the earliest days of a transition, "former administrators who return to the faculty occupy rather equivocal positions" in an educational organization.[61] The encouraging news is that, with time, these anxieties seem to abate. After Mark Mallinger of Pepperdine University had completed his first semester with faculty responsibilities, he concluded, "I began to feel more comfortable in my 'new' role, but the transition was not smooth, emotionally, and I'm still struggling to find my balance."[62] Even Schwarzbach found that leaving the deanship was not without its joys; chief among them, "being surrounded by bright, energetic, and ambitious students; ... engaging with interesting and dynamic colleagues; ... pursuing delayed or brand-new scholarly projects; and ... having opportunities to serve the university when and how we choose."

COLLECTED WISDOM 3

Sharing Your News

A flurry of choices awaits you regarding when and how to share the news of your departure. The more visible and senior your position, the greater the magnitude of your impending absence will be felt: calibrate your approach accordingly.

When others learn of your plans to leave, invariably, many of their first thoughts (and fears) will be about how your departure impacts *them*. Keeping this top of mind will help guide your actions and support your colleagues. Anticipating this will prepare you to meet your colleagues where they are. Knowing that these conversations will be emotionally taxing will not shield you but will help you pace yourself.

Take It in Stages
Many leaders approach their announcements as a series of concentric circles: begin with those closest to you and then gradually inform increasingly disparate stakeholder groups. A president might start with their governing board officers, followed in short order with cabinet members and senior staff, the deans, the faculty and staff, students, alumni, and then, finally, the public at large. Of course, you will also want to share your plans with close friends within and beyond the university.

Informing Others
Leaders might choose to announce their departures using one-on-one conversations, small group announcements, public statements, or some combination thereof. In deciding which route to take, balance your preferred ways of sharing news with others' preferred ways of receiving it. If you choose to do it in writing, avoid sending an email announcement late in the day or just before a weekend or holiday. If you choose to share your news in a speech, a faculty meeting might be a more appropriate venue than overshadowing the focus of a commencement ceremony. Recognize that once information is out there, word travels. If it is important to you that certain people hear it directly from you, you should aim to move faster than the rumor mill.

Give Others a Heads-Up

Beyond your direct reports and closest colleagues, consider giving advanced notice to an extended circle of leaders just before your news goes fully public. Who is in the circle will depend on your role, but it might include senior directors, your fellow deans, or department chairs. Even a small courtesy, like a note that goes to them a few hours before an all-campus email, will be appreciated. Doing this may help these colleagues feel more informed and better prepared to swat the swarm of questions and text messages.

Consider Timing

While there is no best time to announce an impending leadership change, there are certainly worse times. Ideally, choose an opportune moment in the academic year that gives your institution ample time to select your replacement, ideally a year in advance.

Say What You Need to Say

Both of these statements are true: (1) university spokespeople are invaluable assets; (2) your stepping away announcement must be in your voice. Trusted advisers and staff might help you draft the announcement or offer feedback, but this is your chance to tell the campus something important and share as much about your motivations for leaving as you choose. As in all things, be brief, gracious, and humble.

Allow the Institution to Follow Your Announcement with "Next Steps"

An impending change in leadership can make even the sturdiest institution feel wobbly. Your university will probably follow your resignation announcement with a cascade of prepared communications, such as lists of your accomplishments, a notification of your last day, information on the search process, dates for forthcoming celebrations, and whether an interim leader will be named.

Clear Your Schedule, If You Can

The day your announcement goes public is probably going to be an emotional one, both for you and for others. Expect heartfelt notes to fill your inbox and congratulatory phone calls. In the day or two after your news goes public, keep your schedule as open as possible, gifting yourself and others the time and space to adjust. Amid the distraction, it will be hard to pretend that it's business as usual. Your ability to hold a consequential meeting will be challenging. Honor the reality that the day your news goes public will not be a "normal" day. Pretty soon, people will adjust to the impending change, and you can finish out the remaining days of your term doing your job.

Former leaders are quick to give advice about how former leaders should comport themselves after serving in an administrative position. There is little consensus. One camp of experts cautions their peers against meddling or overstaying their welcome. Those who favor the muted stance advise former leaders to "keep a low profile and avoid involvement" in campus life or, upon returning from a sabbatical, to take up residence in an office in a "remote and secluded area of the campus."[63] Those in the opposing camp encourage former leaders to remain visible and engaged within their university communities. In a book about leadership transitions in higher education, Patrick Sanaghan, Larry Goldstein, and Kathleen Gaval recommend that former leaders attend events like faculty assemblies, both to show support for their successors and "to relieve some of the stress of campus stakeholders during a [leadership] transition."[64] Peter Flawn, reflecting on his presidential service at two public research institutions, defined a "successful transition back to faculty life" as finding that "your years as president have prepared you well to chair important university committees and, if you want it, to occupy a place as a senior faculty statesperson."[65] Flawn goes further than most by encouraging former administrators to continue to serve their institutions through service and active participation in campus leadership.

Guidance for Colleges and Universities

There is broadly shared agreement among scholars and practitioners that senior academic leadership transitions are challenging for institutions.[66] Advanced planning and careful management can mitigate some of the potential stress.[67] When abrupt terminations and departures occur, it is likely that turmoil will follow: distracted faculty, a scramble to finalize interim replacements, stalled campus initiatives, and perhaps even damage to the university's reputation. Ideally, exiting leaders will provide an institution with at least a semester of advanced notice before leaving or returning to the faculty, but such a window is not always possible, especially in a competitive job market. Only adding to the challenge, succession planning remains woefully inadequate across higher education, only heightening the effect of sudden departures.[68] Members of governing boards are probably best poised to begin insulating their institutions against these risks. Those who appoint and review presidents—or presidents and provosts who in turn supervise deans and directors—should adopt a regular practice of initiating annual conversations regarding job satisfaction, well-being, and future planning. Boards should hold presidents accountable for ensuring that systems and structures are in place to maintain continuity in the case of a sudden vacancy anywhere in the leadership hierarchy.

Institutions can take steps to both manage and normalize leadership transitions. Academic rituals and ceremonies, including farewell celebrations and presidential inaugurations, can symbolically mark the changing of the guard. These events provide a sense of closure for departing leaders while helping the campus community prepare to welcome a new leader. Beyond pomp, circumstance, and parties, one of the best gifts that an institution can bestow on an exiting leader is clarity of expectations, especially concerning salary and workload.[69] Administrative contracts are often negotiated behind closed doors; often "faculty retreat rights" and post-administrative salaries are established when a new leader is hired. Some states, including California, Tennessee, and North Carolina, have enacted laws enumerating the rights, responsibilities, and pay for presidents and chief academic officers who vacate their positions.[70] Absent such structures, leaders and their institutions can always revisit these agreements. For example, if the goal is to usher out a problematic leader quickly and quietly, a university might strategically cede its bargaining strength and settle the manner at any cost.

Institutions can provide outgoing leaders with material support to ease their return to the faculty. A survey of more than one hundred department chairs identified the resources necessary to help them reprise their faculty roles: a paid sabbatical, start-up funds, or a graduate assistant to help them reengage their research programs.[71] Bear in mind that while some department chairs carry a heavy administrative load, most retain half-time (or greater) teaching appointments. If chairs envision needing time and assistance to resume full-time faculty responsibilities, the case for support seems even stronger for presidents, provosts, deans, and other central administrators.

While benefits like a paid sabbatical and research funding can go a long way in helping a former administrator get back up to speed on their professional responsibilities, it is prudent for institutions to remember that transitions exact an emotional toll as well. Many ex-leaders felt *othered* by their peers: "faculty almost inevitably come to view their former colleagues as administrators, not as fellow faculty members."[72] In addition to feeling isolated at work, some former leaders may struggle with letting go, accepting their changing professional identities, and coming to terms with their professional legacies.[73] To fill these social-emotional gaps, one study advocated for the creation of support groups for former administrators.[74] Given the sporadic nature of administrative departures, professional societies might be best positioned to provide this service for similarly situated leaders across multiple institutions. Such organizations might provide webinars, conference sessions, and even one-on-one coaching to help individuals come to terms with the emotional dimensions of their transition.

Research Design

Studies of administrators' lived experiences remain conspicuously absent in the research about higher education leadership.[75] To bring their voices to the foreground, I adopted a constructivist grounded theory research design to guide the creation of research questions, select participants, analyze data, and ultimately, arrange findings into the Stepping Away Model.

Why Is It Called a Theory?

From the very outset, grounded theorists set out to collect and analyze data to develop a new representational framework for a phenomenon or social process that is understudied or cannot be adequately explained by existing theories. When this is the case, a researcher sets out to develop a new conceptual model to "make coherent what otherwise appears as disparate and disconnected individual events." While that may seem overly abstract, the intent is practical: "theory is the means through which we learn lessons that can apply to situations we have yet to encounter."[76] The methodologist Ian Dey has explained that grounded theorists are often interested in theorizing social processes with a goal to "focus on understanding the intentions and strategies of actors involved in that process; that [the method] proceeds through exploring the process through a variety of settings; and that [the method] involves a systematic analysis of data through categorization and comparison."[77] To improve a theory's trustworthiness and utility, the researcher must develop a sufficiently large and diverse sample to ensure that a variety of perspectives have been consulted. It is expected that a theory can and should be tested against different populations and in different contexts. These future studies help to refine the model by adding nuance and robustness.

Why Is It Called Grounded?

All grounded theory approaches are fundamentally inductive processes in which the researcher seeks to move beyond description and propose a new theory that is "grounded" in actions, events, and personal experience.[78] Grounded theory approaches begin with the collection and analysis of data from individuals with firsthand experiences and "reference specific, everyday-world situations."[79] The methodologist Kathy Charmaz outlines the basic steps of conducting a constructivist grounded theory study: "(1) Begin with inductive data; (2) invoke strategies of going back and forth between the data collection and analysis; (3) use comparative methods; and (4) keep the researcher interacting with and involved with data and the emerging analysis."[80] One of the most important aspects of this approach is that the researcher always begins with the data—letting it guide and inform all subsequent steps in the process. By constantly evolving their research collection on the basis of emergent findings and always going back to their data (e.g., interview transcripts, field notes), researchers will begin to build a representation of study participants' lived experiences.

Why Is It Called Constructivist?

Barney Glaser and Anselm Strauss are generally cited as the founders of the grounded theory methodology. They maintained that research findings are *discovered* empirically through the systematic analysis of data. Their approach maintains that truth is more or less objective—anyone who analyzes the same data will arrive at roughly the same conclusion. Their approach is less compatible with the epistemological tradition of constructivism, which maintains that there are "multiple, apprehendable, and sometimes conflicting social realities that are the products of human intellects."[81] Much like anthropologists, constructivists "attempt to understand the complex world of lived experience from the point of view of those who live it."[82] The design of this study gives considerable weight to participants' firsthand accounts while also recognizing that I, as the lead researcher, play an active role in "constructing data" and shaping the findings.[83] In a departure from the orthodoxy of Glaser and Strauss, for Charmaz, "a constructivist approach means more than looking at how individuals view their situations. It not only theorizes the interpretive work that research participants do, but also acknowledges that the resulting theory is an interpretation."[84] Charmaz's approach acknowledges that research is both personal and subjective. In chorus with other postmodern and contemporary scholars, Charmaz submits that it is impossible to disentangle the self from the research process because "researchers bring to their qualitative writing all that they are, and this includes what many refer to as their 'baggage.' . . . 'Baggage' has some negative connotations—one's 'hang-ups,' aversions, and the residue of one's past unhappy experiences—a legacy that burdens one down and makes progress difficult. . . . [But baggage] is more than a negative impediment. It is also a unique life experience and strength."[85] For Charmaz, "conducting and writing research are not neutral acts" because data and findings are always mediated and filtered by the intervening researcher.[86]

Examining assumptions and personal biases is a critical part of the constructivist grounded theory tradition. Unpacking personal bias begins with accounting for how the researcher's salient social identities will influence the project. Given the diversity of the participants in my study, I found myself somewhere on a continuum. With some participants, I shared multiple demographic characteristics and life experiences, and with others, only a few. In my interactions with participants and, later, making sense of what I heard from them, I endeavored to remain aware of how my personal identities as a straight, married, able-bodied, cis-gendered White woman who is childless by choice influenced my thinking about what I heard them say. Beyond identities, I bring the "baggage" of having worked as a college administrator for almost two decades. Having supported three vice presidents for academic affairs at a small private university and worked closely with presidents at two public research universities, I have developed the ability to shift between being an insider and an outsider when conducting research with this population. My "insider" professional networks undoubtably made it easier for me to recruit participants, and my working knowledge of the norms of administrative life allowed me to establish rapport quickly in interviews. Despite these advantages, my view of senior leaders remains fragmented and fractional; I have never experienced the full scope of responsibility belonging to a president, dean, or provost, nor have I ever worked as a tenure-track faculty member. My professional background disposes me to have considerable empathy for senior academic leaders and to give them the benefit of the doubt. When thinking about what the best administrators contribute to their colleges, I find myself well aligned with the description offered by the longtime college administrator Rita Palm: "For all the negative attitudes about administration, one could make the case that the highest calling of a professor is to become an academic administrator. Our job is to improve the lives and opportunities of faculty and students, alumni, and other supporters of the institution. . . . It is fundamentally a calling to service. Administration is a place for those who are willing to sacrifice their own academic career to further the important goal of high quality in higher education."[87] To be clear, this is not to say that I believe that all presidents, provosts, and deans possess altruistic motives or that the participants in the study necessarily subscribed to this view. In accordance with the foundational principles of constructive grounded theory, it is important for me to account for my underlying sympathies and to be transparent with the reader about how who I am and its potential impact on what I will see in the data.

Study Participants and Recruiting Efforts

The research for this book was conducted between 2016 and 2020 and sanctioned by the Institutional Review Board at The University of Texas. Participants had to meet two criteria to participate in the study. First, the individual must have been employed as a senior academic administrator (e.g., president, chief academic officer, dean) at a nonprofit, four-year college or university in the United States. Second, the individual must have stepped away and returned to the faculty within the past two years or announced an intention to do so. While some study participants ultimately left their institutions for one reason or another, all had accepted a faculty contract at the time of the first interview. Academic leaders who left their universities and began work elsewhere or retired outright were excluded from the study. A future study might consider why some leaders opt not to return to the faculty—but I have left that work for someone else to do.

Aiming to recruit participants to the study who were positioned to contribute information-rich cases, I used purposeful sampling to ensure that a variety of leadership roles, institution types, and motivations for stepping away were represented.[88] In all, I interviewed fifty-two current and former senior academic leaders over a four-year period; nineteen participants were interviewed twice. Striving to cast a broad net, I used my professional networks, snowball sampling, and general internet searches to identify prospective participants. In the absence of any national database, I made extensive use of the *Chronicle of Higher Education*'s "Appointments, Resignations, and Deaths" column (now called "Transitions"). When cold calling, I sent a single follow-up after the initial invitation. Several potential participants declined to participate, citing a lack of time or an unwillingness to discuss the terms of their exit or giving no reason whatsoever. Given the ad hoc nature of my recruiting strategy and reliance on publicly available data, many (surely excellent) potential participants were unintentionally omitted from the study. Several professional organizations—including the Association of American Colleges and Universities, the Annapolis Group, the American Council on Education, and the American Conference of Academic Deans— declined my request to recruit via their membership lists and listservs, citing terms of use concerns.

The demographics of study participants are shaped by the individuals who were willing to speak with me. As I approached the later stages of my research, I intentionally sought out additional women, deans, and people of color to ensure a greater diversity of perspectives. I personalized my recruiting email and made more targeted use of my professional networks. The comparatively large sample size for a qualitative study ensured that many views were considered. Ultimately, I ceased data collection upon achieving what Charmaz calls "theoretical sufficiency," concluding that the data were robust enough to develop a theoretical model that could capture all perspectives and experiences. Characteristics of study participants and their institutional affiliations are listed in tables 2.1 and 2.2.

Table 2.1. Personal Characteristics of Research Study Participants

	Number of participants	Percentage of sample
Leadership role		
President/chancellor	6	12
Chief academic officer / provost	24	46
Dean	10	19
Other senior leader	12	23
Sex		
Female	18	35
Male	34	65
Race/ethnicity		
White	48	92
Person of color	4	8
Marital status		
Married/partnered	46	88
Single/divorced	6	12
Age		
45 to 54	12	23
55 to 64	15	29
65 to 75	25	48
Number of years in administrative role		
0 to 5	10	19
6 to 10	15	29
11 to 15	11	21
16 to 20	4	8
21 or more	10	19
Undisclosed	2	4
Disciplinary identification		
Arts and humanities	14	27
Social sciences	23	44
STEM	12	23
Professional degree	3	6
Circumstances surrounding departure		
Voluntary departure	39	75
Involuntary departure	11	21
Undisclosed	2	4

Table 2.2. Institutional Characteristics of Research Study Participants

	Number of participants	Percentage of sample
Institution type		
Public	20	38
Private	32	62
Degrees granted by institution		
Baccalaureate granting	7	13
Master's granting	14	27
Doctoral granting	31	60
Institution size based on enrollment		
Small (0 to 3,000 students)	20	38
Medium (3,001 to 10,000 students)	8	15
Large (10,001 or more students)	24	46

Nearly half of the study participants ($n = 24$) once served as a chief academic officer, holding such titles as vice president for academic affairs, dean of the faculty, or provost. While nearly all CAOs had oversight for the faculty and curricular matters, there was a great deal of variation across their professional portfolios. Some CAOs managed deans, campus athletics, institutional research offices, and student affairs units. The number of direct reports and budgetary scope tended to correlate with institution size. The role category with the second greatest number of participants ($n = 12$) was "other senior leaders," a heterogeneous group that included roles like assistant and associate deans, special assistants, assistant or associate vice presidents or vice provosts, and specialty roles like registrar. These leaders had oversight for critical university functions like accreditation and research, led academic programs and departments, granted policy exceptions, and usually had some authority over budgets and staff. Roughly one-fifth of participants served as a dean ($n = 10$), providing senior leadership to a unit, such as a law school or a college of education. Title and scope of authority can be misleading; in the study, some deans managed larger budgets and more faculty members than did CAOs from smaller institutions. The category with the fewest participants was president/chancellor ($n = 6$). While the total number of presidents interviewed was small, presidents from both public and private institutions and from small-, medium-, and large-sized institutions were represented, allowing for a variety of perspectives.

Consistent with the national population of senior administrators, men outnumbered women in the study, accounting for 65 percent of the total sample. The gender balance was particularly skewed in the president/chancellor category, as no women presidents could be recruited. Despite concerted efforts to recruit participants of color, nearly all participants (92 percent) identified as White. Across the sample, a majority were married or had a long-term partner; only six were single or divorced. The age of participants ranged from 42 to 76; the mean age of study participants was 61.8 years old, and the median age was 64. Approximately half of the participants (48 percent) were of retirement age (65 or older). On average, study participants had served in an administrative role for 12.4 years; half served between 6 and 15 years. The shortest amount of time that a participant served in a leadership role was an interim associate provost who had served a single year. The participant with the longest tenure was a chief academic officer who had served for 37 consecutive years, bless him.

Nearly all participants had earned the rank of full professor. While not necessarily climbing every rung on Cohen and March's ladder, many participants had come "up through the ranks" and served previously as a department chair, leader of the faculty senate, or associate dean before moving up. Many had also enacted lateral career moves, for example, having worked as a provost at two different institutions. A small number of participants had worked outside of the academy at some point in their careers (sometimes before serving as a faculty member, sometimes during a break from the university). I invited participants to self-identify their disciplinary affiliations. The highest percentage of participants held terminal degrees in the social sciences (44 percent), with roughly equal numbers holding degrees in the arts and humanities (27 percent) and STEM fields (25 percent). The remaining 6 percent held terminal degrees in professional fields, including law and business.

Recognizing the potential sensitivity of the topic, I invited participants to disclose the circumstances leading to their administrative exit and return to the faculty. A majority ($n = 39$) indicated that they had returned to the faculty voluntarily, meaning that they had self-initiated their exit. Roughly one-fifth of participants ($n = 11$) returned to the faculty involuntarily, meaning that they resigned under pressure or were fired. While these eleven participants left their administrative roles involuntarily, they chose to return to the faculty rather than retire or leave the institution. Two participants did not disclose the circumstances that led them to leave their roles.

There was a high degree of diversity among participants' institutional affiliations; they differed greatly in mission, selectivity, prestige, student body, and fiscal resources. The sample included leaders from the Ivy League, state university flagships, R1s, branch campuses, single-gender institutions, minority serving institutions, religiously affiliated and secular institutions, residential liberal arts colleges, and commuter institutions. Their colleges were located in more than twenty states (reflecting all political persuasions) and included a mix of rural, suburban, and urban areas. Participants from private institutions (n = 32) slightly outnumbered participants from public institutions (n = 20). More than 60 percent of participants were employed by universities granting doctoral degrees (n = 31); fewer participants were employed by master's (n = 14) and baccalaureate (n = 7) granting institutions. Nearly half of the study participants came from "large institutions" with a total enrollment of ten thousand or more students (n = 24), while others were distributed between "medium" (n = 8) and "small" institutions with fewer than three thousand students (n = 20).

All participants selected or were assigned a pseudonym to maintain confidentiality. Table 2.3 includes information on each participant; an asterisk notation is included for participants who were interviewed twice (at different points in their transition). The decision to omit additional characteristics about each participant—age, length of administrative tenure, disciplinary training, race, and so on—was made to preserve anonymity.

Data Collection

Upon recruiting a participant into the study, I conducted a one-on-one, "intensive interview" to collect demographic data and explore their experiences stepping away from administration to return to the faculty.[89] I conducted interviews in person, by phone, or by video conference, and initial interviews usually took between sixty and ninety minutes. This flexibility allowed me to construct a sample with considerable geographic, institutional, and demographic diversity without incurring significant travel costs. When possible and the participant was agreeable, I conducted a second interview approximately six to fifteen months later. This allowed me to follow the participant's continued progression, record shifting perceptions, and discuss aspects of the transition that proved most challenging or surprising. Nineteen participants were interviewed twice. Interview protocols are included in the appendix. All interviews were transcribed to facilitate coding and analysis. Given that this project stretched over multiple years, I kept in touch with participants through brief email exchanges and arranged social

Table 2.3. Research Study Participants (Sorted by Role)

Pseudonym	Administrative role	Institution type	Sex	Circumstances surrounding exit
Brian*	President	Private	Male	Voluntary departure
Chris	President	Private	Male	Voluntary departure
Mack	President	Private	Male	Voluntary departure
Ralph*	President	Private	Male	Voluntary departure
Randy	President	Public	Male	Voluntary departure
Ted	President	Public	Male	Undisclosed
Bernie	Chief academic officer	Private	Male	Voluntary departure
Betsy	Chief academic officer	Public	Female	Voluntary departure
Buddy*	Chief academic officer	Private	Male	Involuntary departure
Christine	Chief academic officer	Private	Female	Involuntary departure
Emma*	Chief academic officer	Private	Female	Voluntary departure
Frank*	Chief academic officer	Private	Male	Voluntary departure
Ginsu	Chief academic officer	Private	Male	Involuntary departure
Grace	Chief academic officer	Public	Female	Voluntary departure
Igor*	Chief academic officer	Public	Male	Involuntary departure
Isabel	Chief academic officer	Public	Female	Voluntary departure
Judy	Chief academic officer	Public	Female	Voluntary departure
Kevin	Chief academic officer	Private	Male	Voluntary departure
Luke*	Chief academic officer	Private	Male	Voluntary departure
Norm	Chief academic officer	Private	Male	Voluntary departure
Paul	Chief academic officer	Public	Male	Involuntary departure
Penelope*	Chief academic officer	Public	Female	Voluntary departure
Robin*	Chief academic officer	Private	Male	Involuntary departure
Rosie	Chief academic officer	Private	Female	Voluntary departure
Saga	Chief academic officer	Private	Male	Undisclosed
Sid*	Chief academic officer	Private	Male	Voluntary departure
Steve	Chief academic officer	Private	Male	Voluntary departure
Stuart*	Chief academic officer	Public	Male	Involuntary departure
Wesley	Chief academic officer	Private	Male	Voluntary departure

Pseudonym	Administrative role	Institution type	Sex	Circumstances surrounding exit
William*	Chief academic officer	Public	Male	Voluntary departure
Aaron	Dean	Public	Male	Voluntary departure
Charles*	Dean	Private	Male	Voluntary departure
Felix	Dean	Public	Male	Voluntary departure
Greg*	Dean	Public	Male	Voluntary departure
James	Dean	Public	Male	Voluntary departure
Martin	Dean	Private	Male	Involuntary departure
Nancy*	Dean	Public	Female	Voluntary departure
Richard	Dean	Private	Male	Involuntary departure
Roger	Dean	Public	Male	Voluntary departure
Sam*	Dean	Private	Female	Voluntary departure
Alice	Other senior leader	Private	Female	Voluntary departure
Allie	Other senior leader	Private	Female	Voluntary departure
Ashley	Other senior leader	Private	Female	Involuntary departure
Barbara*	Other senior leader	Private	Female	Voluntary departure
Bill*	Other senior leader	Public	Male	Involuntary departure
Chelsea	Other senior leader	Private	Male	Voluntary departure
Harriett	Other senior leader	Private	Female	Voluntary departure
Horace*	Other senior leader	Private	Male	Voluntary departure
Mildred	Other senior leader	Private	Female	Voluntary departure
P.J.	Other senior leader	Public	Male	Voluntary departure
Rita	Other senior leader	Public	Female	Voluntary departure
Sabrina	Other senior leader	Private	Female	Voluntary departure

visits when we were both attending the same professional conferences. These measures deepened the relationships I built with participants and alerted me to changes (e.g., the participant accepted a new job elsewhere).[90]

I want to offer a brief note on how I approached interviewing senior academic leaders. The research methodologist Lewis Dexter has surmised that many members of an elite or privileged class—those set apart by their power, resources, and status—often encounter feelings of isolation and loneliness in their workplaces.[91] Given that candor might be a professional liability, individuals take on a guarded posture, rarely sharing their innermost thoughts with coworkers; many find it more comfortable to disclose their feelings and experiences to an understanding stranger (such as a researcher, a therapist, or an executive coach). By describing the measures I would take to preserve their anonymity, I aimed to create a space where participants could openly share their anxieties, disappointments, and setbacks. Offered these assurances, participants were remarkably forthcoming, occasionally noting that they were sharing information with me that they regularly withheld from others.

While the interview provided a safe haven where former administrators could be completely honest, the conversations occasionally took on a revelatory tone. Drawing on decades of interactions with university leaders, the higher education researcher Adrianna Kezar has proposed that research interviews can be a vehicle to promote leaders' self-awareness. In particular, she encourages interviewers to call attention to the study participant's unexamined assumptions about power and privilege.[92] I remember a participant discussing the challenges of reintegrating into their academic department, specifically making do with a smaller office and reduced travel funding. My follow-up questions led the participant to reflect on how his rejoining the department might have been a hardship for his department chair and how his resource needs only exacerbated that tension (and what he might do differently moving forward).

From Analysis to Theory

One way that constructivist grounded theory differs from other social science research methods is that data collection and analysis are performed simultaneously in a back-and-forth "zigzag" process.[93] While some qualitative research methods recommend a strict division between data collection and analysis, blurring the distinction allows the researcher to fully benefit from iterative learning and real-time sense-making. For example, after one of my research participants talked about the limitations of the metaphors "stepping down" and "returning to the faculty," I decided to add a question about these metaphors to my protocol for future interviews. As a result, I learned a great deal about how leaders saw themselves and the stepping away process (see Collected Wisdom 1 to read some of the alternative metaphors proposed). Later in the research process, when I was testing out whether to name the process "stepping down," "stepping back," "transitioning," or "stepping away," I was able to run my draft ideas past participants and incorporate their suggestions.

Even by grounded theory standards, Kathy Charmaz's approach to data analysis is among the most organic and flexible.[94] I was fortunate to attend a multiday, in-person workshop with Charmaz in San Antonio in 2017 where she warned us to "guard against forcing our preconceptions on the data we code."[95] In the workshop, she invited participants to use the constant comparative method to identify similarities and differences across our data. We did this by reviewing a small number of transcripts and methodically going line by line to write descriptive statements of any actions in the margins. Charmaz encouraged the researcher to use gerunds—the form of verb that functions as a noun (often achieved by adding the suffix *-ing* to a verb). Some of the initial codes I developed included "picking up kids from school," "moving into a temporary office," or "dressing more casually." In these early rounds, I developed hundreds of codes; some applied to a single transcript, and others were applicable across multiple transcripts. The point of this stage is to be sure that you do not discard an idea prematurely or overlook a potential finding.

Following the next step in Charmaz's process, I switched from handwritten margin notes and used the software program nVivo to continue to code transcripts. With approximately seventy interviews across multiple rounds of interviews, I compiled more than one thousand pages of data. As I developed new codes, I began to group them into categories and wrote memos to help me work out relationships between codes. Eventually, in the focused coding stage, I went back to transcripts from my earliest interviews and whittled down the list to about seventy codes that were "more selective, directed, and conceptual."[96] I created figure 2.2 to demonstrate how I moved from an initial description, through several layers of analysis, to arrive at a finding.

Features of the nVivo software made it quicker and easier to conduct comparative analyses; it allowed me to examine the presence or absence of codes across groups (e.g., participants who exited voluntarily and involuntarily, private and public institutions, and men and women). Sometimes, patterns emerged; the finding *experiencing role and status confusion* was more prevalent among women. For other findings and characteristics, I could discern no meaningful differences. For example, the finding *experiencing and using time differently* was equally prevalent across genders, institutional types, and

48 STEPPING AWAY

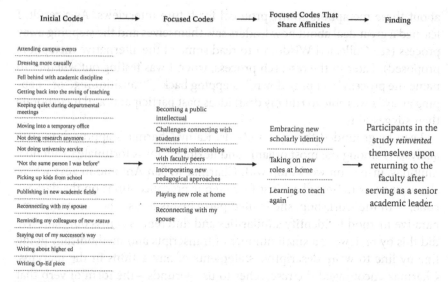

Figure 2.2. Charmaz advises researchers to develop initial descriptive codes and gradually refine them into more abstract statements called "focused codes." This figure represents how I moved through each stage.

participants who left their positions voluntarily and involuntarily. Not only did these queries help me refine the findings, but they helped me organize representative quotations to cite in later chapters.

By the time I had conducted and coded a few dozen interviews, I had already begun to formulate some ideas regarding the design of a model. I used later interviews to test out whether the emergent themes that I had noticed in preliminary data analysis resonated. This was the perfect opportunity to determine whether the patterns I was noticing felt relevant and applicable to others in the study. Engaging participants as sense-making partners allowed me to incorporate their feedback into the model to verify that all claims were accurate and conveyed clearly.

Study Delimitations and Limitations

Like all qualitative studies, the Stepping Away Model is not intended to be broadly generalizable across all populations and settings. What it can offer is an abstract rendering of a social phenomenon (returning to the faculty) within a situated context (at four-year colleges and universities in the United States). Many perspectives may be absent or underrepresented in the findings; for example, academic leaders who signed nondisclosure agreements would have been contractually obligated to decline my invitation to participate. One participant who met the study criteria declined to participate on the grounds that her emotions were still too raw to talk about leaving a job she truly loved.

Research design decisions have a direct impact on the resulting findings. I made a conscious choice to delimit my study to include only senior academic leaders of four-year, nonprofit, postsecondary institutions in the United States. For-profit universities and community colleges were excluded on the grounds that many have a very different understanding of tenure and organizational structure. Originally, I considered including international examples, but after interviewing one participant from the United Kingdom, I decided the contexts were too different to produce a fruitful comparison. (I thanked the participant sincerely and explained why I would be excluding his data from my analysis.) In the future, I would like to expand this research to include global perspectives, seeking to leverage cross-cultural insights about organizational structures.

CHAPTER 3

First Steps

Look as You Leap

Rather than conceiving of returning to the faculty as a single, linear process with a clearly defined start and end, former senior academic leaders in the study proceed through seven, interrelated microprocesses, each possessing its own beginning, middle, and end. These microprocesses can feel like sustained sprints nestled within an endurance race. At the start of the sequence, senior leaders often find themselves *imagining parallel futures* and *experiencing role and status confusion*.

A defining feature of this model (see figure 1.1) is that the microprocesses are *iterative*. Elements, decision points, and feelings will reverberate and resurface from start to end. Over time, many ex-leaders employ insights gained along the way or adapt a strategy gleaned from one microprocess to another. Given the cyclical nature of transition, former leaders are often least equipped to navigate the start: they have yet to perfect their strategies, having acquired little transferrable knowledge and experience. The earliest days can be particularly challenging. At this point in the process, former administrators are least practiced in answering questions, especially hostile questions from those who hold inaccurate perceptions of why a leader is stepping away and what they will do as a faculty member.

Microprocess 1: Imagining Parallel Futures

Returning to the faculty is often preceded by a period of contemplation and quiet plan-making, during which senior academic leaders *imagine parallel futures*. This activity often includes formulating the goals and expectations that will shape their lives after administration, often considering whether those goals can be met as a faculty member at their current institution. At one extreme, Judy expended little effort contemplating her future after voluntarily leaving her post as a chief academic officer at a public institution. She never doubted her plan to spend a few years on the faculty and then move into full retirement living nearby her beloved grandchildren. But other senior leaders engaged a range of strategies to help them develop plans in the moments immediately preceding and following the act of leaving office. Over two decades, Rosie ascended through a series of increasingly senior administrative roles at the private college where she earned tenure and later became the provost. Electing to resign her role after her working relationship with the college president unraveled, she found herself standing at an unfamiliar crossroads when she imagined what to do next:

> There is very little risk in going back to the faculty. I know who those people are. I know I can do it. I'm a good teacher. I love teaching. It would be a good life, and I could do that. It might be a little boring. . . . You know, trying to kind of weigh that risk against the desire for novelty and the sense of wanting maybe one more adventure, that's where I am. . . . It's odd to be at this age and this phase of my career and feel surprised by the challenge of the task of figuring it out.

While Rosie found the prospect of novelty and adventure appealing, she recognized that mid- to late-career job changes pose added complications. The sheer number of factors to be considered left Rosie with much to think about: "I have found it really hard to even decide whether to pursue these [external opportunities], because every one of them is such an enormous shift. Every one of them has the potential to be such an enormous change in every feature of my life: where I live, where I work, what kind of position I have, what my husband's job is—where I live, how close I am to my kids or not, all of those things, and what the culture of that place is."

Imagining a parallel future is doing the emotional and mental calculus of weighing potential risks, rewards, certainty, and novelty. The equation often requires a former leader to analyze their own goals and needs, those of their spouse and family, and institutional needs. While some participants had clear reasons for resuming their faculty career or were ready to embrace full retirement, a handful of participants found that going on the job market was essential to the discernment process. Speaking with a level of candor I did not anticipate, participants talked frankly about assessing the professional opportunities available to them (both at their current institutions and elsewhere).

Strategy 1: Embracing Plans to Stay

Chris talked me through the thinking that led him to return to the faculty at his private college. His board had hoped that he would extend his presidency, but a period of reflection led him to conclude that it was in neither his best interest nor the best interest of the institution to do so. He explained:

> It's a privilege to be able to stop and be at a crossroads and to think, "Who am I, where am I, where am I going?" . . . And so for me, the crossroads was, "Oh, I'll do another two or another three [years]." But it was obvious that our having reached successful closure—on things like the strategic plan, the capital campaign—and having made strides on never-ending things like diversification of the culture, and deepening the well-being of its values, and things of that sort—things that don't come to closure. We had reached a certain point where it seemed to me that either I would commit myself to another seven years or something like that and see itself through another significant phase of self-evaluation and development, or it was important for me to move on. And looking at my age, I realized that if I wanted to be a scholar still, and I want to be a teacher seriously, this was my last chance to do that. There was a day when the decision had to be made. I have to say that when I woke up the next day, I felt really great. I didn't feel regretful. So, I knew it was probably right.

While Chris gave careful thought to the prospect of continuing in his presidential role, for some senior academic leaders, the choice to return to the faculty was more straightforward. Former provost Penelope "never wanted to be a university president," and therefore, when her contract ended, she never seriously considered anything but returning to the faculty at the institution where she had spent several decades of her faculty career.

Similarly, those who planned to transition into full retirement within one or two years of stepping away from their administrative roles rarely gave serious consideration to applying for jobs elsewhere. For leaders like former provost Judy, returning to the faculty was more or less a placeholder. She determined that returning to the faculty temporarily provided a helpful buffer: "I wasn't ready to just stop at that point—stop dead." Given that her spouse was not ready to retire, Judy cited the advantages of earning a few more years of salary while also beginning what she called a "phased fade-away."

When leaders commit to remaining at the institution where they served as an administrator, they often need to take steps to rebuild a faculty life. Most participants in the study, especially those who left their roles voluntarily, invested time and capital to prepare the groundwork for a successful transition. In the final years of Ted's presidency, he allocated greater attention to reengaging the contemporary debates in his discipline to ease his impending return to the classroom. Knowing that being fluent in recent scholarship would be important to build credibility with students, Ted found that this preparatory work had the added benefit of helping him begin to separate his identity from his administrative role. Rebuilding a faculty life often entails more than course preparation. For some, it might include purchasing and or renovating houses. Depending on the circumstances, leaders might smooth the way by attending social gatherings to reconnect with the faculty in their home department or take initial steps to revive dormant research programs. While the forms of preparatory work differed, for many participants, it took an intentional effort to strengthen relationships in their department or discipline, get caught up on a decade's worth of scholarship, and construct a new residence.

Strategy 2: Actively Pursuing Alternative Opportunities

Just as some academic leaders are confident that returning to the faculty at their current institution is the best next step, others are equally convinced that leaving is the preferred option. Ginsu, a provost who left his position involuntarily, was actively pursuing other jobs. He said plainly, "I don't want to be a faculty member." He continued, "While the process of helping students learn is phenomenal and honorable and great fun, it's not sufficiently complex to compare to what I've been working at for the last thirteen years. . . . What really drives me is understanding where an organization is, where it wants to go, what the internal and external environmental factors are, and how to optimize that and then how to make all the systems and people work together." A paid sabbatical allowed Ginsu the time to apply for other jobs. Although Ginsu was something of an outlier in the data set—very few participants were this candid about their intentions to leave their institution in the near or immediate future—his perspective reveals that sometimes the phrase "returning to the faculty" is code for "until I get the job I really want."

While a former senior leader might seek to separate from their institution, some leaders prefer to loosen the connection without severing ties.

54 STEPPING AWAY

While Christine remained employed as a professor, she actively pursued side projects that would allow her to be more closely affiliated with networks and communities beyond the private institution where she had served as a provost for almost a decade. For context, it is important to know that Christine's administrative exit resulted from an unanticipated presidential turnover; the new president told Christine that she wanted to "choose her own provost." Classifying her resignation as involuntary and "ugly," Christine explained, "it is not what I wanted to do." But she obliged the president's request, nevertheless.

Given the tensions Christine experienced with the new president preceding her resignation, she decided that her best course of action was to direct her energies externally. In her first year out of the provost's office, Christine's paid sabbatical provided her the flexibility to give several keynote addresses, join the board of a professional organization, and teach modules in an executive education certificate program (the program was not affiliated with her home institution). She also busied herself with a new venture: "One colleague who was a president who lost his job in a similarly ugly fashion decided to bring together a group of sitting provosts, former provosts, sitting presidents, former presidents as a consultancy. We're working through the beginnings of that." As she readied herself to resume teaching, her focus shifted to preparation, noting, "it's taken a lot of time to develop my courses because I haven't taught for fifteen years." While Christine maintained her faculty appointment, external work provided rewarding outlets for her professional energies. For leaders who felt a level of frustration with their universities or specific individuals within the university, side projects might provide a sense of balance (and escape).

Strategy 3: Achieving Clarity by Examining Choices

Of all the leaders I interviewed, Horace served the shortest amount of time in his administrative role. He returned to the faculty after completing an interim one-year appointment as an associate provost at a private university—declining the provost's invitation to continue permanently. While the length of his administrative service was brief, it was impactful. One of the many insights that Horace gained from his temporary appointment was the renewed confidence to continue in his faculty role. One factor that motivated Horace to accept an interim leadership role was because he felt that his academic career had grown stale, the next link in a chain of inevitability rather than an intentional act: "There's a part of being an academic that feels like—at least that has for me—a little bit like inertia. I used to love to stay in school. I was a good student, so I went to a good college, and then

I did really well in college. I went to a good graduate school. I did well in graduate school, so I got a [tenure-track] job. It feels a little bit like a continuation of the life you've led since you were five." An interim position allowed Horace to reevaluate the trajectory of his career. Deciding that his goals and interests were better aligned with a faculty position, at the end of the year, Horace returned to the faculty with a new attitude: "Just the perspective of having developed in a different way over the course of the year or just that little nudge of feeling, 'No, I really am choosing this [faculty] life.' This is at least one of the reasons why I'm walking away from a job that, in many ways, I found very fulfilling." Horace's realization came about in a temporally compressed cycle—shifting from faculty member to administrator and back again in a single year. The speed by which Horace came to this conclusion was unusual, but he was hardly the only former senior academic leaders who achieved vocational certainty by trying something out and assessing his options.

After Roger had completed the first term of his deanship at a public university, he was required by law to undergo a demanding, yearlong review process to be eligible for reappointment. He entered that review process in good faith, assuming he would continue in this role. He explained what happened at the conclusion of the review:

> The president and provost sat me down. They said, "What do you say to another six years?" And I had a moment of clarity when I said, "Oh, hell no."
> [They asked] "Well, why did we go through all this if you were just going to turn it down?" And that's a fair question. The best I could offer them was, "I didn't have clarity until we went through this. And now having heard your and others' reactions and visions for the next six years, I'm taking a candid look at my own life and priorities. I'm not excited about this."

For Roger, both statements were true: he was interested enough in continuing in his dean role to agree to participate in the review process required for reappointment, *and* the review (while positive) was instrumental in helping him decide to leave the deanship. While I imagine that his president and provost were disappointed by the outcome, ultimately, the review process forced Roger to examine his goals. Both Horace and Roger found that reminding themselves of their choices—that being neither a faculty member nor an administrator was a passive inevitability—provided them with greater enthusiasm for continuing in their chosen work.

The thought processes that led Roger to his "moment of clarity" illustrates the considerable and consequential impact of *imagining parallel futures*. This activity is hardly comparable to low-stakes daydreaming or talking through hypothetical situations. For senior academic leaders, truly weighing their options demands actual labor and even a little risk (on the part of both the individual and their institution). These leaders underwent comprehensive performance reviews, mounted the steep learning curve to learn a new role on an interim basis, and invited the exposure that comes from being considered for a new job.

Among all the participants in the study, Bill's story is something of an anomaly. His return to the faculty at a public university had been abrupt, involuntary, and unexpected. The shock of learning that his position was being eliminated and of his imminent dismissal was compounded by events in his personal life, including the death of a parent and being diagnosed with cancer. The confluence of these events infused Bill's return to the faculty with added emotional charge, launching him into serious midlife reflection. He recalled asking himself, "What do I want to do? How can I make a difference? How can I make an impact? Or, what does that mean?"; he added, "I am also wrestling with that question." For Bill, the discontinuation of his administrative role first led him to explore opportunities beyond his current institution. He applied for several positions; while he had several on-campus interviews, no search yielded an offer. Applying for positions was affirming nevertheless, allowing Bill to exercise his personal agency at a point in his life when many things felt beyond his control: "It really was for my mental health to see whether I was in the game or could be in the game and whether I had choices in that regard—kind of all of that. I think—well, I don't know. Everything seems changed, and I'm a big proponent of pushing change. But it's different now that this change is swirling around." Pursuing alternative job opportunities led Bill to an epiphany:

> I think I decided, "Okay, I'm going to be at [my current institution], or do this work in the department for the next ten years and retire"—something along those lines. But it was really important to me at the time to [apply for positions]. My wife was really stressed out about it, like, "Wait a minute." Actually, she was on board with [me applying for positions], but then when it came to actually possibly something happening, then it was like, "Well, I don't know. Are we doing it?" I said, "No, no, I don't think so." She asked, "But then why are you doing it?" And I said, "Because I need to."

The mental processes associated with applying for a new job—including having to articulate his passions and goals during a job interview—gave Bill the sense of closure and control that he lacked. While Bill's job searches did not result in offers, he explained that choosing to return to the faculty at his current institution was not "settling." Instead, the process led him to recognize that returning to the faculty was a good option. Exploring opportunities brought Bill's goals into focus and inspired him to identify new ways to "satisfy his itch" by making positive contributions in the lives of students. Although Bill would have preferred continuing in his administrative role, exploring his options made him excited about the possibilities awaiting him as a faculty member.

COLLECTED WISDOM 4

To Look or Not to Look: Exploring New Job Opportunities

As soon as you make your intentions to step away known, the inquiries will start. Expect to hear from friends, former colleagues, and search consultants. When the opportunities come calling, you will be pressed to decide whether to take the call and then whether and how to respond. Before you draw a line down a sheet of paper to weigh the pros and cons of a specific job or start looking up real estate prices in a new city, it can be worthwhile to ask yourself if applying for another job is worth it.

Looking Is *Just* Looking

It can be reassuring to remind yourself that you cannot accept a position that has not been offered to you. Reading a job ad or agreeing to speak with a search consultant carries no further commitment. Simplify things by not adding undue pressure. It is entirely reasonable to reassess your situation regularly. You might ignore all the offers for the first year or two and then start looking strategically in the third year.

What You Might (Re)Learn

While rarely framed this way, going on the job market is a learning opportunity that can result in major epiphanies or reassuring insights. Your instinctive response to a job ad is probably a good indicator of whether you have, indeed, accomplished your big goals or whether you have more you want to do professionally. A hiring cycle can help you better understand your strengths, give you a real sense of your stamina, and affirm how others see you. Alternatively, a job search might reveal new ways to use what you know. For instance, in preparing for or participating in an interview, you might realize ways to transfer your university experience into a role in a foundation or another nonprofit.

What You Might Gain

For some people, a job search can restore a sense of agency and worth. If your ego could use some stroking—and it might after an abrupt or difficult exit—gaining external affirmation of your value might do a world of good. Searches can result in

58   STEPPING AWAY

positive outcomes beyond a new job—they can lead to a speaking engagement, consulting work, or a worthwhile new connection. Sometimes, a search helps you see the greenness of your backyard grass. Of course, taking a new job in another part of the country might bring you closer to your family or allow you to relocate to a place better suited to your retirement dreams.

What It Might Cost

The time and energy that a job search demands may not warrant the investment. Every minute spent wondering, "what if . . ." or proofing a cover letter is a minute not thinking about something else, be it your teaching, research, or health. While consultants can promise discretion in the early rounds of a search, public campus visits always bring some reputational exposure. Should you be offered a position, the prospect of an unwelcome cross-country move or the demands on your spouse might stir up inordinate trouble on the home front. Sometimes it is better to make the best of what you have rather than assume the risk.

Strategy 4: Delaying Decisions about the Future, Until, Well, Later

When it comes to *imagining parallel futures*, another common tactic among senior academic leaders who return to the faculty is to attend to immediate decisions and delay those that are not urgent. For example, when Ralph concluded his presidency and vacated a campus residence, he and his spouse opted to move into a home they already owned, some ninety minutes from campus. He characterized their move as "temporary," acknowledging that they had not decided about where to live permanently. He joked, "Here I am, as planful a person you are going to meet, and still uncertain about what to do. Do we keep this place and buy a house [closer to the university]?" Moving into a house they owned made good sense in the short term. Instead of worrying about logistics, Ralph could focus on his scholarly writing and other dimensions of his post-presidency life. Once they had a chance to "recover from the presidency" (his words), Ralph and his spouse would reevaluate their plans.

Former dean Roger—the one who underwent a successful performance review only to realize that he no longer wanted to be a dean—had not abandoned the possibility that he might want to return to an administrative role at some point in his career. He attributed his ambivalence to his relatively young age. He explained that deciding to take a different job in the future would depend on finding the perfect fit: "I've made no decisions largely because I don't think at age fifty there's a way that I could credibly, in the Ulysses sense, lash myself to the mast of a ship. Even if I were to decide—and say I made the decision that I was never going to do it—I could always take the headhunter call next year, right? Or say I made a different decision: 'I'm absolutely going to do it.' It doesn't mean the right thing is going to come along." Immediately upon exiting his deanship, Roger felt little urgency to finalize his career ambitions. In adopting a stance that was both *open* and *selective* about future job prospects, he explained that he would be interested in roles that offered him an intellectual challenge in a location that was agreeable to his spouse and teenage children. He had not yet found such an opportunity.

The same open and selective logic governed former chief academic officer Emma's thinking about her career. For the time being, returning to the faculty allowed her to spend more time with a young child, shed the administrative responsibilities that weighed on her, and find satisfaction teaching and doing research. While she appreciated the short-term benefits, she had not foreclosed the possibility of, one day, casting a broader net. In thinking about her future, she wondered aloud, "Do I stay here as faculty for ten years and then just do something else altogether?" She explained, "Because one thing that has been a product of these [administrative] years is that I have real financial security that I never imagined having as a professor. I really could go do something else altogether in ten years, or similar. There are lots of things that interest me. So, I also wanted to have some time and space to think about that stuff. . . . I'm not sure higher ed is the right place for me."

During our interview, Emma enumerated the many costs of having spent multiple decades in upper administration. The job demanded time away from her family and brought the angst associated with making hard or unpopular decisions. She felt the cumulative strain from navigating workplace cultures that she found to be exclusionary, elitist, and sexist. While these forces exacted a toll, financial savings accrued during her administrative appointment afforded her the freedom to entertain less lucrative job options in the future. When we spoke, she thought that she might enjoy working for a foundation or becoming more involved in social causes that aligned with her values. While Emma hinted at exploring careers beyond traditional faculty roles, she expressed genuine gratitude for the quality of life she enjoyed as a faculty member: "Reaching this moment of being happy and being balanced is more important to me than seeming powerful or seeming to be a change agent while butting my head against the impossible every single day." For Emma, returning to the faculty restored a sense of work-life balance that she was unable to achieve previously. And as she began to envision different professional scenarios, she had ruled out taking another provostship. She was cognizant that accepting a new senior leadership position would threaten her quality of life, and in her fifties, she was no longer willing to make the sacrifices.

Returning to the faculty is but one choice available to experienced senior academic leaders. Many will elect to retire, engage in consulting work, or seek a position at another institution. Deciding when to leave and where to go is rarely easy, especially for individuals who anticipate working for another ten to fifteen years. As you might expect, participants who left their positions involuntarily—and continued to have the interest and ambition to continue in an administrative career—often applied for opportunities beyond their institution. But this is only part of the picture. Some former administrators who left their positions involuntarily—including provosts pressured by their presidents to resign—found themselves unexpectedly invigorated by returning to the faculty. While the timing or the outcome might not have felt ideal at the time, these former leaders relished returning to the classroom, felt energized by their research projects, and felt happier and healthier than they had in years. Even if returning to the faculty was not exactly what they imagined for themselves, they came to delight in how a job change added so much to their lives.

Microprocess 2: Experiencing Role and Status Confusion

For administrators in the study, returning to the faculty means many things. Some welcome the chance to hand over the reins to a capable successor; others lament the loss of salary and sense of importance; a few will do anything for a reprieve from the stress; and many relish returning to the classroom. Given the lack of consensus among senior leaders, it should come as no surprise that many faculty members, staff, students, alumni, and trustees find the arrangement to be utterly baffling. Those furthest from central administration are likely to be least certain of what the former president, provost, or dean *is* doing, why they are doing it, and how to engage with them in their new capacity. After describing some of the misconceptions and challenges that study participants faced upon returning to the faculty, I will name strategies that participants used to navigate awkward exchanges, impolite questions, or hostile acts of outright othering.

During my research, former administrators regaled me with anecdotes about the humorous, bizarre, or even suspicious exchanges they shared with colleagues about returning to the faculty. Perhaps the most common misconception that needed correcting was explaining the difference between stepping away from administration and retiring. Outside academia, there are few parallels on which to draw, so it is unsurprising that others struggle to understand.[1]

Former provost Robin found himself in the position of educating others about this quirky academic tradition: "Trustees would say, 'If you're a chief executive officer, a chief operating officer, when you're done with the organization—you're done.' In their experience, it's almost nothing like what I'm doing now, which is, you go back and have some other kind of position within the organization. Their sense is, 'We have a new CEO. That person has to be given space to be the new CEO.' It's hard to do that if the other person is hanging around or is on the board. It's less clear-cut." Robin's experiences illustrate that it is presumptive to assume that all members of a campus community, especially staff members or students, understand the philosophy and mechanics of faculty retreat rights. Even members of the governing board can have a muddled understanding of this long-standing academic tradition.

Another common assumption that participants confronted is the belief that all administrative exits are involuntary. After Felix had wrapped up his deanship—an exit he initiated after eight years on the job had taken its toll on his health and well-being—his university issued a boilerplate press release announcing his resignation. He explained, "Somebody said to me, 'When you read a press release and it says so-and-so is going back to the faculty, that is code for someone getting fired.'" While his colleague's cynicism might represent an extreme view, I would wager that on every college campus, you could find at least one faculty member who shares this sentiment. Felix took steps to protect his reputation and set the record straight: "I've been very conscious about trying to dispel that notion that this was an involuntary thing. I guess there's a sense of pride there." Unfortunately, this deep-seated misunderstanding could not be resolved easily. Helping colleagues understand his situation—that he served as a leader for nearly a decade and now wanted to do something else—was an ongoing task that Felix would have to address one conversation at a time.

Strategy 1: Coming to Terms with Who You Are Now

While being bombarded with questions, many leaders in the study were still working out the kind of faculty member they want to be. For instance, upon returning to the faculty, former provost Bernie saw himself as "neither fish nor fowl," occupying a status somewhere "in between" a faculty member and an administrator. Former dean Roger said that he felt "professor-ish." Since people will ask, leaders develop an explanation to satisfy the inquiring minds while they continue to work out plans for themselves. Sid, the former CAO of a small private institution, encountered faculty peers puzzled by his present faculty status and his former administrative responsibilities. This is how he handled it:

> I think we're all kind of figuring out how to relate to each other. . . . I think the overlay of being dean, that doesn't go away. A lot of faculty still refer to me as "dean" when they speak to me—or about me to somebody else. They'll catch themselves and say, "Wait a minute, he's no longer the dean." What that means is "he's no longer broken" or "he's no longer carrying the authority," "he's safe." They will catch themselves, and they will kind of laugh about that. All of that is part of the overlay of the relationship with me.

Sid's perception of the "overlay of being dean," an imaginary gauze between himself and others, is a good representation of how an administrative persona follows a leader into their faculty career. Sid noted that as time passed, the way that others viewed him shifted and the gauze began to disappear. When we spoke a year later, I asked Sid how things had progressed. He explained, "It would not be true to say that I have now been fully accepted as a member of the faculty. I'm still regarded by some faculty as an administrative person. I still represent the management, they the labor." The faculty members who had known him the longest were most likely to see him as an agent of the administration—a faculty adversary. As new faculty members were hired into the institution, they only knew him only as a colleague. He continued, "The changing demographics of the institution are lessening the sense of difficulty that I had with a number of my faculty colleagues, some of whom have retired since I shifted myself and some of whom will retire after me. I'll continue to be in this space between two identities. I'll have elements of both for some. I will be a full faculty person for some cohorts and still be an administrator for others. It's a shape-shifter role, in a certain sense, where depending on who I'm with, who I am will be shaped by their experience of me." In chapters 4 and 5, we will revisit some of the strategies that Sid used to shift between these identities and to galvanize his faculty role. Finding ways to reintegrate himself into the faculty and knowing when to hang back proved especially useful.

For Ashley, an associate dean at a private institution, returning to the faculty was complicated because of a fundamental misalignment between her sense of identity and the way others viewed her. In her mind, Ashley believed that she remained true to her faculty values while serving as an administrator. After five years in her leadership role, it became clear that some of her faculty peers doubted her loyalty to their cause. She wondered,

> Why is it that faculty don't see me as faculty? Because I am a faculty member. . . . I've been a faculty member forever. I don't think I was in this position necessarily long enough to be completely not viewed as a faculty member anymore. . . . People would sometimes say, "I don't know. Just that you're an

administrator now, and blah, blah, blah." I think that maybe I felt ambiguity in the role to begin with, not really wanting to let go of being a faculty member. I tried to make it seem like, "Of course, I'm still one of you."

Ashley was not the only administrator who felt *othered* while serving in an administrative role or after it. After Emma had voluntarily left her provostship, she had a telling exchange with a member of her department: "One associate professor told me that he wouldn't feel comfortable having me around until he understood that I wouldn't be making as much money as I made as provost. He wanted to make sure that I didn't take up an office or a future faculty line." The directness of Emma's colleague revealed that some faculty members might harbor deep mistrust and find it difficult to accept a former administrator as a true faculty peer. Emma's colleague dismissed her as a drain on resources and a burden on the department. Returning to the faculty can give former administrators cause to exercise the skills honed in positions of senior leadership: smile politely, give an evasive remark, use humor to break the tension, and resist getting baited into an argument.

Strategy 2: Anticipating and Navigating the Factors That Exacerbate Role Confusion

There appear to be certain circumstances—many beyond an individual's control—that can make it harder to return to the faculty. My data analysis revealed that women leaders were more likely to report experiencing role or status confusion than their male counterparts were. This is consistent with the findings of the study conducted by Luna and Medina.[2] The examples in the previous section underscore some differences that follow the gender line. For instance, women often recounted exchanges marked by hostility and skepticism. While Sid's colleagues enjoyed a lighthearted laugh upon mistakenly referring to him as a dean, Emma was confronted by a (male) colleague who told her that he was not "comfortable having her around." To be clear, not all women felt this way, but many of them did. Not all men were spared their colleagues' wrath, proving that there is no shortage of equal-opportunity jerks.

As a woman of color, Rita felt that both her gender and her race complicated her efforts to integrate into the faculty at a public university. While serving in her administrative role, Rita said she felt "very lonely and isolated—very, very lonely." While many senior academic leaders also reported feeling lonely, Rita's experiences took on a unique quality. Here is an example of how a male participant (Roger) described the loneliness of being a dean: "It's an exceptionally lonely job, even though every minute of my day was filled with other people. None of the other people were people who had my job or my responsibilities or my worries." Like Roger, Luke felt isolated because his faculty colleagues did not understand the daily work of a chief academic officer and, therefore, could not relate to the struggles he experienced upon returning to the faculty. Their inability to understand only added to Luke's feelings loneliness and isolation: "Faculty members generally have no idea what an administrator does day to day. My faculty colleagues . . . are sure that returning to the faculty is not much of a problem because they don't understand the world the ex-administrator is coming from. They picture resuming a faculty career as seamlessly picking up where one left off. Ex-administrators thus can't count on their colleagues understanding their adjustment challenges, not because they're callous but because they aren't aware of the major differences between administrative and faculty culture." This knowledge gap can exacerbate the tensions of a role change. Even when colleagues tried to see things from Luke's perspective, few could grasp it. With Luke having spent close to twenty years as a provost, returning to his department required him to regain his confidence in the classroom, accept having less influence over policies and priorities, and overcome the learned helplessness that comes from having a capable staff (e.g., calendar management, using the copy machine). Just as Luke and Roger felt that few people on their campuses could appreciate the demands of senior leadership, their challenges went unrecognized.

This brings us back to Rita. While Roger and Luke attributed their loneliness to being the "only one" in a position, Rita's feeling of being othered stemmed from her belief that her colleagues thought she had been given preferential treatment as a woman of color. She believed that some of her colleagues thought that she was unqualified, having only been promoted into a leadership role to enhance the optics of the office. Whereas Rita felt the isolation that comes from responsibility (like Roger) and had to relearn some basic faculty responsibilities (like Luke), these challenges were further compounded by being surrounded by professional colleagues who doubted competence. While Rita's "thick skin" helped her confront this discrimination, there is no doubt that her return to the faculty carried challenges that others were spared.

These differences are pronounced enough that women, people of color, and others who possess marginalized identities might prepare themselves for their faculty status being directly challenged and contested. The strategies described in Collected Wisdom 5 might help ease this strain by signaling and reinforcing one's new role to others. I am hopeful that researchers will continue to investigate how gender, race, and identity impact how leaders see themselves and are seen by others in the workplace.

First Steps **65**

COLLECTED WISDOM 5

Helping Others See You Differently

There are few professional equivalents for "returning to the faculty." The relative novelty of this tradition may puzzle others, including trustees, employees on your campus, students, and your brother-in-law at Thanksgiving dinner.

To overcome the predictable confusion, it will take some work to explain your motivations and clarify your new responsibilities. Here are a few strategies that might help you bridge the knowledge gap:

- *Explain what you are doing.* Be proactive and tell them rather than assume that others share your understanding of what it means to return to the faculty. This can be done through official channels like your farewell speech or through other campus communications, like press releases or an alumni magazine interview. Expect to reinforce these formal announcements with informal follow-ups. Be ready with a joke to deflect comments about your impending "retirement." Before you speak in a campus meeting, offer the disclaimer, "I'm not the dean anymore." Regular, frequent, and brief reminders of your new role will normalize it.
- *Set boundaries.* Disentangling yourself from projects and processes, especially those you are deeply invested in, is tricky. Aim to provide your successor with sufficient support while also scaling back your involvement. Creating hard stops—wrapping up your daily work in time for an afternoon walk or identifying a date when you will no longer be available for consultation—can go a long way to curb any tendencies to overstay your welcome or allow the institution to remain dependent on you.
- *Take yourself out of the mix.* Use your administrative leave to buffer the past and the future. Make yourself scarce during a sabbatical. Limiting your interactions with campus colleagues during this time affords everyone an adjustment period.
- *Change how you dress.* Faculty might be inclined to see you as a peer if you ditch the suits, ties, and corporate heels. Plus, wearing comfortable shoes is perhaps the best-earned perk of faculty life.
- *Let it go.* Queen Elsa from the enormously popular Disney film *Frozen* got it right: "Let It Go." It is exhausting, if not futile, to try to correct every falsehood or misconception. Rumors will fly. Fight the battles worth fighting. Let the little ones go. Some people may never fully understand what you are doing or why you are doing it.

Strategy 3: Maximizing the Factors That Alleviate Role Confusion

Senior leaders identified aspects of their campus structures and cultures that eased the strain of role and status confusion. When a leader is fortunate enough to benefit from these conditions, they should use them to their advantage. The size of an institution will impact a leader's trajectory. At a small- to medium-size institution, a provost, dean, or president is likely to interact with faculty members frequently. At a small institution, a provost or dean senior leader might counsel department chairs about personnel matters, interact with faculty on university committees, or socialize with faculty and staff at receptions. At larger institutions, opportunities for routine interaction are more seldom. When Penelope, a former provost at a large public institution, returned to her department, she felt that the institutional context complicated her return in some respects but made it easier in others. We spoke a few weeks after she completed a sabbatical and resumed teaching again. Now that she was using her campus office regularly, she interacted with her faculty colleagues frequently. She described those interactions this way: "They don't know me from Adam! Honestly, it's really funny. [With one or two exceptions] the rest of them, I barely know. I'm sure they're thinking, 'Well, who is this woman who used to send me emails? Wow, this is weird.'" Penelope found herself entering a department as a stranger, more or less. While many of her faculty colleagues knew her name from emails, they did not know her as a scholar or much about her as a person. This dynamic meant two things. First, she had to work to establish relationships; she had to share information about herself and allow others to get to know her. Second, she was afforded a high degree of anonymity, meaning that if she wanted to remain peripheral, she could. In other words, she had a choice about whether to become involved in the culture of the department.

By contrast, a leader in a small institution—especially one who had spent decades working as a professor before stepping into an administrative role—has arguably less freedom to make a clean start. Past relationships and familiarity can make some aspects of reentry easier; the ex-leader will have the benefit of some friends and a lot of acquaintances. At the same time, in a small place, a well-known leader may find it hard to distance themselves from lingering grudges or hurt feelings. Depending on the kind of faculty member you want to be at this point in your career, either familiarity or anonymity might be better matched to your desired outcomes. Additional information on how the insider/outsider dynamic impacts a return to the faculty can be found in Collected Wisdom 12 (in chapter 5).

Institutional culture is another factor that exacerbates or dampens role and status confusion. One former law school dean in the study felt confident about his prospects of reintegrating within the social order of his school because of how he and his colleagues related to one another. He explained, "I think that they will see me as a peer. . . . I think that's how they view me now. I think that's very typical of law schools. We tend to be very, I think, collegial and not hierarchical kinds of places. I think that they will view me as just a colleague. That's effectively, I think, how many view me [as a dean]: just as a colleague who has access to money." The nonhierarchical culture might be common among law schools or specific to this one institution. The larger takeaway is the same: institutions with less formal and flat structures are more suited to reintegration than are those with more calcified hierarchies.

The nature of the department a former leader returns to can also impact the degree of role and status confusion they experience. Upon stepping away from being the provost at a large, public research institution, Grace found it beneficial that her faculty line was housed in an interdisciplinary research center. Not only did this arrangement better suit her intellectual interests, but the fact that the center was relatively new offered added benefits. The center's affiliated faculty "haven't formed much of a culture that would resist anything new coming in or going out." Grace felt optimistic that she would be more readily welcomed and accepted in a new interdisciplinary center rather than a traditional department, where established relationships and norms might be hostile to an outsider's arrival. Other dynamics might play a role in how easily a former administrator is accepted into a department: the ratio of tenured to untenured faculty members, whether the culture is competitive or collegial, or whether the department is sufficiently resourced to support faculty needs. Some departments will prove to be softer places to land than others. Collected Wisdom 13 (in chapter 5) and Collected Wisdom 16 (in chapter 6) identify some questions and considerations that can make your arrival as undisruptive as possible.

Ashley expected that the nature of her administrative role at a small private college would mitigate against status confusion. She recounted to me some advice from a colleague who formerly served as dean of the faculty; while his advice helped her prepare for her upcoming role change, she contrasted his experiences and the ones she anticipated for her future: "[My colleague] always calls himself a 'recovering dean.' The deanliness never washes off. . . . I don't necessarily feel that way because this role I was in was so new—it's not like I was a dean or something that's more defined. This role was kind of fluid, I guess. Yeah, I won't feel that way. I feel like the 'associate vice president-ness' will wash off. . . . These kinds of roles, associate vice president, I think are a bit more ambiguous than a dean or a vice president, a provost." Ever an optimist, Ashley anticipated that her impending transition would be eased both by what she saw as the "fluidness" of her role (somewhere between faculty member and senior leader) and by only having served in the role for a short time (less than five years). She posited that these considerations would make it easier for her to return to the faculty compared to her former dean.

In the end, the jury is deadlocked on whether role and status confusion ever fully dissipate upon stepping away from a position of academic leadership. Echoes of these early conversations about belonging continued to surface in former administrators' ongoing interactions with campus peers. A leader's ability to "wash off the deanliness" (indeed, even if they want to wash it off) is determined by how successfully they engage Microprocess 5: *becoming reacquainted* (to be addressed in chapter 4).

Putting It into Practice

In deciding to return to the faculty, a senior academic leader encounters profound questions: *Should I continue to serve in this administrative role? Should I pursue new professional challenges beyond this university? What kind of faculty member do I want to be at this point in my career? How can I explain what I am doing in a way that others will understand?* Depending on how an administrator answers these questions, the period of discernment might be quick and easy. For those who need to step back and evaluate their options, these processes can feel protracted or even unresolved.

Table 3.1. Strategies to Navigate Early Challenges

Microprocess	Useful strategies
Imagining parallel futures: Formulating goals and expectations for life "after" administration	*Embracing plans to stay:* Welcoming opportunities to return to teaching, resume research, and immerse yourselves in personal and professional communities.
	Actively pursuing alternative opportunities: Applying for other jobs and working with a headhunter can provide an academic leader with the kind of challenges they find most rewarding..
	Achieving clarity by examining choices: Actively pursuing other positions can be an important step in the discernment process.
	Delaying decisions about the future: Returning to the faculty in the short-term need not prevent you from considering other positions and administrative opportunities in the future.
Experiencing role and status confusion: No one quite knows what to make of an administrator who returns to the faculty	*Coming to terms with who you are now:* Defining what returning to the faculty means to you is often necessary before you try and explain it to others.
	Anticipating and navigating the factors that exacerbate role confusion: Like it or not, some circumstances can make it harder to return to the faculty. Try to anticipate and limit the impact of these factors if and when you can.
	Maximizing the factors that alleviate role confusion: Some circumstances reduce role and status confusion—use these to your advantage if and when you can.

CHAPTER 4

The Messy Middle

Making a Transition Is Making Choices

During an episode of the *Unlocking Us* podcast, the researcher and best-selling author Brené Brown described a concept she called "day two." The episode aired in September 2020—roughly six months into the COVID-19 pandemic—a fraught time when the prospect of mass vaccination felt impossibly far off, tensions ran high amid protests following the murder of George Floyd, and daily news coverage was dominated by the upcoming presidential election. The episode centered on the pervasive feeling of angst, impatience, and exhaustion felt by many Americans in that moment. Brown drew a parallel between her assessment of the nation's collective consciousness and something she had observed from delivering three-day intensive professional development workshops. Brown explained that the challenging content of the workshop's second day always coincided with a wave of fatigue for both workshop leaders and participants. Whereas day one was marked by excitement, by day two, everything became "dulled. And now you're in kind of this dense fog where you don't have the shiny possibility of day one or the running toward the finish line of day three. . . . The middle is messy, but it's also where the magic happens, all the tension that creates goodness and learning. There's interesting research that says, 'If learning is not uncomfortable, you're not really learning.' Like this is the seat of discomfort, is in day two."[1] Whether the metaphoric "day two" is contained to a twenty-four-hour period or the plodding discomfort extends over multiple days and weeks, for Brown, none of us achieve the sense of resolution that comes on day three without confronting the resistance, avoidance, and uncertainty of day two. The football legend John Madden put it this way in an offhanded remark: "the road to easy street goes through the sewer."

Brown's characterization of the "messy middle" is a good shorthand for the three microprocesses that constitute the bulk of the work of returning to the faculty: *experiencing and using time differently, reinventing the self,* and *becoming reacquainted.* These processes are set into motion upon exiting an administrative role—coinciding with the start of an administrative leave or surfacing post-sabbatical when an ex-leader resumes full-time teaching. This portion of the process is rich with opportunities for administrators to think and act differently and to give them cause to practice becoming a faculty member again and anew. Within the larger contours of the Stepping Away Model, these three microprocesses occur in the temporal middle. Yet, each microprocess also has its own beginning, middle, and end. Each often starts with feelings of novelty, experiment, and excitement (Brown's day one), moves into a messy middle (day two), and eventually arrives at a sense of fulfillment and accomplishment (day three).

What strategies does Brown offer to help people navigating the emotional turmoil of "day two"? She proposes that individuals "name it, normalize it, put it in perspective, and reality check against it."[2] When stuck in the middle, the best way to get unstuck is to describe their feelings, to recognize that these feelings and experiences are neither abnormal nor unique, and to use these insights to guide choices and actions. Different individuals move through social-emotional processes at different paces and arrive—justifiably—at very different destinations. For most former administrators, the middle can stretch on for a year or longer, demanding considerable patience, stamina, and acts of self-kindness.

Stepping away from a position of academic leadership is at its core a process that is shaped by making choices, learning from them, and living with the consequences. Of all the choices that former senior leaders made, those made during this middle period are highly determinative. It can be a delicate dance to renegotiate a relationship to time, which new roles to take up (inside and outside the workplace), and how to signal these changes externally. Indeed, much of the labor of returning to the faculty is bound up in figuring these things out.

COLLECTED WISDOM 6

Identifying, Following, and Breaking the Unwritten Rules

As you reprise your faculty role, some expectations will be easier to anticipate than others. For instance, some specific job-related details may be agreed on during exit negotiations, like the number of courses you will teach, your office or lab location, and salary. Still, former academic leaders report finding it challenging to know what is expected of them during and after the transition.

There is an old adage in boxing: the punch you don't see coming is the one that knocks you out. Giving advance thought to how you might navigate the murkier expectations can help you avoid the blow. Navigating the written and unwritten rules is often an exercise in awareness, improvisation, asking clarifying questions, compliance, and at times, principled resistance.

Engaging with Stakeholders, Donors, and Friends of the University

Some expectations are clear. A former administrator-turned-faculty-member will no longer be expected to prepare a written report for the trustees or attend semiannual meetings. Yet, interacting with trustees, donors, and friends of the university is rarely this clean-cut. Ask yourself,

- What happens if the former president sees a trustee at a social engagement?
- What if a donor calls with a question, a complaint, or gossip?
- What, if any, discussion topics are off-limits with stakeholders like alumni or community partners?
- How will you know whether your behavior is appropriate?
- Should you resign from the boards of all civic organizations and nonprofits? After stepping away, to what extent do you continue to represent the university when acting as an engaged private citizen?

The Power of Precedent

Many former administrators I interviewed found that the "unwritten rules" on their campus were heavily influenced by local precedent. If your predecessor did something one way, members of your campus community would assume this to be the default. For example, if a former president opted to attend departmental meetings, your colleagues may expect the same from you. There is no reason to assume that leaders are obligated to follow their predecessors' footsteps, but it will take intentional effort to interrupt past practices. Ask yourself,

- Are there specific ways you wish to emulate your predecessor?
- How will you let others know that you will do things your own way?

- How might you learn about the full range of options open to you?
- How will you weigh your preferences against the needs of others?

Service Is a Minefield

Conversations with dozens of former administrators led me to conclude that service expectations are especially challenging to decode. There is a healthy tension here. On the one hand, many former administrators recognize that as faculty members, they share some responsibility for helping the college fulfill its mission through committee service (and in some cases, their new contracts demand it). On the other, they worry that service might be viewed as a desperate grasp for power or prevent another from gaining valuable leadership experience. Rather than general principles, your minefield is probably best navigated in light of the nature of your university's governance structure and your circumstances. A few questions that might better prepare you to make these assessments include the following:

- Are there committees on which you should not serve (e.g., promotion and tenure, senate)?
- Are there committees that might benefit from your administratively derived knowledge, skills, or relationships (e.g., alumni board, IRB, the university press)?
- If and when you participate in campus service, where should you sit, and when should you speak?
- Is it appropriate for you to serve in a leadership role on a committee, in a department, or in a college or school? Whom might you consult before agreeing to be a chair? Who gets to decide?

Microprocess 3: Experiencing and Using Time Differently

A majority of participants in this study were eager to discuss how returning to the faculty altered their sense of time. Stepping away often results in a jarring shift: one day is highly structured and demanding, and the next is relatively open and self-determined. Former president Randy said that such a change gave him "withdrawal pains." With this change came an equally dramatic shift in where and how former leaders spent their time. For the most part, participants welcomed these changes: they engaged a variety of coping strategies to align their time with new and evolving goals. In rare cases, major life events, such as being diagnosed with a serious illness, impacted how former leaders experienced time.

When I asked participants to describe how their lives changed upon concluding an administrative appointment, nearly all pointed to their schedules. Most traded days of constant meetings for an unencumbered year of administrative leave. Participants told me that as leaders they regularly worked between seventy and ninety hours per week between campus commitments, required attendance at evening and weekend events, business travel, and answering email. When summarizing a typical week as a provost at a public university, Betsy explained, "Last week, every day I came in at 6:30 a.m., and not one night did I get home before 10 p.m. because I had dinners, I had meetings, I had rallies. During that week, I had forty-one meetings scheduled on my calendar." While some participants also had significant fund-raising and friend-raising responsibilities that demanded considerable travel, Betsy's description is largely representative of what I heard from all participants. Sam, a former dean who was on the verge of beginning a sabbatical when we first spoke, told me that she most "looked forward to" getting off "the thirty-hours-of-meetings-per-week treadmill." Having fewer scheduled commitments was one of most appealing parts of stepping away for the administrators I consulted in my research.

Not only did the volume of meetings take its toll, but many leaders also grew to resent the obligations foisted on them. One of Mildred's least favorite parts of being an administrator was the "loss of autonomy and especially the loss of time autonomy." When serving as an associate provost, Horace often felt like "the day was laid out" for him, and he "just had to sort of put out the fire." Kevin, a former provost at a private university, explained that he learned to cope with the lack of control over his time. Rather than resist, Kevin learned to accept it: "You have no choice of what you do. You are driven by your calendar. I got very good at it, so I wouldn't know what I was going to do the next day, but I would get up in the morning and look at it and say, 'Oh, okay, here's what I'm doing today.'" Their schedules meant that Kevin and Horace rarely had the luxury of looking ahead or planning how to use their time; they were left to react to the task immediately before them or attend the meetings that appeared on their calendars. Going on sabbatical brought some immediate relief to Kevin's calendar, but it also introduced new challenges, namely: "You go from where you're constantly driven by your calendar to having a calendar that's entirely open. You're back in the old faculty mode, where you're figuring out yourself what you're going to do and what you are going accomplish that day. It's remarkably difficult to make that transition."

Strategy 1: Breaking the Cycle

Facing the prospect of a completely open schedule, participants often expressed a sense of relief tinged with angst about beginning an academic leave. Steve, the former chief academic officer at a private university, described his anxieties: "I'm discovering that I'm really having to structure my time to make certain that I'm just not blowing off all this time and frivoling it away. I am not used to not having a load of stuff in front of me that has no deadline." Serving as an administrator pressured Steve to keep up with a high volume of work, but the unstructured nature of a sabbatical tested his resolve to be productive. Steve admitted that he had not yet learned to guard his newfound time; rather than focus on his priority projects, he found himself accepting invitations to meet with his successor and was prone to losing track of time.

Noting how often exhaustion and lack of control surfaced in conversations with former administrators, several study participants had high hopes that sabbatical would cure their burnout and mounting resentment. For many, reducing their responsibilities did indeed bring immediate relief. While welcome, relief alone often proved insufficient to teach a former leader how to apportion their time as a faculty member. Judy explained how sabbatical helped her transition from provost to faculty member:

> I think it's important to have a sabbatical break to just decompress, to get all of the nonsense out of your head—you know, the people that have been niggling at you—and to finally get them out of your mind. It takes a while to get back into thinking about whether you're writing a book, whether you're doing research, whatever it may be, that's going to be your principal thing that you do for the next few months. It takes a while to wrap your mind around that and really absorb it and work it through. I think it is important to have the sabbatical, and I think it's important that at the end of that sabbatical, it be a little bit like with junior faculty first coming in, that there's a bit of slack for that first semester before you become a full-time and fully contributing member.

Judy explained that change was not automatic; the onus is on the individual to guide the process: "Different people will respond differently. Some can just switch from one to the other, but I think most people will need that transition time because it is a different world. Depending on how difficult the circumstances were—if somebody was stepping down without lots of bouquets and parties and things but where they're kind of 'you're out'— then that's very hard." For Judy, sabbatical provided a buffer to help her, as an ex-leader, move between "the different worlds" of faculty and administration. She found that sabbatical had therapeutic benefits because it gave her time to clear her head.

Strategy 2: Transferring Energy into the Next Thing

While some participants gave themselves generous space to adjust to a new way of being, others continued to structure their time rigidly after stepping away from an administrative role. Ralph found that writing a book was a "good virtual placeholder for the presidency," as it consumed the totality of his waking moments. Paul, a former provost at a public institution, also adopted a highly structured daily routine centered on research. He found the initial adjustment between his academic calendar and the freedom of sabbatical jarring: "My life has been lived in ten- or fifteen-minute increments for twenty years. Can I sit down at my desk, and my Outlook calendar says, 'from 9:00 a.m. to 5:00 p.m.: Write Book'? And I mean, that's terrifying. But so far, I wouldn't say I've mastered it, but it's better than I feared that it might be." While Paul was still adjusting to having blocks of uninterrupted time, he found that keeping a set daily routine where he worked full-time was integral to his success.

Emma was one of the few participants in the study who elected to delay taking an administrative leave upon completing her provostship at a private institution. Immediately upon leaving office, she shifted to a part-time schedule for one semester: she taught one course and scheduled designated blocks of time to onboard her successor. This arrangement appealed to Emma because she preferred to take her transition more gradually. This schedule allowed her to wind down her professional responsibilities, ramp up her teaching, apprise herself of contemporary debates in her field, and have more time with her family. She explained, "I signed up for a Monday-Wednesday-Friday teaching schedule, which is the opposite of what I would have done in my provost role. I like to stretch out the shorter class periods but across more days. I think I'm looking for ways to help me manage the strangeness of time." Emma sought to avoid the abruptness of going from an all-consuming administrative appointment directly into a sabbatical. Enjoying the freedom of a part-time schedule, she worked to make sense of what she called "the strangeness of time." After one semester of this schedule, she took a leave, during which she fully stepped away from the university. She reflected that she was more productive during her sabbatical because her part-time semester allowed her to shake off some of her administrative stress and begin to adjust to being a faculty member again. While most participants found it advantageous to take a leave immediately upon leaving their offices, Emma's more gradual withdrawal shows how a scaffolded exit can be a good alternative.

Trying to identify the best schedule for a former senior academic leader is essentially a chicken-or-egg problem. Self-selection comes into play. The kind of faculty members who find that they need uninterrupted blocks of time to do their best writing and thinking would be least inclined to voluntarily step into an administrative role. But those who are wired to excel under busy, highly structured, deadline-driven conditions that demand the ability to multitask might be drawn to leadership positions in which such skills are prized. People who identify with the second camp might see limited value in changing their daily routines despite stepping away from a leadership role. Former dean Nancy told me that she spent the first few days of her sabbatical sitting on her porch reading a mystery novel. Upon finishing the book, she said to herself, half jokingly, "Okay, that was fun. Now it's time to get back to work." When I reconnected with Sam—the former dean who described wanting to get off the "treadmill" of constant meetings—she told me that, after her sabbatical, she was (happily) putting in long days managing a team carrying out an ambitious new research study. While her calendar was almost as busy as when she was a dean, Sam did not mind because she was on a treadmill of her own choosing.

Strategy 3: Attending to Self and Others

Stepping away from academic leadership can present the opportunity to pay more attention to one's physical and mental health or invest in personal relationships. Multiple participants explained that their health improved upon stepping down from their administrative positions. The relative flexibility of their faculty schedule allowed them to make positive lifestyle changes, like exercising more and eating healthier. Several participants lost weight and reported that they slept better. Nearly all reported that they felt less stressed, had more energy, and felt more present when interacting with others.

Several leaders found that their administrative responsibilities made it impossible to unplug. Steve, a former chief academic officer at a private university, compared the vacation he took during his sabbatical with previous trips:

> We went on a vacation just recently to the beach. It was the first time I had done that in years in which I didn't feel as though there was this gnawing in the back of my mind of things that needed to be done or emails that needed checking. Literally, every vacation, I'd have to carve out an hour or

two hours every morning [to read emails or talk to a member of his staff]. Whether you're on vacation or not, [as an administrator] you just have to deal with these things. [This time] I didn't have to do that. It was just a wonderful experience.

Steve's experience is representative. Stepping away allows former leaders to clear their minds, enjoy their leisure time, and relax.

Not only does stepping away from an administrative role change how a former leader experiences time, but many of the benefits extended to the members of their household. Upon stepping down as president of a public university, Ted noticed immediate changes: "The presidential position is clearly a 24/7, 120 percent speed position all the time for both myself and my spouse. You're in the public light constantly, and that's certainly not the case as a faculty member. You know, that's kind of a nice change, actually. I'm not talking to the press. I don't need to go out and talk to legislators, things like that. It's quite a different lifestyle—very busy but far, far, far less of a public life for both of us than it was before." Stepping down from his executive role not only gave Ted the freedom to resume teaching and delivered relief from an unrelenting schedule but also provided a level of privacy that he and his spouse rarely enjoyed previously.

It is not only that ex-leaders and their families have more time for themselves but also that their experience of time is fundamentally different. Returning to the faculty allowed many participants to reconnect with their spouses. For Wesley, the freedom of a sabbatical paired with the flexibility of his teaching schedule afforded him the opportunity to spend more quality time with his wife. He explained, "There's a dimension added to our lives that we didn't have time for because we had busy jobs because we are raising kids, etcetera." Former dean Roger appreciated that exiting the deanship gave him more time with his high-school-aged children; he knew "the window was closing" before they left for college. Former provost William captured it nicely: "The biggest change has been going from a highly structured and highly scheduled life to one that is fairly unstructured and fairly unscheduled. It means that I actually have more opportunities to gather with friends and more opportunities to do the sorts of things around the house that we let go for eight years. I get to take on projects of my own choosing and not projects that are of necessity to the institution." William's experience underscores how multiple factors related to time converged—a less structured schedule, regaining personal autonomy, and reconnecting with his spouse—and added up to significant changes. It sometimes takes stepping away from a big job for leaders to recognize just how neglectful they had become in other domains of life.

Strategy 4: Reprioritizing

Life factors, especially those that are unforeseen or tragic, can magnify the disorientation of returning to the faculty. Sobering crises prompted some study participants to make significant choices. Five participants in the study (roughly 10 percent) told me that their return to the faculty coincided with the death of a parent. Not only did these losses bring about feelings of grief and practical responsibilities, but they were instrumental in leading many former administrators to (re)prioritize their goals. The death of Ashley's father was one of many factors that led her to step away from her associate dean role at a small private university. While she had once envisioned staying in her administrative role for a second term, her father's death made her reevaluate this plan. She explained, "I want my nine-month contract back because I want my summers. I want to spend time with my mom while I can." Familial considerations convinced Ashely to step away from her administrative role and increased the value of having greater autonomy over her time.

Several participants in the study disclosed having been diagnosed and treated for serious illnesses. Dealing with an unexpected health crisis prompted participants to shift their priorities, sometimes prompting them to delay, abandon, or reframe professional goals. When I first spoke with Robin at the start of his academic sabbatical, he told me he planned to "work for a few more years." We talked about some of the classes he was preparing and the challenges of reviving a dormant research agenda after devoting his full energies to the provostship. When I checked in with him a few months later to clarify some points from our initial interview, he told me that he had been diagnosed with an aggressive form of cancer. This prompted Robin to accelerate his retirement: "My decision to retire was partly based on health. If I weigh all of the things that I'd like to do or I have time available to do, I feel like I've accomplished most of what I want to do as a professor. It's not like I have other kinds of hobbies or other things I want to devote myself to. It's more being able to focus on the things that matter most." Of course, a personal health crisis or the death of a loved one need not be part of stepping away from an administrative role, but participants discussed these matters with such frequency that it is important to recognize their potential impact. When they co-occur, these milestone events of midlife become entwined with professional role change. Institutions can do little to guard against the risk that a leader will cut their administrative service short should their personal circumstances change.

Bill had an unusually tragic few years, capped off by being told that the administrative role in the provost's office that brought him so much satisfaction was being eliminated. He explained, "There just has been a lot going on.

My mother died a month ago; [my spouse and I] lost three parents in the last fifteen months. My involuntary change of job. Our dog died just before Christmas. And my cancer diagnosis and a surgery. There's a lot that has been going on. That is kind of mixed up in this [time of change], too. . . . It's all part of the swirl." Being in a "swirl" of different emotions and challenges, Bill was committed to finding a silver lining. He shared his plans: "I will take the year to think about what I want to do. . . . There might be some opportunity to look for other positions if I want to. I wasn't going to make that decision quickly. I'll take this year to think about what I wanted to be when I grew up." Setting aside for a moment the personal anguish and grief that Bill experienced in the concentrated span of a few months, it appears that the confluence of transitions prompted him to reflect on his goals in a more significant way. Had these losses happened in isolation, perhaps he might not have undertaken such a deep examination.

Another participant—who shared details about a recent medical diagnosis under the provision of complete confidentiality—explained how experiencing two major life events simultaneously intensified the challenges of adjusting. The participant explained how strange it felt returning to faculty spaces. Not only did they experience the lingering "gauze" of otherness that some described, but the illness also only added to the awkwardness of returning. "I still feel a little bit under the looking glass—not a lot, but just a little bit. I think that will dissipate over time. Part of the reason is also because people know I've been ill. They are often looking at me just to see how I'm doing. People have been really kind and generous in dealing with me. Again, the two things have sort of become intertwined and influenced each other." Many people, both in the study and in other domains of life, who have undergone treatment for a serious disease have told me how much they dread interactions with those who do not know what to say. When stepping away is prompted by or accompanies a health crisis, it is impossible to disentangle where one identity change begins and another ends. Though when the trials of midlife intersect with workplace transitions, the combination may prompt a person to reprioritize how they use their time and energy.

80 STEPPING AWAY

COLLECTED WISDOM 7

When Transitions Collide

For too many senior academic leaders, their administrative exit is prompted by or coincides with another major life event, such as the death of a parent, a significant illness, moving house, or the retirement of a spouse. In ordinary circumstances, stepping away from administrative duties carries its own challenging mélange of adjustment, relief, and in some cases, grief. When a professional transition unfolds alongside another significant midlife event, the resulting disorientation is likely to be amplified. Concurrent life transitions might result in moments of clarity, but unfortunately, these insights might come at an inconvenient time. When difficult transitions in work and life collide, getting through the day can be cause enough for celebration.

In Your Own Time

One immediate benefit of resuming a faculty role is that your calendar will be more flexible and self-determined. The ability to apportion your time and attention is a small mercy during life's hard seasons. Concentrating your teaching to a few days a week can make it easier to schedule medical appointments or to flex your schedule around the needs of an ailing parent. Be grateful that capable hands are guiding the ship now, and you can detach from work.

Embracing "For Now"

When my father died, one of the most helpful things I learned from a grief counselor was the power of the phrase "for now." For example, "we're not making any decisions about selling the house, for now," or "for now, our family will not celebrate our usual holiday traditions." More than a phrase, I came to value "for now" as permission to declare a moratorium on making consequential decisions until I was better positioned to make them. When the big, somewhat impolite questions came—and they did, often more quickly than expected—answering with "for now" allowed me the gift of being noncommittal. When my family was ready to make decisions, we did. Until then and as long as we needed it, we always had "for now."

Will This Ever End?

One of the greatest frustrations of any major life transition is the pace. Few of us have the patience or energy to dwell in liminal spaces for a few days, let alone a year or more. Concurrent transitions can extend feelings of unsettledness. Days can feel like an exhausting blur where little to nothing was accomplished, at least in the traditional sense. Sadly, acknowledging that the interplay of complicating circumstances will further delay a return to normalcy does not make it easier to endure the time. Still, sometimes, acknowledging your impatience makes it easier to wade through the muck.

Perspective

For all the tumult brought by major life events—such as the death of a parent or a cancer diagnosis—they often come carrying the gift of perspective. Attending to the urgent needs of yourself or others can blot out petty concerns and minor anxieties. Should you find yourself in an unenviable position of managing multiple transitions at once, one small upside is that you might spare yourself the unwarranted energy spent worrying about trivialities.

"You Are a Different Person Now"

In chapter 1, I quoted advice from Ron Ehrenberg, formerly of Cornell University, who says, when returning to the faculty after an administrative tour of duty, "remember that your administrative experience has fundamentally changed you; you are a different person and you have to do different things."* The same is true for any major life transition; cancer survivors and the recently bereaved often acquire a new sense of self that impacts how they move through the world. Embrace how these experiences have changed you.

---

* Ehrenberg, "Being a Quadruple Threat Keeps It Interesting," 18.

Microprocess 4: Reinventing the Self

More than half of the leaders I interviewed portrayed themselves as becoming "new versions" of their faculty selves. Although few went so far as to say that they had become a wholly new person, role change promoted a significant adoption of new habits, behaviors, perspectives, identities, and conceptions of self. Returning to the faculty enables leaders to blend aspects of their pasts with emerging interests; these couplings often result in vibrant and inventive combinations.

Degrees of Change

The concept of reinvention was familiar to senior academic leaders. In talking about how they made sense of returning to the faculty, many drew explicit comparisons to how becoming an administrator prompted them to become a new version of themselves. Stepping into a position of senior leadership entails reformulating how you see yourself and how others see you. The scholarly literature about administrative transitions maintains that while faculty colleagues might accuse a leader of "going to the dark side," administrators rarely see themselves as turncoats. Many believe that they retain their faculty identity, augmenting it with administrative responsibility.[3] The degree to which a senior leader continues to see themselves as a faculty member—and the extent to which they continue to be involved in the faculty pursuits of teaching and research—has repercussions later. In other words, leaders who continue to identify with the work and roles of a faculty member have a smaller gulf to traverse than those who commit fully to being an administrator.

There are many ways to keep a faculty identity alive. Despite working as a chief academic officer, Stuart maintained an active research laboratory and steady external funding. Despite the considerable demands of being a university president, Ted stoked the intellectual fires by staying apprised of the current debates in his discipline. While serving as a chief academic officer at a private college, Norm attended social gatherings hosted by his department and other faculty colleagues; in such settings, he let his guard down and presented himself as a colleague (rather than an official representative of "the administration"). Leaders who maintained a strong connection to their faculty selves—doing the work of a faculty member or maintaining faculty relationships—were likely to characterize their reinvention as less dramatic than were participants who had given themselves over to the demands of a senior role.

Just as some administrators brought their faculty identities and perspectives into their leadership roles, many took skills and insights from their administrative roles with them into their reprised faculty roles. Penelope described herself as a "different person" after being a provost, noting that the personal growth and learning she experienced was "transformational." Although Horace served in a senior leadership capacity for a relatively short time, he recognized how profoundly he was changed by a one-year interim appointment as an associate provost at a private institution. He explained that he had already acquired a "different perspective": "The things I really liked about being an administrator: working with other people, collaboration, even just having meetings. . . . My [academic] discipline is extremely solitary, and so I'm sort of curious about going back into the work and trying to think of ways to both honor the parts of the work that just have to be solitary. What are the ways in which I can kind of enact a little bit more of that collaboration mind-set into my everyday work life?" Upon returning to the faculty, Horace planned to actively seek out more opportunities for collaboration to achieve the best of both worlds.

For Mildred, the greatest challenge of returning to the faculty was resuming a role that demanded different things from her than her administrative job. Mildred approached returning to the faculty as a true *return*, in that she felt she preserved her faculty identity throughout her administrative service. While her core sense of self remained stable, she noticed perceptible shifts: "I feel like I'm a different kind of faculty member now." She continued, "in some ways, that [leadership] experience is still with me, or it sort of informs who I am in this professor role, in a way." Bill also noticed how he had changed: "I am a faculty member with a different kind of experience set," continuing, "A different lens is what I mean." Many other participants also portrayed themselves as having a "different lens." These participants often said that an administrative role equipped them to see the bigger picture. Former provost Isabel noted how leadership changed her; after seeing how the university functions, she stated, "You can't *unsee* it. Once you know it, you can't go back." In stepping away, participants like Bill, Mildred, and Isabel struggled to connect with their faculty peers who had a narrower or, to use former provost William's phrase, more "parochial view." They had no choice but to adapt.

Strategy 1: Developing a New Scholarly Identity

Participants often expressed new dimensions of their "post-leadership" identity through their scholarly projects. Some reaffirmed long-established identities, while others built new ones. Some forms of scholarship that ex-leaders engage in include (a) publishing original research in their academic discipline; (b) contributing to their academic discipline in other ways; (c) publishing about higher education; (d) cultivating an identity as a public intellectual; and (e) engaging in little to no scholarly activity.

About a third of study participants expressed an intent to publish in their academic discipline. A few participants remained productive scholars throughout their administrative appointment. For example, Stuart, a former provost at a public institution, stood out for having maintained continuous extramural funding to operate his lab. Returning to the faculty provided him with time to devote greater attention to the research program he had kept simmering across multiple decades of administrative service. For others, returning to the faculty provided the time and space to reignite a dormant scholarly project or return to familiar content and disciplinary methods to begin a new one.

A few participants in the study intended to pursue new forms of scholarship upon returning to the faculty. Former provost Judy decided against publishing in the peer-reviewed journals that had been the mainstay of her work as a professor. Instead, she set to work to produce an open-source textbook for a popular introductory class she regularly taught, making the online resource available for free. The project appealed to Judy as it would make a true contribution to her institution (students could access the material free of charge). The short-term nature of the project was ideal, as it could be completed before her impending retirement. Frank, the outgoing provost of a private college, also drew a distinction between the type of scholarship he did early in his faculty career and the scholarship he did now:

> As I come back for my last decade or so as a professional, I'm going to leave [traditional disciplinary scholarship] behind. I think I've done what I feel I wanted to do there. I'm going to try and move in what is, for me, a kind of radically different direction. . . . I think, in the next phase of my career, rather than doing sort of cultural history, I'm going to be really trying to build my work as an artist. . . . It's a big shift for me. I would say, I have a long way to go in terms of getting any good at it, but I'm also really quite excited by the prospect of it.

While his primary disciplinary training prepared him to analyze literary texts, Frank had become an accomplished amateur artist. He intended to make his art the focus of scholarly activity moving forward. For former provosts Frank and Judy, there was little appeal in doing the same kind of scholarship that they had done earlier in their career. They welcomed the chance to "shift" and redefine the nature of their scholarship after leaving their administrative roles.

The third type of scholarship that participants pursued was the study and practice of academic leadership and writing about contemporary topics in higher education. Participants discussed plans to write books and opinion pieces for venues like the *Chronicle of Higher Education*. Paul, a former provost at a public university, used his sabbatical to write a book about higher education that drew on what he learned as a senior leader. He had not necessarily set out to write this book, but having left his job abruptly after encountering irreconcilable differences with his president, he found himself with (unanticipated) free time. He explained,

> And as I thought about retirement or transitioning into retirement, I thought it would be fun to write another book. I played with various topics. And the PR consultants who advised our campus during a scandal suggested that I leverage [my expertise as a leader]. Being a provost didn't really give me the time to do that. But as I started to think about what next, it occurred to me

that I could really perform a service by writing a book like this that not very many people really were in a position [to write]. . . . I thought, "Why not?" And in addition to the fact that I am surprisingly interested in doing this, it's also therapeutic.

The kind of writing that Paul was doing differed significantly from the disciplinary research he conducted previously. He clarified that he had never written about leadership or for a "mass audience."

Other leaders sought to capitalize on their higher education expertise too. Some former leaders agreed to teach courses about higher education leadership at their universities. These former leaders redirected their energies to share the expertise they developed on the job (such as higher-ed finance or governance). A significant number of participants planned to lead workshops for aspiring leaders or do some consulting to leverage specialized practical knowledge. Recognizing that their status as former leaders afforded them greater visibility, a handful of participants warmed to their new standing as public intellectuals. They sought to build on their national reputations by contributing op-eds intended for nonacademic audiences, writing mass-market books, and appearing on panels and talk shows. Participants often embraced this strategy in conjunction with publishing in an academic discipline or writing about higher education.

Finally, some of the participants in the study did not expect to spend much time or energy doing scholarship or publishing. Although many of these participants had distinguished records of research and had been promoted to the rank of full professor, they were content to let this aspect of their identity go. Faced with the prospect of returning to the faculty, former provost Wesley described his intentions: "I made a very conscious decision not to create a research agenda. I didn't feel that it would be fair to grad students to take them on and explain that I didn't really know the literature because I had been out of a classroom for a dozen years. I didn't want to write grant proposals." Wesley's position is representative of participants who hold terminal degrees in STEM disciplines. For many, the pressures associated with securing external grants was a deterrent against reinvigorating their research programs in the late stages of their careers. Wesley acknowledged that he had lost some currency in his field of study: "It doesn't seem like that's where I should put my energy in the last five years of my career. I think there are people coming out of grad school who will contribute more to the body of knowledge than I will." Since he believed it was futile to try to catch up in research, Wesley structured his contributions accordingly; he volunteered to teach the introductory courses that many of his faculty colleagues deplored teaching.

86 STEPPING AWAY

COLLECTED WISDOM 8

Thoughts on Office Space

You can take the president out of the office, *but where should the former president office?* Academic leadership transitions nearly always involve a physical exit—relocating from one workspace to another. Moving to a new office is, for some, a meaningful representation of their changed place in the university. For others, it is little more than an inconvenient chore.

Almost invariably, your faculty office will be smaller and less august than the one you had as an administrator. Your new space will probably be the physical manifestation of "stepping down."

How you approach your workspace will signify to others how you approach your transition and how you see yourself. Your behavior will speak volumes about your willingness to balance your needs with the needs of others.

If an office is very important to you, then it is advisable to settle the matter as part of your exit negotiations, when you have the most leverage. If the location, square footage, and decor of your new workspace are not a primary concern, it can be advantageous to graciously accept whatever space is offered.

Former academic leaders fall into two camps when it comes to office space:

"Among the People" *Take up residence in a traditional faculty office within the departmental suite*	"Away from the Action" *Occupy an office that is geographically distant from your home department*
• Signal to faculty that you are "one of them" • Be easily accessible to students and colleagues • Prime yourself for informal conversations in the hallway and at the water cooler • Embrace the opportunity to downsize your library and files	• Move into a space befitting your status as a former senior leader • Come and go freely and unnoticed by others • Avoid the awkwardness of displacing someone else by taking their office • Position yourself in a location where it is easy to meet with off-campus stakeholders (e.g., alumni, donors) • Surround yourself with the full inventory of your books and awards

Regardless of *where* a former senior leader's new office is located, they also have choices about *how* to use their workspaces. Some put in full days; others pop in briefly between classes. Keeping the door open or closed sends signals about your willingness to interact with others. If securing your dream office means that others will be displaced or that classrooms or conference rooms are commandeered for your personal use, then ensure that you use that space appropriately. Nothing screams "lousy neighbor" or "clueless ex-administrator" more than demanding a handsome space only to let it sit vacant.

Strategy 2: Adopting New Roles at Home

Participants described how stepping away from their administrative jobs altered their roles in their families. Parents of young children stated that the newfound flexibility in their faculty schedules permitted them to be more involved in their children's lives. Mildred described how stepping away from her position at a private institution allowed her to be "more present" with her children, a change she welcomed. During her administrative tenure, Mildred's spouse played a more active role at home while she put in long hours on campus. Mildred recounted how the change in her work schedule altered things:

> He kind of *held down the fort,* as we called it. He kind of did all the house stuff and all that kind of [domestic] stuff. And so, my younger kids were used to [Dad] doing everything. And I can remember when I went on sabbatical and I got home from campus—I still went over to campus every day—but I got home around maybe 3:45 or 4 o'clock or something. And my youngest, who was probably like a sixth grader or seventh grader at the time, she said—she was talking to [Dad] about, "Oh I need to go . . ." I said, "Oh, I can take you." She looked at me, and she went, "You can?" I was like, "Yeah, I can run you over there." And that for me was sort of an aha moment, where like, "Oh, yeah, I can take my kids places after school." I wasn't coming home at 5:30, 5:45 p.m. or whatever, with [Dad] already having sort of done all that kind of stuff.

While Mildred's primary desire to leave her administrative role was not specifically to enable her to spend more time with her family, she was glad with the result. The new flexibility of her faculty schedule allowed Mildred's family to renegotiate roles and responsibilities in ways that everyone found to be positive.

Mildred's experience stands in contrast to Stuart's. For some added context, Stuart is older than Mildred and had served in senior administration considerably longer. Stuart had maintained a research lab while serving as the provost at a public research-intensive institution. Although most of my conversation with Stuart focused on his career and his professional accomplishments, the end of our interview drifted toward the personal. Looking back, Stuart reflected,

> Just now, I should have said these two things in my *professional* life. I had the *personal* life too. I was a decent father to our grown-up children but not a great father. . . . I think, too often, [I focused on] things in my professional

88 STEPPING AWAY

life. I don't know if it's common or uncommon, but in these really demanding jobs, we had the salary that we could have a traditional nuclear family, traditional roles, and so my wife was involved in much of the child rearing. I experienced the consequences of that and that my grandchildren are much closer to my wife than they are to me. . . . I've tried to address it, but the seeds are sown in spring, and you reap whatever fall gives you. Forty years doesn't change, like, "Well, I'm free on Tuesday nights now, if you want to hang out" kind of thing. That doesn't change as quickly.

Whereas the relative youth of Mildred's children permitted her to take on a new role, Stuart found it much more difficult to make up for lost time. Simply having more time in his post-administrative schedule was insufficient to change the relationships with his adult children. Stuart was not optimistic that such a change was possible. While returning to the faculty can create opportunities for reinvention, these opportunities are bound by the lingering consequences of decisions made decades earlier.

COLLECTED WISDOM 9

You Mean It's *Not* Just about Me?

Even the most well-intentioned and self-aware leaders might benefit from being extra sensitive to limit the adverse effects their return to the faculty will have on the VIPs in their lives.

From Home Rarely to Home *All* the Time

The people in your household have probably managed while you were putting in long days, nights, and weekends on campus. Your new "faculty hours" may result in significant shifts in your presence, availability, and moods. Just because your schedule permits you to be around more often, the former dean of liberal studies at New York University Fred Schwarzbach warned, "to be blunt, your family is used to not having you around, and they may not really want you around *all* the time."*

Seemingly trivial things, like where you work and eat lunch, will impact others. Even if you have frequent and candid conversations with your spouse about your transition, remember that your children could be adjusting to new pickup routines or doing their best to forgive the novice grocery shopper who bought the wrong cereal again.

---

* Schwarzbach, "Back to the Faculty."

Your Former Colleagues Will Feel Your Absence

Should you desire to do so, it will take some thought and care to maintain ties with your "work family." Your former colleagues will probably find themselves adjusting to a new leader and welcome the chance to process that with you. Your team might need a pep talk or some advice from a trusted source if your successor's transition has been a bumpy one.

Working Out New Dynamics

Eventually, after your sabbatical, returning to the faculty will introduce new power differentials, especially with your department head or dean. It can take time and patience to feel one another out as these relationships change. Finding ways to exhibit your deference, support, and understanding will be welcomed warmly.

Here are a few questions to ask yourself (and others) before, during, and after returning to the faculty:

- What do others expect from you? When do they want you around (and when *don't* they)? How often should you revisit these expectations?
- In any transition, some things will change; others may stay the same. What will you *keep* doing and what will you *start* doing and *stop* doing around the house, the department, and the campus?
- Knowing it can take a year or more, to establish new habits and routines, what have you already decided to change? What have you yet to decide? How will you let other people know the difference?
- How will you solicit feedback to help you make course corrections?
- How will you stay in touch with and show your appreciation for those who supported you during and after your administrative career?
- When was the last time you said, "Thank you. It has been a challenging/hard/confusing/self-focused year for me?"

Strategy 3: Modifying Outward Expressions of Identity

After a period of change and personal reinvention, it is common for people to find ways to alter their outward appearance, seeking to make internal shifts perceptible. Some participants reported losing weight, but most former administrators registered their changes by dressing differently. While many participants stated that they innately preferred dressing more casually, they found that a wardrobe change helped reinforce their status as *former* administrators. Luke, a former chief academic officer at a private university, told me that his colleagues often comment about how he looks and seems different now. He said, "They universally say they've never seen me without a tie, and they say they've never seen me so relaxed." Not only did Luke look less like a provost dressed in a polo shirt and sneakers, but his relaxed demeanor made him less recognizable as a stressed-out, overscheduled administrator dashing between meetings. Consciously altering your appearance—your hairstyle, the way you dress, or how you carry yourself—can be an important signifier of internal reinvention.

COLLECTED WISDOM 10

It's a Big Change for Them Too: Advice for Spouses and Families

When an academic leader returns to the faculty, they know that many things in their lives will change: the work that fills their time, the clothes they wear, and in some cases, where they live. The changes can be equally profound for their spouses and family members.

Offer Support, Acknowledge Your Needs

As your spouse, parent, or partner concludes their service in preparation to return to the faculty, you can expect a lot of extra attention. For most "first ladies" and "second gents," all those years of hosting receptions, making small talk with strangers, and managing a busy social calendar will have prepared you for the gauntlet of farewell receptions.

Life after administration is likely to feel less familiar. It's reasonable to assume that you might feel lost or left out, not having to play ringleader to a circus of events and personalities. Adapting to the contours of a new schedule—one that will undoubtedly include fewer scheduled commitments—will be an adjustment. Some spouses delight in returning to a quiet, anonymous life. Some extroverts feel undersocialized and unfulfilled after years of being in the mix. It is also possible that you will feel surprised by your feelings. Acknowledging your perspectives will help you begin to build a new fulfilling routine.

Take a Well-Deserved Break

Almost all the senior leaders I talked to agree on one thing: the first chance you get, take a vacation. For some, this was the first "real," restful, away-from-it-all vacation they had taken in years. A vacation offers the perfect buffer between one chapter and the next. Ideally, the sooner you can leave, the better. Remember, spouses, you've earned this break too.

Allow Things to Change

As your spouse steps away from their senior role, expect that many things will change at home over the next two years—and sometimes change and change again.

Grant everyone in your household some extra grace as things settle down. Part of this process will include you trying out new habits and routines—some will stick, some won't. Another skill you will practice is delegating the chores and responsibilities that former-leader-in-residence might take on (and if you don't give them something to do, they'll probably make a mess of something you'd rather they stay out of). Recognizing that this transition period is temporary will serve you well.

Maintain the Connections You Want, from Afar
It can be helpful to discuss how you and your spouse will continue to connect with your former campus. A fundamental component of stepping away from a position of leadership is the being away part. Unfortunately, this might also include being away from things you truly loved—like rooting on the basketball team, interacting with student leaders, and forming strong bonds with faculty members, other campus leaders and their partners, and members of the facilities staff. You may find that the worst part of stepping away is creating distance from cherished communities.

In my own career, I formed strong bonds with the spouses of the vice presidents I worked under. And I am pleased that we have continued those relationships after their spouses retired or returned to the faculty. I enjoy meeting them for lunch and catching up on our birthdays. I am genuinely grateful that we have stayed active in each other's lives.

Build New Traditions
For the families of senior academic leaders—especially the children who spent formative years living in a campus-owned residence—leaving campus is leaving "home." As you celebrate holidays and life milestones in a new house, take care to establish new traditions and memories, too. It can be nice to visit the campus as a family from time to time.

Find New Outlets
Now that your life does not orbit around a college, you can channel your time and energy in new ways. This slack might be well invested in your career, volunteer service, travel, hobbies, or grandchildren. Upon returning to the faculty, many former academic leaders embrace the sense of reinvention that comes with this phase of their lives. I hope you can find equally rewarding pursuits for yourself.

Share What You've Learned
Should you choose, you might extend an invitation to your university's new "first spouse" to join you for a lunch or coffee. They are probably experiencing a transition and would appreciate the advice, discretion, and understanding of a friend who intimately knows the responsibilities they are coming to inhabit.

Microprocess 5: Becoming Reacquainted

Stepping away affords administrators a chance to try on new routines, habits, and roles. These experiments can begin during a sabbatical leave and continue into the first few semesters of full-time faculty work. Mildred charted her progression, explaining, "the first year [back on the faculty] felt like a trial, a probationary period, if you will. Second year not so much. This year I haven't really noticed it at all." By settling into new routines, committing to scholarly projects, and redeveloping her confidence in the classroom, Mildred grew increasingly comfortable with the version of the faculty member she would be at this stage in her career. The microprocess of *becoming reacquainted* starts with a leader getting back up to speed, reminding themselves how to perform routine faculty activities, and achieving a sense of clarity about who they are. The microprocess continues as others become reacquainted with them.

In total, Sabrina spent seven years away from her home department, six as an associate dean followed by a sabbatical year. Describing what made her most excited about returning to the faculty, she expressed enthusiasm about her new colleagues, especially getting to know those who were hired while she was away from the department: "I'm thinking of myself as somebody who wants to support [early-career colleagues]. I want to get to know them better than I've been able to. I do feel like they know me in a way, but there's another way. We need to get acquainted." Sabrina recognized that many of her colleagues knew her by name—or they were familiar with the initiatives she led—but they did not really know *her*.

When it comes to *becoming reacquainted*, ex-administrators found that using a short-but-intense strategy could be effective, but it also had limits. For example, a wholehearted, deep dive into reading scholarly articles might help a former president or dean regain command of their discipline in just a few months. But the strategy of hitting the gas hard can be counterproductive to developing relationships; others find the intensity off-putting. Becoming reacquainted with people—and allowing them to become reacquainted with you—often entails a careful balance of being seen and heard in just the right measure.

The question of how to respond to a request—or making the conscious choice *not* to—is one that former administrators face almost daily upon returning to the faculty. Ex-leaders must decide whether to attend public events, such as a faculty meeting, where their actions (and facial expressions) will be on full display. Innocuous small talk with a colleague in the hallway might invite comment about the latest sin committed by "the administration." After their third offer to take the department chair to lunch is declined, an ex-leader might find another way to signal their willingness to help. In deciding how to navigate these trickier moments of reacquaintance, former leaders are frequently trying to find the sweet spot between coming on too strong and being seen as aloof.

Strategy 1: Stepping Up

In chapter 3, I noted that women participants in my study were more likely to report *experiencing role and status confusion* than their male counterparts were. While this confusion was present early in the process of returning to the faculty, it was not limited to the start. A few women participants offered examples of how calling overt attention to their new status shut down positional challenges. Although Rosie had wrapped up her provost appointment at a private institution, she agreed to oversee one project through to completion. She had begun an academic leave and was no longer the provost, but she continued to attend meetings related to this one task. Rosie explained how she approached this hybrid arrangement:

> Sometimes it's in those really finite things, like, "I'm doing this, but I'm not doing that" or "I'm not wearing the clothes I used to wear to go to this meeting" or something like that. How do you signal to others that something is different? You know, you weren't just going to continue to work at your normal pace and then suddenly not be there anymore. This is the transitioning out, and I can understand why that makes people uncomfortable. I think just the direct strategy is sort of what people need to hear and be continually reminded of, because for them, they're seeing it in a different way that they don't quite understand either.

When she encountered situations in which the expectations were fuzzy, Rosie found that a direct approach was best: she dressed more casually, exercised strategic visibility and invisibility, and offered verbal reminders of her new role. Another woman in the study, Barbara, used similar strategies when meeting with her department: "I preface a lot of comments now, particularly since I still do have some administrative responsibilities. 'I don't have any special inside information on this. It's just my opinion, but [here's what I think].' And no one has ever said, 'You don't have to say that' or 'Of course you don't' or something like that. I think it's still they're still just getting used to the idea of my being a faculty member again." The reaction from Barbara's colleagues is a reminder that returning to the faculty is an adjustment for both a former leader and their colleagues. Calling attention to the changes helps them register.

Beyond offering clarity, there are other compelling reasons that former leaders make themselves seen or heard. Buddy, who left his role as a provost at a private institution at the request of his president, generally stayed away from the campus during his sabbatical. He made calculated exceptions: "I've only been back twice since school began. I did go to the opening reception because I wanted people to see me. I wanted them to know that it's not like I had been banished because I did something wrong, that I was in jail or something. I thought it was important just to show up, so I went to the opening meeting and the reception." He reflected on the potential consequences of choices: "I hope it hasn't been a mistake being so absent from campus. You always worry that people will think that you had some big blowup with the cabinet or the president or you did something wrong—you embezzled or sexually harassed or something like that. None of that is true in my case. Tactically, maybe I shouldn't have made myself quite as scarce, but I did want to give everybody some breathing room." The prospect that his absence might have fueled additional rumors that might have been avoided haunted Buddy.

Stepping up need not be limited to campus interactions. Nancy, a former dean at a public institution, described how she felt after publishing an op-ed on a politically charged topic: "As a dean, I feel I could never have done that without damaging the institution or bringing unwanted attention. Maybe I'm wrong, but I wouldn't have written it. I wouldn't have felt comfortable doing it." While academic freedom extends to senior campus leaders, many of the former leaders I spoke with had voluntarily self-censored. While a dean at a public institution, Nancy had chosen not to weigh in on policy matters, even when her scholarly expertise made her a credible expert to do so. Taking a public stand in the newspaper enabled Nancy to reassert—both for her own benefit and for others—that she was no longer the dean.

Another domain where proactive effort can help an ex-leader become reacquainted is teaching. After teaching on and off for a decade, former provost Buddy likened himself to "Rip Van Winkle coming back to your academic home." While the learning curve was steep, he found the return to be "fun" and "invigorating." Stuart, a former provost at a public institution, also described feeling energized by what he called his "assistant professor workload," teaching new courses "from scratch" that required extensive preparation. Several administrators struggled to connect with current students, gain expertise with educational technologies, and execute modern pedagogies (e.g., flipped classroom, equity pedagogy).

> ### COLLECTED WISDOM 11
> # "Teaching Is Harder than I Remembered"

Many senior leaders in the study cited returning to the classroom as a primary motivation for stepping away. While many found teaching to be "rewarding," a "good challenge," and "refreshing," it was also "time-consuming" and "harder than [one] remembered." Across the nation, many faculty members have reported an uptick in the demands associated with university teaching since 2020. Even adept faculty members were challenged to become proficient at hybrid teaching modalities, support a growing number of struggling students, and make classrooms more equitable.

You are wise to anticipate challenges related to *what* you teach, *how* you teach, and *whom* you teach. How do you set yourself up for success?

Apprise Yourself of Changes in the Field
Many administrators take steps to (re)immerse themselves in their disciplines, whether by attending meetings of their professional societies or catching up on their reading. Returning to the classroom can be an opportune moment to "decolonize" your syllabus by including a greater diversity of scholars and topics in your course.

Connect with a New Generation of Students
After an extended break, stepping back prompts many a former leader to remark, "students have changed." You might notice differences in high school preparation, life experiences, diverse identities, heightened social awareness, accommodations for learners with exceptionalities, and the increasing role of technology in students' lives. It may take time and effort to match your pedagogy to your learners' evolving expectations.

Learn from Your Colleagues
Much has been written in the business world about the emerging practice of "reverse-mentoring." Seasoned professionals are now seeking the council of younger colleagues on matters ranging from technology to diversity and inclusion.* Engaging graduate student teaching assistants or picking the brains of your early-career faculty colleagues might help you acquire new mind-sets and skills to ease your return to the classroom.

Avail Yourself of Campus Resources
Unlike twenty years ago, most colleges and universities now have robust support systems to support instructors in the areas of pedagogical development and

---

* Jordan and Sorrell, "Why Reverse Mentoring Works and How to Do It Right."

classroom technology (in fact, you might have helped to create these structures as an administrator). Consider attending workshops on antiracist pedagogy, flipped classrooms, transparent syllabus design, active learning strategies, and using the learning management system (LMS).

Apply Insights from Your Administrative Experience
Kevin Pickus transferred the skills and insights acquired during two decades of administrative service at Kansas State into the classroom. Being a dean taught him to "let his guard down" and acknowledge when he lacked expertise. His administrative experience led him to make adjustments when problems arose. Moreover, being an administrator taught him how much context matters when communicating: he knew to describe course policies and articulate the reasoning behind them.*

Be Patient and Forgiving with Yourself
We all know that college teaching is far more art than science. Give yourself a generous on-ramp and celebrate your improvements every semester. You won't always be perfect, but you can always get better.

---

* Pickus, "Teaching Lessons That a Professor Learned as an Administrator."

Strategy 2: Hanging Back

In a seminal article, the nursing researchers Chick and Meleis identified "disconnectedness" as a defining characteristic of transitions.[4] Many leaders responded to disconnectedness by checking out, avoiding interactions, or removing themselves from situations that felt confusing, uncertain, awkward, or difficult. By far, the most frequent tactic used by former administrators to ease the strain of their transition was to play a less visible, even an "under-the-radar," role through physical absence and psychological detachment. Former provost Emma called it "lying low" and being "incognito." Former provost Wesley said that he took his place "on the sidelines" while giving his successor ample space to get settled in. Many participants in the study, including former president Mack, offered this justification for being physically absent from campus during sabbatical: "There's only one president and it's no longer you. . . . Not that there was any real awkwardness in [continuing to live near the university], but [my wife and I] made considerable efforts to keep a low profile and not, in any way, to play much of a public role in the life of the college, because that just wasn't our place anymore."

Former provost Judy provided this rationale for keeping her distance during her sabbatical: "I think it's an advantage for the institution that I'm not there and looking quizzically or critically at something that's going on or even appearing to be pushing an agenda still from the background. I think it is important to be gone." Nonengagement proved to be an effective way to let role confusion resolve itself.

Hanging back is not limited to avoiding campus—it is a posture that can guide all interactions. Bernie, a former chief academic officer, said that as a faculty member he was taking a more "mellow" stance regarding university matters, adding, "I don't feel the need to insert myself in things or become involved in the kinds of issues that people are concerned about at the moment." The same approach proved useful for Robin, who often reflected on "how to moderate [his] own participation": "when to speak, when not; what to say publicly, what not." Being physically present but choosing not to speak can help an ex-leader blend into the background, allowing campus life to carry on.

Former provost Penelope found it most challenging to hang back when the campus rumor mill distorted her intentions or past actions: "It's hard when people start talking about things that you had a hand in or worked on or initiated or were instrumental in, and you know how information travels when it moves through the levels of the university. . . . The temptation is to put your hand up and say, 'Well, really, actually, this is kind of what was supposed to happen.' The dean persistently misrepresents everything that came out of my mouth. You know, I would never *say* those things, but I was *thinking* them." Despite her efforts "not to bring that [administrative] persona into the departmental dynamic," Penelope often found herself in situations that tested her resolve. While she was tempted to defend her past actions and set the record straight, she believed that clearing her name would bring few long-term benefits. She explained, "It's just not going to help you integrate into the group if you're always acting like you used to be the provost. It's not helpful." So instead of inserting herself into every conversation, she adopted the code that sometimes it's better to say nothing at all.

Putting It into Practice

In returning to the faculty, former senior academic leaders face numerous decision points, including how to balance visibility and invisibility on campus, what (if any) kind of scholarship to do, and how to allocate their time. In the middle stages of stepping away, leaders learn to integrate new roles and behaviors with aspects of their pasts. Many find that transferring what they learned in one domain of life can help lessen the strain in another. For instance, a former senior leader who enjoys some success reinventing themselves as a scholar might feel empowered and better equipped to take on a new role at home (or vice versa). Much as a sabbatical can give a former administrator cause to develop a new structure to their day to manage their abundant "free" time, these lessons prove vital to returning to balancing the demands of full-time teaching.

Table 4.1. Strategies to Navigate the Messy Middle

Microprocess	Useful strategies
Experiencing and using time differently: Exchanging a highly structured, demanding schedule for a more flexible, self-determined one.	*Breaking the cycle*: Embracing the discomfort that comes from trading a demanding schedule to a more open one. *Transferring energy into the next thing*: Despite having the ability to spend less time working, leaders elect to keep to a full-time schedule. *Attending to self and others*: Devoting one's newfound free time to health, exercise, relationships, and other responsibilities. *Reprioritizing*: Taking stock of what is most important to you and allocating your time and energy proportionately.
Reinventing the self: Taking on new roles and identities in your professional and personal life.	*Developing a new scholarly identity*: Whether returning to disciplinary scholarship or taking up new projects related to higher education, returning to the faculty affords new possibilities in research. *Adopting new roles at home*: Having a more flexible schedule and cultivating new routines can shift the balance of responsibilities at home. *Modifying outward expressions of identity*: As you begin to take on new roles, dress the part.
Becoming reacquainted: Relearning how to perform your faculty responsibilities and allowing others to become comfortable with you.	*Stepping up*: Working hard to assert your new place in the social architecture of your campus. *Hanging back*: Allowing these things to sort themselves out by keeping your distance and exerting little effort.

CHAPTER 5

"Working for Myself"

Life after Administration

Previous chapters have examined some ways that administrative service left an indelible imprint on senior leaders—changing how they perceived themselves, how they experienced and used time, and how they interacted with others. As administrative leaders become different versions of themselves, their behaviors also change. Apart from the occasional personal essay, the professional experiences of former academic leaders are largely invisible in the scholarly research.[1]

There is no one way, or right way, to go back to the faculty. Former president Randy confidently said, "I don't want to assume a full faculty kind of role. I want to do a lot of things to the community." In his new capacity as chancellor emeritus, Randy often performs acts of service that would be somewhat atypical for a rank-and-file faculty member. He represents his university at Chamber of Commerce breakfasts, attends college presidential inaugurations as a delegate, and does fund-raising for local social service agencies. He clarified that he only represents the university at official functions at the direct request of the current university's current chancellor and that his community volunteerism is something he does as a private citizen. Randy underwent many transformations informed by his administrative experience. For example, he no longer teaches courses in his academic discipline and instead teaches graduate classes about higher education leadership. He continues to regularly attend sporting events on his campus as a fan, and while no longer obligated to, he enjoys mingling with current administrators, alumni, and donors at some of the games. He has continued to work into his midseventies; he finds that this mix of activities suits him well.

Randy's choices illustrates the two microprocesses that constitute the end of the stepping away process: *adding value* and *negotiating autonomy*. Ex-administrators *add value* by performing tasks and stepping into roles that advance the mission of their universities or further the general welfare. Leaders have considerable freedom and latitude to determine what causes to advance and the best means to advance them (*negotiating autonomy*). For many former senior leaders, joy and fulfillment are achieved by expertly balancing *adding value* and *negotiating autonomy.*

Theorists have long posited that anticipating a role transition is categorically different from living through one.[2] My data bear out this finding. When I compared study participants who were in relatively earlier stages of the process (that is to say, those who had announced an intention to step down but had not yet done so or those who were currently on sabbatical), I saw marked differences between their perspectives and behaviors and the study participants who had advanced to progressively later stages in the process, including those who had been teaching for a semester or more. This signals that, at best, departing leaders can only speculate what their post-administrative work will look and feel like. Many participants accurately anticipated that specific tasks, such as resuming progress on a dormant research agenda or returning to the classroom after a prolonged absence, would paradoxically demand a great deal of energy and energize them to do other things. Yet, even for the most planful former leader, returning to the faculty included unanticipated and pleasant surprises, including finding rewarding ways to serve their campus, disciplinary, professional, and civic communities.

While returning to the faculty was not without its challenges, it proved to be a vibrant and productive time for many former senior academic leaders, one that often exceeded their own hopes and dreams. When former leaders approach returning to the faculty as becoming a new kind of faculty member—and fully embracing the possibilities now available to them—they are finally able to integrate a lifetime's experience into a new post-leadership identity.

COLLECTED WISDOM 12

Insiders and Outsiders: How Your Past Shapes Your Future

Whereas upward of 80 percent of university presidents are hired from outside their institutions, about half of chief academic officers are promoted from within.* Upon returning to the faculty, senior leaders always face conditions that are, in part, shaped by where they came from. "Insiders" begin their jobs possessing deep institutional knowledge and preexisting relationships, while "outsiders" bring fresh perspectives and are not haunted by the ghosts of past words or deeds. These dynamics often resurface, sometimes in unexpected ways, when an administrator returns to the faculty.

How Trajectories Matter

In a collection of published speeches and essays, Keith Brodie, president emeritus and James B. Duke Professor of Psychiatry of Duke University, reflected on having spent the bulk of his career at one institution—holding positions from faculty member to president and just about everything in between. Brodie explained, "the single-institution career trajectory had advantages and disadvantages."† The implied inverse is probably also true.

I have spoken to leaders in both camps—those who, like Brodie, "climbed" the ranks in one institution and those who moved up by moving around. Based on what I heard, one path does not make it categorically easier or harder to return to the faculty.

Individuals who were long-serving faculty members at a single institution were grateful for "faculty friends," who helped them stay grounded before, during, and after transitioning roles. Administrators who worked at multiple institutions also relied on their social networks to provide critical support during moments of change (whether those friends were affiliated with their current institution or not). The bigger takeaway is that friends—regardless of where you made them—help ease strain and stress during life's transitions.

Mitigating Factors

Other factors, like the length of service or the circumstances that precipitated an administrative exit, are better predictors of the relative ease or difficulty of returning to the faculty. For instance, a beloved president who completed a decade of service having achieved great things would probably find it easier to return to the faculty than a provost who resigned after a vote of no confidence after two years

---

* Selingo, "What Presidents Think," 9; King and Gomez, *On the Pathway to the Presidency*, 8.
† Brodie and Banner, *Keeping an Open Door*, 5.

on the job. Though, in my research, I was surprised to learn that this was not always the case.

It is entirely possible for externally hired administrators to gain insider status, regardless of where they began their careers. This can be achieved through longevity of service and intentional relationship building with faculty colleagues. Conversely, a faculty member who "rose through the ranks" at one institution might become ostracized and alienated by their decisions and leadership style. Current administrators are wise to recognize that these statuses are earned rather than determined by where you started your career.

Microprocess 6: Adding Value

In my attempt to describe what late-career, post-leadership faculty work looks like in the modern US academy, a few patterns emerged. Nearly all late-stage study participants portrayed themselves as "adding value" to their campuses and communities by engaging in a new behavior that they did not do as an administrator. These behaviors often began after sabbatical was over. Many former academic leaders approach sabbatical as a self-focused time: reading, resting, exercising, writing, traveling, reconnecting with others, and formulating new goals. Being self-focused and protective of their time is both appropriate and necessary. To work through the three microprocesses described in chapter 4 (*experiencing and using time differently, reinventing the self,* and *becoming reacquainted*) requires a leader to disconnect from campus and focus on themselves. An individual cannot skip these crucial decisions or thought processes, as they position a former leader to approach the challenges that still await them.

Returning to faculty work presents former leaders with new opportunities to use their time and talents to benefit others. One arena where leaders direct their service is on their campuses. After Chris had stepped away from his presidency, he described the sense of duty he felt toward his college: "I'm also well aware that I'm being paid a lot of money still to be a faculty member. I have to add value. And I think I have value to add." Chris was not the only study participant who disclosed the terms of his post-administrative employment contracts with me. While we rarely discussed exact numbers, several ex-leaders told me that they had been treated generously by their institutions. In some cases, ex-leaders continued to draw a salary that was close or equal to their administrative salary. (Additional thoughts on this can be found in Collected Wisdom 19.) Others had been awarded named professorships, given research funding, or awarded other desirable perks (e.g., a spacious office, season basketball tickets). Many former leaders, like Chris, believed that their compensation, broadly construed, warranted an elevated level of professional service or heightened research productivity.

Other participants also felt called to service but not because it was a tit-for-tat transaction; they felt a deeper calling to serve their institutions anew. When attempting to explain this impulse, many participants reflected on their origin stories as leaders. Some recalled that they first became a department chair or a dean to advance a cause larger than themselves and that this commitment never waned. It seemed only natural for ex-leaders who had been called to leadership as a form of service to give back upon stepping away. Adding value can be achieved harmoniously in concert with other faculty responsibilities, like performing thankless administrative tasks with little fanfare or teaching the course sections that others saw as undesirable (e.g., large intro courses). Some former administrators sought to satisfy both forms of motivation—one more transactional, one more altruistic—by performing the duties that came as natural extensions of their interests and talents.

Former senior leaders expressed that there are appropriate and inappropriate ways to add value to their universities and other communities. While these differences were rarely spelled out in any official way, nearly all the former leaders I spoke with abided by an unwritten code. Former leaders believed that their contributions should be invited or, at the very least, modest or understated. Guided by this code, participants described adding value in many ways, ranging from serving in visible leadership positions (e.g., chairing a department) to engaging in uncompensated informal mentoring (e.g., graduate students, junior faculty colleagues). To this end, some former leaders explained that being invisible, or playing an under-the-radar or incognito role at their university, is also a way to add value. Ex-leaders described many acts of beneficial deference, such as not weighing in on a controversial department vote, not indulging in watercooler gossip, or aiming to put as few demands on their department chair as possible. They saw adding value as exercising self-control, giving others a chance, muting the ego, not expecting special treatment, and letting things go. In striving to serve and support others, it is critical to recognize where the boundaries of one's potential contributions end.

Strategy 1: Exhibiting Project Leadership

Many former senior academic leaders found that playing a significant role in a major project or campus initiative allowed them to leverage their institutional knowledge and administrative abilities. For example, former CAO Sid agreed to play a central role in the university's reaffirmation of accreditation process, explaining, "The dean asked me to take on, with the help of another person, the collection of data and composition of our [accreditation report]. I think that's just kind of the right thing for me to do. I know the institution inside and out, and now, in a faculty role, I can bring a certain kind of perspective to the writing of that report that probably nobody else in the college could do." For Sid, this project allowed him to apply his institutional knowledge without undermining the provost's authority. At the same time that Sid framed his efforts as helping the institution, the work helped him navigate the "blurry" process of returning to the faculty:

> The role differentiation, which is blurry here, is in part caused by the multiple hats we wear. It's supported by that. In a sense, while I characterize it being in betwixt, I don't find that to be a necessarily uncharitable place to be. I have these skills, I have these experiences. I have to figure out, as everybody does, whether they're negotiating between being a new parent and a new faculty member or being a new associate dean and also being a faculty member. Those negotiations are taking place in different ways for different people. I'm just doing it with a different set of experiences.

In this passage, Sid likens the dimensions of his role change to other life transitions—such as becoming a new parent or taking on a new role at work. Although being between roles can be unsettling, Sid explains how being "betwixt" enabled him to bring multiple perspectives to writing an institutional report. Sid added value to his institution by drawing on these perspectives.

While Sid agreed to play a role in accreditation, Penelope thought she could be of greatest value liaising with external partners. Upon completing her term as provost, Penelope continued to serve as the university's point person for an international partnership that she had been instrumental in creating. Although her successor now served as the official representative to the group, Penelope agreed to travel overseas to lead the campus delegation. Although Penelope was no longer involved in the day-to-day management of the partnership, her participation in the summit had symbolic value, and she added value by freeing the new provost from having to travel to Asia in the middle of the semester. Many participants expressed a willingness to assist in fund-raising and "friend-raising" efforts on behalf of the university. Only time will tell if these offers are accepted, but these individuals believed that they could serve their institutions by interacting with donors and alumni to complement the work of their successors.

While supporting an initiative is one tangible way that participants continued to serve their universities, others contributed by stepping into midlevel leadership roles or major service obligations. At least four participants in the study agreed to become a department chair not long after stepping down as a senior leader. After Mildred had completed her term as an associate provost and took a year's sabbatical, she returned to her academic department as the chair. Feeling some initial trepidation, she acted cautiously to gain the trust of her faculty colleagues. She recognized that some people in the department continued to view her with the skepticism that they reserved for "the administrator," but she used a "casual" and "transparent" leadership style to establish credibility and rapport, especially with the pre-tenure colleagues who had only previously known her in her former capacity. Once she overcame the initial awkwardness, Mildred credited her administrative experiences as equipping her for success as a chair. She listed the many transferrable skills and lessons she acquired as an associate dean:

> I can get things done so much better than I used to be able to. . . . If I hadn't had the associate dean experience, I wouldn't have been able to perform that way. So, I think that my service has just been really enhanced by that. And knowing what it takes to—like just, first of all, who are the right people, and what is the university's larger administrative process for getting, say, remodeling done, and what are their concerns going to be, and here's how I can speak to them to head that off at the pass and get approval for things.

Having been an associate dean, Mildred saw herself as a better advocate for her department, citing her success in negotiating for an additional tenure-track faculty line. Her expanded understanding of institutional procedures allowed her to function more efficiently and effectively. When senior leaders return to the faculty, academic departments gain a deeper bench of prospective midlevel leaders.

In addition to serving as a department chair, participants leveraged their leadership experiences and institutional knowledge through committee appointments. Barbara continued to play an active role on the Institutional Review Board (IRB) after leaving her post as an associate provost. She justified her continued involvement, saying, the "university put a lot of resources into training me on matters related to administering the IRB," and by continuing to do this work, she helped the university comply with federal standards. Barbara appreciated that remaining involved in the IRB allowed her to transition more gradually to the faculty. In exchange for serving as chair, Barbara was awarded one course release—she appreciated having a lighter teaching load while getting back up to speed after a prolonged absence from the classroom. Being able to wind down her administrative job while ramping up her teaching made Barbara's transition "manageable" and "comfortable." In other words, it was a win-win.

Not all leaders who returned to the faculty were as eager as Mildred and Barbara to get involved in quasi-administrative work. Chelsea, a former associate dean at a private university, limited his participation to "low-profile" forms of university service, avoiding groups like the faculty senate and promotion and tenure commission. He particularly enjoyed serving on committees alongside his former administrative colleagues; he liked maintaining contact with them, and their jobs often prevented them from interacting much on a social level. When it came to performing university service, former dean Felix took a similar approach, noting, "I'm a little cautious [because] I'm resigned that my words carry more weight than really they should." For the time being, he preferred focusing his energies on personal pursuits and sidestepping potential awkwardness.

Strategy 2: Making Scholarly and Service Contributions

Participants explained how their post-administrative activities raised the profile of their universities. While it is challenging to quantify reputational benefits, participants explained how their external service and their contributions as scholars enhanced institutional prestige. Several study participants were appointed to named professorships upon returning to the faculty. Such positions typically provided supplemental funding and carried the expectation of maintaining a distinguished research profile. Former CAO Luke appreciated that the terms of his faculty appointment were broadly cast to include service expectations as well, explaining, "[My endowed professorship is] broader than just departmental. . . . I was really grateful for it and really appreciative. It's something that appeals to me intellectually. It gives me a role that I think is kind of a midway point between just being a professor and being an administrator." Luke's professorship not only provided him with an elevated status that made him feel valued but also included an expectation to do cross-disciplinary work, such as strengthening partnerships within and beyond the institution and curating a speaker series. For Luke, this replicated some of what he most loved about being a chief academic officer: interacting with colleagues from across the university, advocating for the relevance and value of the liberal arts, and interacting with visiting scholars. Stepping into this kind of endowed professorship provided Luke with a platform to pursue his own scholarly projects and for the university to reap the benefits through new programs and special events.

Another way that former leaders described adding value to their institutions was by volunteering beyond the university, such as on a nonprofit board. When former president Ralph discussed his service to a local organization, he explained, "Apparently, I still feel the organizational impulse. It's the collective impulse, and I'm chairing the board. . . . All these things are part of the same kind of mind-set and the skill set, I think, that the presidency offers. On the one hand, I have the book [I'm writing], which was the opposite of the scatteredness that being a president involves. I love the focus and the control and the concentration. But on the other hand, I think if I had only been writing a book, I would have been unhappy." Upon completing his presidency, Ralph gravitated toward diametrically opposed activities: writing a book and advising nonprofit organizations. For Ralph, the combination provided him a desirable balance. Writing a book allowed Ralph to concentrate on a single topic, demanding a level of focus that was incompatible with the demands of the presidency. But to overcome the isolation of writing, serving on community boards satisfied his "organizational" and "collective" impulses that he previously satisfied as a university president. Just as Barbara found that serving on the IRB eased her transition to the faculty by allowing her to engage in work that was familiar, Ralph found meaning in doing service that was reminiscent of his presidential leadership. Amid a professional transition, service can become a thread of coherence.

Former leaders identified many forms of service in which their participation positively benefited their institution, including serving on regional advisory boards, accepting an officer position in a disciplinary society, reviewing grant proposals for groups like the National Science Foundation, or giving guest lectures. They sought to add value for their institutions through their scholarly contributions and advisory work. Many of these activities had the added appeal of providing the former leader with a venue to help others and exercise their skills.

Strategy 3: Mentoring Others

Informal mentorship was one of the least visible but most common ways that participants supported their university's academic missions. Most frequently, this entailed an ex-leader working behind the scenes to support and encourage faculty members and midlevel leaders. Former provost Robin's primary contribution took the form of mentoring his junior faculty colleagues. This activity allowed him to leverage his knowledge of administrative structures and his scholarly experience:

> The young faculty member who's really good at doing the research and gathering the materials and then not as good yet at figuring out her idea or what the gist of her argument is—and so being able to sit down next to a person

and say, "Here's where the strength really is in your argument," that sort of thing that all of us do when we start to review manuscripts. . . . A lot of it is coaching at this point. I feel like I'm sort of a consultant in that way when people want to use me, and my feelings aren't hurt when they don't want to use me.

A handful of participants in my study told me that they were glad to have spent their sabbaticals doing an off-campus fellowship, sometimes taking up temporary residence at an interdisciplinary center or a leading research university. Former president Chris enjoyed the chance to live in a new place and identified some of the other benefits that a semester "in residence" provided: "I was mostly surrounded by younger scholars, and I was able to engage their work and act as a sort of mentor to them, as well as a friend and a colleague. And that was just extremely invigorating. I really was lucky because instead of staring just at a blank piece of paper, I was able to have other people's pieces of paper in front of me all the time." For Chris, completing a residential research fellowship provided him with the structures, community, and geographic diversity he needed to be and feel productive after leaving his presidency. While he might have struggled to make such inroads working on his own at his home, Chris found the opportunities presented to him, including mentoring the next generation of scholars, to be "invigorating."

Senior leaders noted that many of their former colleagues seek them out for advice about advancing in their administrative careers. Former provost William explained, "One of the things that I actually find very rewarding is that I still have former colleagues, former direct reports, that come to me for advice now and then and want some mentoring, and I have always felt good about being able to help them." Maintaining these relationships increased William's professional fulfillment and gave him the satisfaction that his perspective had enduring worth.

Upon returning to the faculty, former administrators also described becoming a resource for students. Former dean Greg explained how the flexibility of his new schedule allowed him to mentor students more frequently than he had previously. Given his plans to retire soon, Greg did not take on any doctoral advisees, but he often interacted with grad students, "not as their primary advisor but, you know, helping them think about their research projects." Much in the way that Robin saw himself as a "consultant" and a "coach" to his junior-faculty colleagues, Greg offered his expertise to students as a tertiary advisor. Harriett regularly interacted with students in crisis in her administrative capacity. As a result, she identified how her administrative role prepared her to be a better advocate and resource for students now:

I saw students a lot because I was advising a lot, but I had a different relationship with students than I had had as a faculty member. You see students in a different light when they're outside of class and when you're talking to them about finishing their degree and stuff like that. I think coming back to teaching after that, I really feel like I have an easier relationship with students. I don't feel like I'm trying to prove anything, but I also feel like I understand students better. I feel more open to asking them how they're doing or finding out what's going on in their lives. I just feel more relaxed around students.

Harriett gained an ability to see students holistically—she now feels comfortable talking to them about all aspects of their lives, not only about their academic performance. This enhanced perspective changed Harriett's approach to teaching as well. She explained that she was "a little more aware of what's going on outside of the classroom with students, that they have so many other obligations and so many other things, and a lot of them have other personal things going on that you don't always realize if you're just seeing them in class." While many participants in the study explained that their administrative experiences make it more challenging for them to connect with students, Harriett's administrative experience increased her empathy for students and fostered a greater awareness of the complexities of students' lives. In addition, her increased understanding of the university's policies and inner workings made her a better advisor; she was now able to direct students to the proper channels when challenges arose.

In some cases, mentorship can also take the form of translation—helping people within the same institution communicate across silos. These former leaders embraced being dual citizens, those rare individuals who are able to bridge the gap between faculty and administrative cultures. Ex-provost Wesley felt that he could improve a sense of understanding among his faculty peers: "I'll often sit in faculty meetings and hear people speculate about what the administration is thinking. And I'll realize that I used to have the same speculations, but now I know the answer. It's interesting to be able to provide that kind of insight to the department. . . . I'm able to say, 'When you're dealing with them, this is how they do things. We don't have to do things that way, but we have to understand where they're coming from.'" While former leaders shared their insights, many offered their mentorship with the caveat that it was on a purely voluntary basis. Former dean Greg characterized his take-it-or-leave-it intentions this way: "I think my experience as an administrator has been useful because I can put a perspective on questions that the department has that they would have difficultly coming to themselves, simply because they haven't served in that role and seen the situation from the point of view of an administrator. I try real hard to let the department find its own way, but if they come to me and say, 'What do you think?' then I'm more than happy to share what my experience would help with." Greg's willingness to advise—but his self-control in waiting to be approached—is a common posture for ex-leaders. Nearly all the former leaders in my study were cautious not to overstep the boundaries they perceived to surround their faculty roles; they did not want to undermine the authority of the campus leadership or to come across as know-it-alls.

COLLECTED WISDOM 13
Sharing Your Skills and Honoring New Boundaries

As you approach onboarding your successor, consider former Princeton University president William G. Bowen's advice: "To be sure, new presidents may seek advice from their predecessors, but it should be entirely up to the new president to decide when—if it all—such advice is needed."* In practice, some former leaders (and their egos) might find this advice hard to follow.

- *Ask how and when you might help.* Don't presume that your successor needs what you needed upon starting your job. Consider if they process information the same way you do.
- *Remember your new role.* If you find yourself slipping into "decider-in-chief mode," pull back. Instead of telling them what you would do, ask clarifying questions or fill in relevant institutional history.
- *Ask your successor to bring the agenda.* You may be tempted to make lists of things to tell your successor, but the conversation might go better if you let them drive.
- *Consider context over legacy.* Rather than deliver a monologue on the soundness of a past decision, your successor will probably appreciate an understanding of why and how it came to be.
- *You might offer to make introductions or to identify people,* on campus and off, who could support a new leader's learning and acclimating to a new place.
- *Tread lightly when speaking negatively about colleagues.* Give your successor the freedom to form their own opinions and afford your colleagues the gift of a clean slate. If pressed, stick to factual, descriptive statements rather than evaluative ones.
- *Identify any roles you might be willing to play.* If you are inclined, it would be appropriate to suggest ways that you would like to continue to support the institution (e.g., serving on the board of the university press, attending alumni gatherings).

---

* Bowen, *Lessons Learned*, 143.

It is your successor's prerogative to accept your offer, but if you don't mention it, it probably will not come to be.

Respect Boundaries (Yours and Theirs)

It is reasonable to set guardrails on when and how you will be available to help. Keeping in mind that your perspective is probably of greatest value at the start of a new administrator's appointment, you might designate times when you are available. After that date, make it your primary goal to prepare to return to the faculty. It will be harder to disconnect if you keep getting roped back in.

Just as you might want some limits, your successor is eager to get going. If your offers to help go unacknowledged, take it as a sign that you did your job well. You bequeathed your successor a talented and capable team that will provide all the required knowledge and support.

Thicken Your Skin

Your predecessor will do things differently than you did. In some cases, they were explicitly hired to do things differently than you did. Try not to take it personally when the institution moves in a new direction without you. Institutions need different things at different times.

Strategy 4: Hanging Back

In chapter 4, I made the case that returning to the faculty requires straddling the paradox between hanging back and stepping up—learning to recognize when a goal is best achieved through direct action or through passive patience. In my data analysis, I discovered that for many former senior academic leaders, the code *hanging back* often co-occurred with *adding value*. Participants often rationalized that playing a less visible, low-profile role in their communities was a positive contribution. For instance, while Brian continued to play an active role in the life of the campus in his capacity as president emeritus and professor at a private university, he established clear boundaries about where and when to exercise his presence. During his sabbatical leave, Brian stated that unless he had "an invitation from the president to do something specific," he and his wife did not attend the event or play a role.

Former provost William described how he tried to add value by holding his tongue. He gave this example from a recent department meeting he attended:

> Where the department is facing some problem or some challenge or some roadblock, and rather than speak up in a meeting with all of them to say, "Well, I know the way to fix this," my approach has been to just speak privately with the chair and say, "You might try this, and here is a person that you could talk with to find out more." I don't do the work for him. I don't tell him, "You got to do this." I make suggestions. He can follow it if he wants and not if he doesn't want to. I feel like this is a way that I can help the department in a very unobtrusive way. How do I want to say it? I'm not trying to exercise any authority—I'm just trying to smooth the path or something.

William carefully modulated his participation in the department, striving not to overstep what he perceived to be the boundaries between his former role and his current one. By speaking with the department chair in private, William felt that he could offer value but in a way that did not challenge the chair's authority in public.

Participants believed that they could add value by being flexible in their teaching assignments, deferring to the needs and stated preferences of others. By offering to teach introductory courses, former provost Penelope created opportunities for other faculty members to teach specialized, upper-division courses. She explained,

> Our department consists of not very many senior people; they're more junior and also some lecturers and non-tenure-track faculty, of course, who are trying like crazy to get jobs but, realistically, may never get tenure-track jobs because of the job market. And all of these people are young and ambitious and very eager to teach a lot of courses and to teach courses at the upper division, especially, and where available, graduate courses. My feeling was that they should have those opportunities and that, again, I just wanted to be of service. So, both semesters, I taught [a lower-division course]. . . . And so, somebody got a break because I did that, which was nice.

Penelope recognized that one of the most valuable contributions she could make to her department was agreeing to fill any unmet curricular needs, thus allowing junior-faculty colleagues to gain valuable teaching experience.

Whereas ex-provost William held his tongue in department meetings and Penelope accepted whatever teaching assignments remained after others had taken their pick, former CAO Sid explained how he gradually came to play a more visible role in the social order of the university. This suggests that the decision to step back need not be a permanent one. When I contacted Sid to clarify some points from our initial interview, he had stepped away from his administrative role approximately three years prior. He explained how he comported himself differently over the years, pointing out some symbolic shifts: "[During the] first two years, I did not make a comment in our faculty meeting. We meet twice a month. I made a point of attending. We have two places where you can sit: you can sit around this table that seats thirty-five people, or you can sit in the ring of other chairs around it. I first started in the ring around it. Then last year I moved—because I had no reason not to—to the table along with my other colleagues." As he came to feel more established as a faculty member, Sid shifted his position within the concentric circles of chairs. While Sid made a symbolic shift, he continued to characterize his public expressions as "carefully choreographed": "I've spoken half a dozen times, but they're very carefully choreographed. I think that happens outside the formal meetings too. I've just become comfortable finding a way to translate what I see the institution is perhaps experiencing in terms that might make more sense to faculty who don't have the vocabulary for it, particularly newer faculty." Sid explained that he was only confident to speak up when he was certain that others recognized and accepted him as a faculty peer:

> My comfort is increasing as the audience that I'm engaging with will hear me as a faculty person and not as the former administrator that I was. I think that it's also part of my own self-caution: to be careful that I know what's motivating and what's at stake when I speak, neither as a longing to be back in that position where I have the inside information and therefore can speak with authority—but more the way in which I'm engaging my colleagues is as a peer, one who may be older with a sense of professional or social experiences but somebody who lives in that tribe with them. That's the comfort. It is both comfort in terms of the external location I find myself, but also it is about comfort in my skin.

In this passage, Sid equated how being seen as "faculty person" facilitated his decision to play a more visible and vocal role in campus governance. Like many of the other leaders I interviewed for this project, Sid continued to abide by unwritten rules—such as not challenging his successor's authority or appearing to come across as a know-it-all. But as his peers recognized his legitimate belonging in the "tribe," Sid gained the confidence to step up and speak up.

STEPPING AWAY

COLLECTED WISDOM 14

Advice for Entering or Reentering an Academic Department

Stepping *away* from administrative service often means stepping *into* an academic department. Here are some suggestions to make your entry—or reentry—smooth and collegial.

Bring Clarity and Resources into the Department
As you finalize the negotiations for your administrative exit, take responsibility for ensuring that these details have been shared with your department chair. Chairs often get left out of the communication loop and may not know your contractual teaching load, responsibilities regarding graduate students, and research funding expectations.

To the extent possible, include in your negotiations any resources that will ease your transition—travel funds, research support, a new computer—so that your department is not left to bear unanticipated expenses.

Allow Others to Get to Know You as a Faculty Member
Your department chair, and indeed your faculty colleagues, might not know much about you as a faculty member. Offer to take your new chair to lunch to talk about your research interests, your teaching style, goals for the future, and some classes you want to teach. Help them see you as more than the administrative office you once held.

Recognize Lingering Power Differentials
Whether it be salary, experience, knowledge, discretionary funding, or relationships, you will come into your department equipped with privileges and assets that others, including your chair, lack. Work to cultivate self-awareness of how your social and material capital influences your place in the department. Wear these advantages lightly and use them for the common good rather than personal gain.

Support Your Early-Career Colleagues, Be a Counterweight to Bullies
Like it or not, you are now a senior statesperson in the department. By lending support to pre-tenure faculty colleagues, you off-load some emotional labor that might otherwise fall to the chair. You can help them earn tenure by becoming a research collaborator or co-author, making an introduction to a senior colleague in the field, or demystifying the promotion process. Your status can also come in handy if senior colleagues are behaving badly; calling them out can put a quick end to bullying and wanton self-centeredness.

Respect Your Chair's Authority Above All

Being a department chair is a notoriously difficult and thankless job; do all that you can to make it easier. Never jump the chain of command and leave your department chair out of a formal process or request. While you might not always agree with a decision or outcome, respect your chair's authority. No good ever came from tattling to the dean or balking when something did not go your way.

Strategy 5: Realigning Your Vision

As ex-provost William was preparing to begin a paid administrative leave—a leave he delayed for a year at the request of the president—he described his unease: "I just have this general gnawing feeling of being unutilized. . . . I think I have a greater capacity to do things compared to what I am currently doing. The real question is how long it will take for me to figure out how to fulfill that." For William, the kinds of contributions he should make as a faculty member was not immediately clear. At the time of our interview, he had not yet resolved how to bring his administrative experience and capacities into alignment with his university's expectations and his own desire to help. For William to add value, he needed to work out what he wanted to do and how best to do it.

While participants wanted to add value to their institutions using a variety of means and approaches, some struggled when their offers were not accepted. Isabel explained that after she concluded her term as provost, her institution expected little of her beyond the relatively modest teaching, research, and committee service requirements spelled out in her faculty contract. Her offer to continue to help to raise the funds for a passion project was declined by her successor. Reflecting on what she saw as a missed opportunity, she explained, "I think there are things where they might have been able to use me, and I would have been able to see things happen, things that I had started. But that was their choice, and they didn't want to do that. . . . I got it as close as I could [to the goal], and the building is under construction now. I would have been happy to have been involved in further fund-raising for that because I think it's really important for the students to be able to have [this space]." Although Isabel was willing to continue to support this effort, her transition to the faculty was occupied with the mental and emotional work of overcoming the disappointment that came with being told that her services were no longer needed.

116 STEPPING AWAY

Like Isabel, Steve found himself having to realign his vision for how to add value after his offers to help were rebuffed by the provost who succeeded him. Despite having offered to meet on multiple occasions, Steve explained,

> I'm a little surprised—I have been from the very beginning—how uninterested he is in anything that I have to say. In fact, it worried me a little bit. . . . [Previously,] he had had several administrative appointments, and so he probably had this whole administration stuff figured out. We were coming up to the first day of his appointment, his first day of being on the job, and I did mention to the president that it seems a little odd that [he] hasn't reached out and asked me about anything, like, "Are there any things that I should know?" I was particularly concerned about his understanding of our relationships with external groups. . . . [Eventually, we had lunch.] I had a couple of things that I felt like I needed to share with him and got my thoughts organized. He didn't ask me any questions.

Steve was keenly aware that the new provost was brushing him off; not only did it make him feel underappreciated, but he worried about the larger harms for the institution:

> I had always thought about succession planning. This was an important part of who I am, and whether it was a committee that I served on, I wanted to make certain my successor had all the materials that they had, that the house was in better order than when I left. I kept always thinking about, "Are we wired up in such a way so that if somebody got hit by a bus, we wouldn't be disadvantaged?" And that was sort of a culture that I tried to impose on a lot of my subordinates and myself included. I was the beneficiary of that. I left things in pretty good enough shape and access to information and records so that they wouldn't have to come calling on me. But neither one of them—the provost or the dean—really has reached out for any information.

Steve's conception of succession planning clearly differed from his successor's expectations and onboarding needs. Steve's story presents useful takeaways. If a university or a new leader decides not to make use of their predecessor's talents, the onus is on the former leader to find a way to accept this outcome and move on. While being underutilized or overlooked might sting, one way to add value is to come to terms with the fact that your institution has moved on and work to find ways to move forward in your own life and work without harboring resentment.

Seeing the larger picture might help former leaders recognize that their future contributions might take on a more muted tone. Former president

Mack contributed a useful perspective when thinking about the role that a governing board might play in a transition to align expectations for both outgoing and incoming leaders. For Mack, boards can help set the tone and ensure that universities put plans in place to aid the new leader's integration:

> I think institutions have a far stronger obligation to the person coming in than to the person coming out. Where institutions often fall short is that once they brought the new guy in, he's on his own or she's on her own. Integrating someone—particularly someone coming in from outside the institution or from outside academia and, even more particularly, as is increasingly the case, somebody coming in from outside, who is not in academia—I think governing boards and administrations have a special obligation. They don't need to worry about the guy going out: he'll be okay. But the guy coming in, there's one they need to worry about.

Former leaders are keen to recognize that offering to help—and then stepping back graciously if such offers are declined—is in and of itself an act of service. In addition to fielding emails from the former president/provost/dean, the new leader is probably receiving solicited and unsolicited advice from members of the board, their new administrative colleagues, and the very talented staff bequeathed to them.

And finally, while the larger arc of stepping away encourages former leaders to find ways to add value in alignment with the university's needs, Steve's and Isabel's experiences contain cautionary lessons for newly appointed leaders. While the first few weeks of a new job may present merciless learning curves, carving out time to meet with your successor will be read as a symbolic expression of gratitude for a valued colleague's work and service (and may yield a useful resource). Waiting six months or a year is probably too late—what began as a good-natured willingness to help is likely to have denigrated into hurt and frustration.

The participants in my study believed that they contributed to their institutions by sharing their leadership expertise, institutional knowledge, and original scholarship. Participants were conscious of having reinvented themselves upon returning to the faculty—part of that reinvention included becoming a mentor and translator by providing context for the actions of senior administrators. Some believed that playing low-key and unobtrusive roles in their departments allowed them to keep the peace. Often motivated by a sense of duty, participants welcomed the change to add value to their colleges and were soured when such offers were rebuffed.

Microprocess 7: Negotiating Autonomy

In chapter 4, I examined how former administrators experienced and used their time differently upon stepping away and returning to the faculty. Recall that former administrators used a variety of strategies to adjust from having a busy, highly scheduled calendar to the relative freedom of sabbatical and, later, the characteristic flexibility of a professor's schedule. Acclimating to this enhanced sense of self-determination—both what to do and when to do it—is a defining characteristic of fully inhabiting a "second" faculty career. All tenured faculty members, including those who never serve in a leadership role, are entrusted to use their professional judgment to define and carry out their work as teachers and scholars. Some former administrators felt that they possessed even greater latitude than their typical faculty peers in determining what activities constitute their work, by having the ability to negotiate their teaching loads and engaging in the research projects that interested them. Although Derek Bok's analysis of the economics of the US workforce is dated in some respects—written before the widespread adoption of the internet and before the 2008 financial crisis—it remains prophetic about the self-directed nature of contemporary faculty work:

> As things now stand, professors on many campuses are among the least accountable professions in America. Although most faculty members are quite conscientious, every campus has professors who devote much time to outside activities that could be better spent on teaching and other academic duties. Carnegie surveys show that scheduled office hours are declining. There is also a worrisome growth of anecdotal talk about the difficulty of finding faculty to take on committee assignments and other normal administrative tasks. . . . All these signs suggest that keeping faculties committed to their institution and to the needs of their students will be a major challenge on many campuses. . . . Any prudent university, therefore, should be thinking about ways to improve incentives and safeguards to protect the central functions of the institution.[3]

Despite Bok's call to action, within the academy, there remain few systemic levers to mandate the behavior of tenured faculty members. Given that some universities can go several years without awarding a merit raise, these institutions must rely on faculty members' intrinsic motivation. Affirming Bok's worst fears, former administrators recounted having few demands placed on them as they returned to the faculty—most had the autonomy to define their roles and work and established salary levels. Some participants employed by public institutions encountered more "accountability measures" than did their colleagues employed by private institutions. Still, a faculty career is at its core largely self-defined: at the end of the day, the individual is only accountable to themselves, whether they revise their courses, crank out another article, or raise their hand to join a committee. Illustrating this point, Horace talked about the appeal of returning to the faculty: "[As tenured professors,] we're very lucky not only because of the security but also because we too have genuine flexibility within how to define the job, like designing new classes. I mean, there are very few parameters on the academic job." Since so much of faculty work is self-determined, there is an almost infinite number of ways to feel inspired, rewarded, and challenged. But like so many things in life, the knife cuts both ways: every benefit brings drawbacks. For those who thrive on clarity and structure, the lack of parameters amounts to a staggering degree of freedom. Former provost William's newfound professional independence unsettled him. The undefined nature of his faculty role led him to question things that he had previously taken for granted:

I am used to saying to people, "I'm still trying to figure out what I want to be when I grow up." It feels odd. Part of what feels odd right now is going through [college and graduate] school—I can't say I really knew what I wanted to do. But you just sort of follow the path. You're on the path. You follow the path. It leads you to a certain place, and then once there, you have ambitions about what you're going to accomplish as a professor. Maybe you get some administrative responsibility. So what are you going to accomplish there? There is sort of a well-run route that takes you up through administrative ranks.

Up until this point, William believed himself to be following a path that was designated for him—one step leading to the next, etcetera. "This is the first time in my life I've been at a point where I don't feel like I'm on a particular path. I'm just kind of hanging out and dabbling in this and that and have some ideas about things I might want to create, but it's totally self-generated. I don't know a good analogy to compare that to, but that's kind of what it's like." Stepping down from his senior leadership role erased the perceived structure that had heretofore given William's career momentum. Whereas Horace embraced the "self-generated" quality of his post-administrative career, William's footing was less sure. The implied casualness of "hanging out" and "dabbling in this and that" suggested that William had not yet found a sense of purpose in his unstructured faculty role.

Strategy 1: Working for Yourself

Barbara contrasted her limited faculty responsibilities with the more expansive administrative portfolio that she previously oversaw, describing the difference this way: "It feels more like I'm working for myself, even though I'm still working for the same institution." A prime benefit of returning to the faculty is recovering the professional autonomy and intellectual freedom to pursue endeavors of one's choosing. As Harriet talked about her post-administrative work, she said, "I just feel liberated, not from responsibility but just from an administrative role. As I said, I'm not on a lot of committees right now, so I can focus in on what I want to be doing right now." While Harriett continued teaching and meeting her professional obligations, having greater control over her time and fewer demands left her feeling "liberated."

Whereas many institutions require faculty members to submit a proposal to qualify for a paid sabbatical, most of the participants in the study were granted an administrative leave pro forma. Since they did not have to commit to specific goals as a condition for receiving a leave, participants were essentially free to use their time however they wanted. For example, former provost Wesley approached his sabbatical as an extended "vacation," which allowed him to travel, relax, and exercise. Even upon the conclusion of sabbatical leaves, participants continued to enjoy a relatively high degree of autonomy over their time and tasks. Planning to retire within a few years, former dean Greg felt little pressure to conform to others' expectations: "The department has been extremely supportive of me and my work. I couldn't ask for a nicer way to put one foot into retirement. They've been just great about, for the most part, giving me the time that I need to do the things that I want to do." Part of what made Greg's transition to the faculty so "easy" and "tension free" was that his colleagues put few restraints on him. After years of service, Greg found that being self-focused allowed him the ability to conclude his career doing the things that brought him the greatest meaning. He appreciated this flexibility as a gift.

One of the things that Bill came to appreciate about returning to the faculty was the ability to take advantage of unexpected opportunities. Recall that Bill left his position involuntarily when his immediate supervisor decided to restructure the office. This chain of events prompted Bill to engage in extended self-reflection, applying for other jobs elsewhere, and to care for himself during cancer treatment. When I interviewed him a second time, he was transformed. Whereas he seemed a bit lost when we first spoke, the intervening months made him focused and energized. He was serving as a department chair and coauthoring a major grant proposal. By returning to the faculty, Bill said, "Things change. And things change in ways that you don't always expect—or even this [granting agency] preproposal. If I had [left the institution] and something like that had happened, then I don't know. I don't know, I just sort of leave things open now and say, 'Well, I don't know what might come.'" Possessing the autonomy to become involved in new projects enhanced Bill's professional satisfaction. In fact, he remarked that had he left the institution, he might have missed out on valuable opportunities. While Bill was initially concerned that stepping away from his administrative role meant that he would have to stop doing the things that brought him joy—collaborating with others and launching programs to support student success—he found that these things were still possible returning to the faculty.

Strategy 2: Shaping Your Own Performance Criteria

While participants described having more professional and time autonomy as faculty members than they did as administrators, a few participants described structures and policies that curtailed some of their freedom. Participants who were employed by public institutions were, on average, less likely to characterize their late-career experiences as unstructured due to post-tenure review and statutorily defined terms in their faculty contracts. By comparison, participants who worked at private institutions often customized their post-administrative roles to meet their preferences and goals. Some negotiated for having no research expectations; one former president negotiated to be free of teaching responsibilities.

Undergoing a post-tenure review added pressure to some faculty members who would be rejoining departments with considerable research expectations. With respect to research productivity, Bill did not appear overly anxious about his upcoming post-tenure review. He explained, "I am just kind of taking time. I am kind of chilling out, on [research] right now. My post-tenure clock won't start until fall, actually, so I actually have a reprieve in that sense for a semester, nine months at least. I've got to get that into writing. I have a number of research projects in mind and a grant proposal that I will probably work on this summer with another person at the university." Whereas a leader who was not subject to post-tenure review might feel justified in delaying their research projects indefinitely, Bill allowed himself the brief "reprieve" of a summer off before revving up his research engines. As he navigated the demands of his university's post-tenure review, P.J. felt he needed to move on from the grant-funded bench science he had done earlier in his career. He explained, "No one can expect me to go back into a lab and get funding to do research. That train has left the station. I think for some administrators, you couldn't go back if you wanted to. You're just not in the loop on that anymore." Given that his discipline had changed, P.J. pivoted his approach both to satisfy his dean's mandate and to fulfill the expectations of post-tenure review. Moving away from discovery research, P.J. planned to direct his energies into the scholarship of teaching and learning. Not only could he complete these projects without significant external funding, but P.J. found himself gravitating to topics that drew on the work he had done as an administrator: "more educational research, the technology involved, outcomes assessment, those kinds of things." While institutional structures exerted some pressures on P.J. to remain active in research, he felt that he had the latitude to interpret this expectation to suit his current preferences.

While post-tenure review might entail a more rigorous review of faculty research, nearly all universities periodically review the performance of tenured faculty. Acknowledging that it can sometimes take a few years for a former administrator to find their footing in the classroom and reignite their research programs, the private university where Mildred served as an administrator agreed not to review her for five years (this was a slightly longer window than usual). She noted, "Not that it really mattered a whole lot, since I'm a full professor, but I just appreciate that." While the merit review process at Mildred's institution created some incentive for her to strive for excellence, she appreciated that the stakes remained low. Provided that she demonstrated a reasonable degree of effort, she remained confident that she could meet her university's expectations while pursuing her self-determined goals and priorities. For long-serving administrators who are anxious about their readjustment, requesting additional time before being reviewed can relieve some pressure.

The broader lesson is that while leaders who return to the faculty will be expected to make contributions to their campuses, they enjoy the latitude to be creative in how they meet those expectations. Whether by establishing their own timeline for future publications or reinventing themselves as scholars, former administrators find closure to the stepping away process by doing work they deem to be authentically rewarding and meaningful.

COLLECTED WISDOM 15

Finding New Joy

In "I Was a Dean, Now I'm Not," a candid personal essay published in the *Chronicle of Higher Education*, George Justice recounts how, upon involuntarily leaving his deanship at Arizona State, he encountered "a mix of emotions": "a lower salary, a loss of visibility and professional status, and bittersweet recognition that in all likelihood, this is it. I will spend the rest of my career as a professor, a job I enjoyed but hadn't anticipated resuming." Justice's imposed job change led him to lament all that was lost.

The phrase "stepping away" might imply leaving behind a Technicolor Oz for the humbler delights of black-and-white Kansas. But like Dorothy, learning to embrace the overlooked comforts of home can be one of the best gifts of returning to the faculty.

Good Riddance

Looking to the bright side, Art Shriberg, a dean for more than two decades at Xavier University, offers, "Now when I go to parties at the university, I only talk to people I want to talk to. Now I find myself saying *yes* most of the time; I used to say *no* most of the time."* Many former leaders are quick to name the aspects of their administrative jobs that they don't miss, such as the inability to set their own schedules, having their decisions scrutinized constantly, nagging headaches caused by personnel issues, or being at the beck and call of the institution.

Less Is More

There is value in exchanging the din of constant demands for a more intentional and focused life. As Kate Northrup argues, reducing the sheer volume of tasks can result in a person being more present and content in their daily lives.† By resisting cultural pressures to value quantity over quality and learning to divorce feelings of self-worth from productivity, Northrup observed that personal satisfaction increases. Once you begin to clear away the clutter of your administrative life, you might find yourself making meaningful progress in the areas of life that you most value.

Serve Thyself by Serving Others

While ceasing annoying activities can bring happiness, taking on new roles and routines can also produce real contentment, especially when those efforts benefit others. In *The Happiness Lab* podcast, Yale professor Laurie Santos points to many

---

* Shriberg, "From Deaning to Teaching," 37.
† Northrup, "Want to Be More Productive?"

124   STEPPING AWAY

psychological studies wherein small acts of kindness, service, and expressions of gratitude yield outsized dopamine boosts.* It is no wonder that many former administrators derive such pleasure from offering advice to early-career scholars or serving as a sounding board to a novice administrator. For those who prefer to get their kicks off campus, similar joys might come from being an officer in a disciplinary society, joining an editorial board, mentoring aspiring leaders through professional groups, or getting involved in the local community.

Delighting in Delight

In *The Book of Delights: Essays*, the poet Ross Gay offers many well-observed musings on the sheer "delight of inefficiency," be it "lounging, sipping coffee, listening to the oatmeal talking in the pot," or "not getting the groceries in from the car in one trip."† Many overscheduled leaders who have grown accustomed to mile-long to-do lists may have fallen out of practice when it comes to the innate pleasures of the scenic route or smelling the proverbial roses. Half jokingly, former dean Nancy told me that she spent the first few days of her post-administrative sabbatical sitting on her porch reading a mystery novel. Upon finishing the book, she said to herself, "Okay, that was fun. Now it's time to get back to work." Even if a former administrator clings to some old habits, it can be useful to remember, every now and again, that in small doses, unhurriedness can be a joy.

---

* Santos, "Season 3, Episode 6: The Kindness of Strangers"; Santos, "Coronavirus Bonus, Episode 5: Help Others to Help Yourself."
† Gay, *Book of Delights*, 5–6.

Strategy 3: Accepting the Prospect of Retirement

Without much prompting, participants' thoughts, plans, and fears about retirement often surfaced in my interviews. Some participants, including former provost Steve, looked forward to retiring: "I've worked with a number of faculty and seen how they [work] into their late sixties, into their seventies, and even those that are in their eighties. That kind of long-term engagement just never really had any appeal to me. I felt as though I worked very hard. I got into college teaching very early on in my life, [and] I'm thinking, 'Enough's enough.' I want to ultimately retire and enjoy and be able to do things I see other retirees doing, and I felt like there could be a life after [this university] that I could really enjoy." While Steve embraced a vision for the future that did not include work, the very notion of ceasing professional work incited considerable anxiety for others. P.J. would only make whispered references to the "R-word." Former CAO Norm was enjoying the comforts of his post-administrative appointment—a generous salary, supportive colleagues, and the freedom to explore his teaching and research interests—and felt no urgency to rush into retirement.

Equating the end of work with the end of life, talk of retirement often took on a saturnine undercurrent. Without mincing words, former president Ralph said, "It kind of feels like I'm getting ready to die. All these things are coming together, and I will have done them, and it's like, 'Okay. Now what?' I'm unsettled, unconfident that I'll think of stuff to do. I don't really have as clear a plan as I've had for the last twenty years." Not having developed a plan for what might follow his working years, Ralph sought to prolong deciding when to retire or what to do with his time.

Apart from a pressing desire to do something else or lacking the financial resources to retire, several participants lamented the absence of clear indicators that it is time to retire (while some public universities enforce mandatory retirement ages, most do not). Former leaders' impulses to delay retirement were often rooted in indecision. Ex-provost Wesley put it this way: "I haven't decided when to retire. One of the oddities of academia is that it's my choice and there's not a lot that the institution can do to influence my choice. If this were industry, we'd be having a very different conversation. Realities would be very different." Although former provost Rosie was still in her fifties and not in a financial or an emotional position to retire, she agreed that universities could do more to give faculty members the tools to come to terms with retirement: "I think maybe it's especially challenging in academia. I think most of us go into academic careers motivated by a sense that 'This is who I am.' This work is often very tied to our identities." She continued, "If you hated your job, you'd be like, 'Whatever, I'm done.'" But most academics like their jobs, and as a result, ceasing work takes on added symbolic meaning.

Whether a leader has already formulated a plan to retire upon exiting their administrative role or whether it takes another ten years to develop one, the final stage of returning to the faculty is reconciling yourself to the prospect of leaving it for good. To this end, much can be learned from former chief academic officer Sid, who intentionally approached returning to the faculty as a chance to prepare for the transition into retirement. He explained that in the next few years, he saw himself "transitioning to something that's a little more scary, which is post-professional work or at least post-teaching institutional work." He continued, "I see it as this fluid transition both in time and role that's going to take me to that point. I think [returning to the faculty] is going to give me some capital as I make this other shift." Learning to inhabit a professional identity apart from his administrative title, regaining autonomy over his time, and completing his professional goals would play an important role in helping Sid overcome the fear and indecision he felt about retirement. Illustrating the third tenet of Schlossberg's transition theory, individuals are more likely to adapt to change when they have past experiences to draw on. Approaching your return to the faculty as a trial run for retirement—a chance to try out different strategies that allow you to develop new routines and identities—is giving your future self a wealth of tools to make the next transition.

Delaying retirement rarely benefits the individual or their university. Many study participants reflected that only after they stepped away from an administrative role could they more clearly recognize the signs of burnout in themselves. They realized that they had been exhausted and found diminishing satisfaction in their work. A few pledged not to repeat the mistake of delaying a beneficial role change by staying too long in their faculty role. They pledged to themselves that while the day to retire might not be today and it might not even be next year, they would work up the courage to recognize that day would come.

Putting It into Practice

As we have seen in this chapter, senior leaders who return to the faculty are capable of exercising both their abilities and their restraint to advance the mission of their universities (as well as the greater good). And yet, it is difficult for former leaders to always get the balance right. Former leaders define and perform their "second faculty careers" according to very different and even contradictory impulses. Some perform their post-administrative roles as inward focused: they mentor colleagues and serve on university committees. Others direct their energies externally: they volunteer with local nonprofits, take on a service role in their disciplinary society, or busy themselves with consulting work. No matter what activities consumed their time, the majority of former senior leaders I spoke with saw the lingering challenge of stepping away as learning to balance adding value and negotiating autonomy.

Table 5.1. Strategies to Navigate Your "Second" Faculty Career

Microprocess	Useful strategies
Adding value: Former leaders possess specialized knowledge and skills to advance their universities, disciplines, and communities	*Exhibiting project leadership*: Invest institutional know-how into a campus initiative or service role (e.g., committee chair, department head). *Making scholarly and service contributions*: Orient your service outside the institution by publishing in your academic discipline or advising a nonprofit organization. *Mentoring others*: Pass on what you know and use your networks to invest in the next generations of scholars and campus leaders. *Hanging back*: Sometimes the best way to contribute to the greater good is to not interfere and let someone else take the lead. *Realigning your vision*: Your vision of adding value may conflict with your successor's or your university's vision of the roles you should play. Process the disappointment and find ways to fulfill your goals.
Negotiating autonomy: Faculty work is largely self-determined; challenge yourself to find work that continues to inspire you	*Working for yourself*: Engage in forms of teaching, research, and service that you find meaningful at this late stage of your career. *Shaping your own performance criteria*: If your university has specific performance criteria, define them in ways that align with your timeline and interests. *Accepting the prospect of retirement*: Indecision and equating the end of work with the end of life can prompt some people to delay retiring; do yourself and your institution the service of being brave enough to accept the prospect that one day, your time on the faculty will end.

CHAPTER 6

Reimagining Leaders, Reimagining Leadership

The lived experiences of more than fifty senior leaders who stepped away from administrative posts at a variety of four-year institutions across the country reveal that few of those institutions use a strategic or intentional approach to shape the process of returning to the faculty. A former leader's ability to assimilate into faculty life is left largely to the individual to sort out. While some highly motivated and self-aware individuals will manage just fine under a laissez-faire mentality, much more could be done to ensure that future transitions are managed well and former leaders become strategic assets. By leaving much to chance, institutions make themselves vulnerable to a former academic leader becoming a financial liability or a loose cannon.

Across sectors, we have at best an impartial and imperfect understanding of what *should* become of a leader who relinquishes their title. At the federal level, we have watched former presidents go on to lead global foundations, write voluminous memoirs, return to their Texas ranches to paint, and play a lot of golf. In corporate America, ex-CEOs might take up advisory duties on a corporate board, but we generally expect them to pay little attention to the day-to-day operations of a company, leaving them to explore new passion projects, to engage in charity work, or to play a lot of golf. Academia provides an unusual test case to explore how an individual can transition from senior leadership to a more ordinary, anonymous, and low-authority role within an organization.

Keeping these bigger dimensions of post-leadership in mind, in this final chapter of the book, I offer some targeted recommendations designed to improve the process of stepping away in universities. Two solutions emerge: more time and less money. By creating more time for sitting senior academic leaders—by both reimagining their daily duties and providing uninterrupted blocks of time to allow them to remain rooted in the noble faculty pursuits of teaching and research—we will make leadership roles more appealing and sustainable. The second solution concerns money. As the job demands for the presidents, provosts, and deans have swelled to include not only the management of academic programs and personnel but also fund-raising, data analysis, legal standards, federal compliance reporting, managing semiprofessional athletic teams, and institutional marketing, salaries too have soared. A study by the American Council of Trustees and Alumni determined that between 1993 and 2007, administrative spending at 198 leading public at private colleges increased 61 percent, compared to a 39 percent rise in instructional spending.[1] Arguably, any increase is too high, as the cost of a four-year college degree feels increasingly out of reach to middle- and low-income students. Pointing to unsustainable growth, many scholars and politicians have decried the adverse effects of mission creep in higher education and the true cost of institutional "striving."[2] While it may not be the silver bullet, committing to pay senior leaders who return to the faculty like faculty members (instead of as former administrators) is a small step toward managing costs.

These recommendations for how to rethink senior leadership roles to bridge the gap between administrative and faculty cultures have implications for individuals (e.g., trustees, new presidents) as well as professional organizations (e.g., the American Council on Education). At the individual level, there is a need to help former senior leaders to calibrate their expectations and take steps to prepare for rewarding faculty careers. By listening closely to what former senior leaders have to say, we can learn how to direct former administrators to add value in specific ways and give department chairs better guidance to manage senior leaders who return to the faculty. Even a few small tweaks will go a long way toward reducing ambiguity and stress. At the same time, policies, practices, and a commitment to address underlying issues can address the macro issues and better shield institutions from the high costs of leadership turnover. Members of governing boards who negotiate the employment contracts for top administrators must recognize their important role in the stepping away process. When it comes to how they structure the contracts of new presidents or how they expend resources to support the university's mission, trustees, advisers, and regents have significant responsibilities.

What Former Leaders Want

I ended each of my interviews with former senior leaders by inviting participants to identify the ways their institutions supported them to successfully transition to the faculty and what, if anything, else might have helped. The themes of time, money, and symbolic acts of appreciation figured prominently in their responses. Nearly all participants cited the importance of receiving a paid academic leave of at least a year after they left their role. They identified how this time enabled them to destress, to reacclimate to faculty work, and to stay away from campus while their successors established authority. (These efforts are examined more closely in chapter 3.) Specifically, many appreciated that their leaves came with few strings attached. While faculty might be expected to produce something like a publication at the end of a research leave, administrators appreciated that they were free to be as productive (or unproductive) as they chose to be during their "year off."

Former leaders pointed to other forms of institutional support that eased their transition and improved their quality of life as they navigated new roles. Nearly all senior leaders talked about how much they appreciated the celebrations that their campuses hosted to mark the end of their appointment. In general, leaders appreciated it when the tenor of these events matched their personalities; those who were uncomfortable with lavish displays preferred smaller affairs with a relatively small number of speakers; others liked it when the size of the assembled crowds measured in the hundreds. No matter the format, these events provided a sense of closure for leaders, allowed them to reflect on the contributions of their service, and enabled them to share information about what they planned to do next.

Former leaders appreciated the opportunity to step into faculty roles that reflected their interests and strengths. Many former senior leaders, especially those with long research careers, felt flattered to receive a named professorship or honorifics. Whether these titles carried any additional salary or operating support, their symbolic value was most important (but frankly, a little discretionary funding was appreciated too). Some individuals talked about specific requests that they included in their exit negotiations. This ranged from securing a desirable office to favorably structuring their teaching responsibilities in their academic discipline or elsewhere (e.g., higher education leadership graduate programs, interdisciplinary centers). Having agency over what they taught and where they worked was very important to some former leaders; others were fine with taking whatever was offered.

The final category of recommendations named by former leaders includes many no-cost and low-cost forms of interpersonal support that made their transitions easier. Some of these recommendations have been discussed in previous chapters, such as provost Emma's decision to teach part-time prior to beginning an administrative leave (chapter 4) or Mildred's ability to delay her first faculty performance review for five years (chapter 5). In addition to measures that gave them time to adjust to a faculty role gradually, former senior academic leaders were deeply appreciative of individuals who helped them navigate potentially awkward and difficult circumstances. Former dean Felix, for example, explained how his successor played a vital role in his return to the faculty: "'I am not going to let you fall off a cliff,' I guess are the words he used. He has been extraordinary in the ways that he has been able to support my time. He let me pick and choose some of the activities that I want to continue to do [as a faculty member]." Compared to former senior academic leaders Isabel and Steve, who felt that their institutions underutilized them in their faculty capacity (chapter 5), Felix was grateful that his new dean empowered him to do a limited amount of quasi-administrative activities. Not only did Felix find satisfaction in the familiar tasks, but he was also grateful that his successor asked him to contribute in a way that made him feel valued.

Former senior leaders shared ways that their home departments and new department chairs made them feel welcome. General onboarding or being invited to lunch by their new chair to talk about teaching and research interests had an outsized effect to reassure former administrators that they were returning on good terms. Unsurprisingly, small acts of kindness and professional courtesy go a long way, sometimes having a greater impact on the individual's transition than more costly investments. Whether or not it is fair to do so, former leaders often conflate the actions of an individual actor with the stance of the whole institution. For example, when a new administrator gives the former leader the cold shoulder at a social event, former leaders are left feeling slighted by "the university." But when a department chair is generous—say, by giving a former leader a plum teaching time—an ex-leader may interpret this move as the college expressing its gratitude for past administrative service.

It is beyond the scope of my research to say how much guidance department chairs received from central administration about "how" to welcome a former administrator into the fold or just how generous to be. Anecdotally, I have spoken with chairs who received little, if any, information beyond being told that "X person is returning to your department." Sometimes, the new chair is left in the dark about any promised arrangements, including what the former senior leader will teach, how much funding or research support they will receive, or guidance on how to evaluate their performance. Since conversations with former senior leaders suggest that these individuals can really make or break a transition, universities ought to ensure that chairs get more consistent guidance.

132 STEPPING AWAY

COLLECTED WISDOM 16

Advice for Department Chairs Who Supervise Former Senior Leaders

Just as your institution might have offered you limited guidance regarding your return to the faculty, your chair probably received even less direction. You have my permission—and encouragement—to share this list of considerations with your new department chair as the first step to establishing a healthy working relationship.

Ask Questions

Administrators return to the faculty for complex and varied reasons, and their post-leadership goals differ significantly. Don't assume that you have the full picture. The best way for a chair to support a new faculty colleague is to welcome them back sincerely and ask questions such as the following:

- What might you want to teach?
- What are your research goals? How can I help you achieve them?
- What forms of service might you want to engage in?
- What questions do you have about the department?
- What do you need from me as your chair to be successful?
- Based on your past experience, what, if anything, would you like to bring to the department?
- Are there things, within reason, you would rather not do?
- What else am I missing?

Recognize that Your "New" Faculty Colleague May Benefit from Onboarding

Bear in mind that your new colleague might have never served as a traditional faculty member at this institution. Even if they did, policies and processes have probably evolved considerably in the intervening decade(s). An administrator who returns to the faculty might benefit from the same practical information as any other new hire. Offer a tutorial in using the copier, guidance on placing textbook orders, and a primer on completing travel paperwork; order a new box of business cards, and introduce them to the support staff and student workers.

Be the Chair

Being a good chair sometimes means looking out for an individual; other times, it means looking out for the collective good. Welcoming a former administrator into the department will probably call on you to do both as you assign courses, award travel funding, and field routine requests. Treat your new colleague the same way you treat others to the extent possible.

Recognize What You Have Gained

While a former senior administrator coming into your department might give you some managerial angst, be empowered to make your new faculty colleague a thought partner, sounding board, and resource. Their relationships and insider knowledge might make your job easier when you want to make a more persuasive case to the dean for a new faculty line. You might also want to tap a former administrator's wisdom about legal standards, interpreting complex financial reports, managing difficult personalities, or handling a crisis.

Time: The Problems of Burnout, Languishing, Summit Syndrome

Participants in this study painted a vivid picture of what it means to lead a college or university. They experienced high amounts of stress, worked upward of sixty hours per week, and regularly sacrificed time with family and their physical well-being in the name of their jobs. None of this is new information. Scholarly research about senior academic leaders has long warned of the high likelihood of burnout and declining physical health that comes from having a demanding leadership position. Mary Ann Swain warns of "the administrator's thirty," the propensity for a new leader to gain weight from long days on the job, the lack of personal time, and expected attendance at catered events.[3] Added to this, the job rarely stops upon leaving the office; leaders bring these demands home with them.[4] Apart from the commonsense triumvirate of self-care practices to curtail these negative effects—eat right, exercise more, and get more sleep—there is much less talk about systemic solutions to reimagine leadership roles and make the culture more humane. In a sense, the senior leaders in this study are the canaries in the coal mine—pushing themselves past the point of exhaustion to advance a fiction that universities can do it all and be all things to all stakeholders. In the quest toward such unsustainable and amorphous ends, a postsecondary institution's insatiable appetite to grow larger, increase prestige, and compete for students and research dollars may no longer justify the costs. Restoring balance and realigning our ambitions needs to be a paradigm shift, not a quick fix.

My research could not pinpoint when a formerly exciting task became stale; this threshold depended entirely on the individual's constitution, campus-level factors, and external pressures (e.g., state politics, the financial crisis, the pandemic). Many participants had the self-awareness to name the precursors that contributed to their burnout: centralizing functions, piling on responsibilities, adding direct reports, and being pressured by their institutions to extend their contracts beyond an agreed-on departure date. On their own, each of these small accumulations may seem manageable, but over the course of many years, they become unsustainable. Failing to heed these signals can be catastrophic. When a leader is burned out, they are more likely to "cut corners," accept the status quo as good enough, and shy away from tackling big challenges. Peter Flawn advises his fellow university presidents that "early retirement as a successful president" is a better outcome than the consequences that come when the "institution get[s] away from you."[5] In recognizing the potential harms of ratcheting up the expectations for senior leaders, universities can ensure their long-term success by proactively taking better care of their leaders.

Added to all of this, the COVID-19 pandemic only accelerated the high stakes and nonstop nature of administrative service. The pandemic pressured senior leaders to continually pivot their campus operations, manage financial volatility (sometimes making drastic spending cuts or staffing reductions), and lose sleep over ensuring the health and safety of their campuses. In one of the year's most read articles in the *New York Times*, the columnist and Wharton School of Business professor Adam Grant described the collective feeling of distraction and despondency, the inability to focus, and the lack of motivation that plagued many workers: "Languishing is a sense of stagnation and emptiness. It feels as if you're muddling through your days, looking at your life through a foggy windshield. . . . Languishing is the forgotten middle child of mental health. It's the void between depression and flourishing—the absence of well-being. You don't have symptoms of mental illness, but you're not the picture of mental health either. You're not functioning at full capacity." For Grant, one of the greatest disruptions the pandemic had on the American workforce was a communal "dulling of delight" and "dwindling of drive."[6] Whether senior leaders were languishing specifically because of the pandemic or because of their already-demanding jobs is somewhat immaterial. The takeaway is the same: failing to address the root causes of chronic stress leads many people to check out. Grant points to a few strategies that an individual can use to stave off languishing, providing glimpse into how higher ed can take better care of its leaders. The first strategy is to name the experience and to talk about it. Leaders who cannot recognize the signs will not be motivated to change. Second, he advises that achieving "flow," the "elusive state of absorption in a meaningful challenge or momentary bond where your sense of time, place and self melts away," can help an individual find their way back to happiness and engagement.[7] The conditions of senior administrative work may make "flow" even harder to achieve: dashing between more than forty meetings per week, skimming hundreds of emails each day, and being pressured to respond quickly are antithetical to deep mental absorption. Or, as Grant explains, "it's hard to find flow if you can't focus." Alternatively, Grant offers that focusing on small achievable goals or "giving yourself some uninterrupted time" could also whack back some of the effects of languishing.[8] Again, given what we know about the daily and weekly calendars of a senior academic leader, blocks of uninterrupted and unscheduled time are nearly impossible to come by. Even when a leader can cordon off a rare morning or afternoon on their calendar, urgent meetings, calls, and emergencies always seem to come up.

Despite knowing these pitfalls, one of the most disconcerting things I heard from study participants is that they rarely had opportunities to speak candidly about their professional challenges or express their frustrations in ways that could address the structure or nature of their work. While we expect many things from university presidents—and we probably ask too much of them—perhaps we have overlooked their importance as managers of other senior leaders. By cultivating trusting relationships in which other senior leaders can speak candidly, the president does the university a great service. When warranted, presidents should take the lead in restructuring roles or reallocating responsibilities for their direct reports (and, in turn, governing boards should invest equal care in presidents). Too many participants in this study harbored long-simmering feelings of burnout, frustration, disengagement, and isolation that might have been prevented or alleviated by more attentive and generous management. If not a university president, then perhaps an independent career coach or consultant might provide confidential support and give sitting leaders the formative feedback and spaces for compassionate listening that is currently lacking at many universities. If presidents fail to initiate conversations with their subordinate deans and provosts about their career goals and professional satisfaction, I fear that this systemic problem will continue. No one in the organization will feel comfortable airing their vulnerabilities if the behaviors are not modeled by the people at the top.

This is not simply about allowing a senior leader to vent, though that might help every now and again; it is a call to create spaces for conversations about holistic well-being and workplace satisfaction among those who support and mentor others. Few study participants were given formative feedback on their job performance, and several had gone multiple years without undergoing a formal professional review, even in public universities where such reviews are mandated by law. Not only do reviews provide an opportunity to evaluate an individual's past performance, but they serve as a protected space where an employee can set future goals and brainstorm ways to make their job more fulfilling and productive. The fact that such reviews are not prioritized or framed in this way reveals a strategic vulnerability.

It is unreasonable to expect senior leaders to stay in their positions indefinitely—and it is high time that institutions recognize this. Expanded institutional supports can help ensure that senior academic leaders have terms that are productive and balanced rather than stressful and exhausting. When leaders invariably leave or step down, institutions must be better prepared to move forward without disruption. Unfortunately, one way that institutions try to preserve stability is by asking other senior leaders to stay in their roles longer than they might like. For example, if a president leaves to take another position, the institution might ask a provost to delay retirement, perhaps even offering financial incentives to stay on. Data from this study show that extending a senior leader's service by a year or more often comes at a cost to both the individual and the institution. The handful of individuals who agreed to this kind of arrangement regretted it later. Here is what one of those leaders who agreed to extend their services said:

> Since this study is anonymous, I'll just come out and say it: I'm not the kind of faculty member that I was desirous of having on the faculty when I was provost. I'm a little bit of a slacker because I've been there, done that, and I'm willing to cut the corners in a way that wasn't true certainly when I started my career. . . . My department is doing a lot of searching for new faculty members, and I'm not involved in any way. I'm on the sidelines. I'm happy to offer advice to the chair when asked, but I'm not going and banging on the chair's door and saying, "You have to do this, and the department needs this." I feel like I'm here for a few more years. I don't know how many that is, and then I will retire.

While an institution might be tempted to squeeze out another year from a leader in the name of stability, it increases the chances that the professor will drift for the remainder of their career. When they eventually did go back to the faculty, these individuals were often far less engaged in research, less committed to teaching, and wholly uninterested in service. Agreeing to spend another year or two in administration forced them to use up what little gas they had in their tanks.

If institutions continue to ignore these persistent issues by delaying performance reviews and failing to address the root causes of burnout, then it remains incumbent on sitting academic leaders to recognize in themselves the symptoms of mental and physical exhaustion. Sitting leaders must be attentive to the early warning signs described by the participants in this study: losing interest in performing the core functions of the job, noticing when once-interesting tasks become mundane, leaving health issues unaddressed, and losing patience. Considering that many faculty members get into administration (and then decide to stay) because it provides novelty and intellectual challenge, the moment that their work starts to plateau should be cause for action. Participants who explicitly or implicitly acknowledged having stayed in their positions for too long exhibited the telltale signs of what the corporate world calls "summit syndrome," a feeling of emptiness that can follow achieving a major goal. Summit syndrome is most common among "overachievers who thrive on challenge," a common personality type among ambitious leaders. Those who build their identities around overcoming daunting challenges will find that as they "near the summit of a job's learning curve," their performance dips, their enthusiasm fades, and they feel cynicism and anger.[9] If and when a leader recognizes the onset of growing disengagement—be it languishing, burnout, or summit syndrome—then it may be fruitful to imagine and pursue a parallel future (chapter 3). Leaders might find renewed purpose by seeking out a more senior position at another institution, making a lateral move that provides unfamiliar problems to solve, or reinventing themselves as a professor (or in another domain of life).

I think that all will agree that colleges and students deserve leaders who are fully engaged in their roles. By removing the stigma of "stepping down" and ensuring that administrative contracts do not incentivize continuing past the point of burnout, we help leaders gain the confidence to leave when their interest begins to wane. If anything, the testimonies of former leaders in this study demonstrate that there is life after administration. Participants were often invigorated by returning to the classroom, found service rewarding, and loved how the availability of free time allowed them to think clearly. Hopefully this finding will help future leaders gain the confidence to initiate a professional change before languishing sets in.

Restructuring Leadership Positions

Few of us would encourage new college graduates or our own children to accept a job schedule that would, almost inevitably, lead to burnout. As higher education finds itself facing a wave of presidential retirements, talented faculty leaders may not want to fill these anticipated vacancies, at least not the way the jobs are structured now.[10] In addition to reducing the stigma around burnout, another way to make administrative jobs more satisfying and less demanding is to cut back on the scope of responsibilities currently assigned to any one individual. This could be achieved by crafting more faculty positions with fractional leadership responsibilities. For example, why not divide an associate dean's role into two, each with a more discrete set of responsibilities? Whereas a current administrative role might require the totality of a forty-hour workweek, dividing these responsibilities among individuals might demand fewer sacrifices from any one person in the areas of teaching and research. If administrative stipends and course releases were divided between two candidates, there need not be much added costs for institutions. In fact, the leaders might even stagger their service in the summer so that each one is able to get a real break while business carries on. Simply reassigning administrative responsibilities to surrogates or adding more subordinates does little to address the root problem: expanding the number of mid- and senior-level administrators puts an even larger burden on leaders at the top.

Some law schools, including Rutgers, the University of New Mexico, and Case Western Reserve University, have recently instituted a co-dean structure, implicitly recognizing the benefits of divided executive responsibilities. Case Western selected a collaborative leadership structure because "neither [candidate] wanted to give up their roles—and if they ran the law school together, they wouldn't have to."[11] Some law schools are pursuing these structures to recruit stronger candidates, to increase productivity, to divide the burdens of fund-raising travel, and to foster a built-in support network for individuals who occupy positions known to be isolating. Assuming that co-deans do not step down at the same time, the structure affords continuity in a time of leadership change.[12]

Allowing faculty members to take on some administrative responsibilities without wholly ceasing their professorial activities might have other benefits as well. While such jobs may not appeal to all faculty members, some individuals might find such an appointment to be a worthy new professional challenge, giving them cause to develop and flex new muscles after hitting a career plateau. Whereas many senior leadership roles demand twelve-month contracts, perhaps shortening such appointments to ten or eleven months could restore some balance. Why shouldn't we encourage provosts and deans to use a month or two during the summer to write an article or take a brief sabbatical to develop a new skill or knowledge base? By temporarily delegating responsibilities during such periods, institutions will build their internal leadership pipelines and give leaders a needed break. Encouraging senior leaders to reconnect with their academic disciplines (e.g., attending a conference, teaching a seminar) or to attain the restorative benefits of a sabbatical (e.g., coauthoring a paper, extended rest) are also great long-term investments.

In 2020, Colorado College made the somewhat unusual move to appoint two individuals to serve as acting co-presidents: Mike Edmonds, dean of students and vice president for student life, and Robert G. Moore, senior vice president for finance and administration. Granted, the circumstances were somewhat unique—not only were we in the first semester of the pandemic, but President Jill Tiefenthaler was planning to leave the college to become the CEO of National Geographic, and the interim president (former provost) Alan Townsend was also leaving to begin a deanship elsewhere. Combined, the acting co-presidents possessed over forty years of experience at Colorado College, and they would benefit from the guidance of an Academic Advisory Council whose membership included six tenured professors.[13] While this structure was presumably adopted to provide continuity during a particularly trying time, higher education might consider the benefits of such a design. Moore shared some of the perceived benefits in an alumni publication: "Mike and I had worked together for 12 years and knew each other really well. That allowed us to share and rely on each other's strengths. When we had to make hard decisions, like whether to send students home, we talked."[14] Not only did the acting co-presidents have a high degree of trust in each other, but they also leveraged their combined strengths for the good of the institution. A similar model was adopted at Mount Union College in Ohio, where two longtime administrators were appointed to serve as interim, co–vice presidents of academic affairs. In an email to the campus, interim president Robert A. Gervasi described instances when one leader would have primary authority (one individual overseeing academic policies, while the other would make decisions regarding hires and promotions) and the areas where the pair would have shared oversight (e.g., piloting a new program review system, regional accreditation matters). He praised the collaborative arrangement as providing the campus with "increased productivity and responsiveness during the interim period."[15] In addition to campuses gaining leaders with broad domains of expertise, this shared arrangement might reduce some of the common challenges facing senior leaders. Many leaders have discussed how lonely it can be at the top and the emotional toll of making hard decisions; co-leaders are able to approach some of the hardest decisions together and find comfort in confiding in someone who intimately understands the realities of their working life.

If not a co-administrator model, colleges could think more creatively about the administrative calendar to build in periodic breaks for presidents, provosts, and deans to recharge their mental batteries. Might it be possible to provide mini-sabbaticals during the lulls in the academic calendar—such as after Thanksgiving to mid-January or late May through mid-July? Institutions might award leaders four to six weeks off in which they could visit other institutions to get new ideas, catch up on their reading, learn a new skill or certification, engage in professional development, or enjoy prolonged blocks of uninterrupted rest. Several senior leaders regretted that their positions prevented them from taking a traditional semester or yearlong sabbatical, but surely a shorter leave might give senior leaders the freedom to rest, think, and lead. And the institution benefits by providing others an insider's view of what a senior leader's days are like.

Another productive shift that colleges and universities could make is to stop perpetuating the notion that taking on an administrative appointment is akin to crossing over to the "dark side."[16] Instead of structuring positions that demand a decisive identity shift, we should find ways to increase the fluidity between faculty and administrative roles. Several participants in the study championed administrative term limits in principle, including participants who were employed by institutions that used them and those who were not. The clearest advantage of fixed-term contracts is that they offer clarity and certainty. They ensure that periodically there is "fresh blood" and "new energy" to confront institutional challenges. The transparency of the timeline can nudge leaders to begin quietly tapping possible successors on the shoulder. Proponents of term limits reasoned that leaders who serve for shorter terms stay truer to their faculty values and perspectives. Normalizing the understanding that leaders step into and out of administrative roles with some regularity allows an institution to feel less shaken when transitions happen. Term limits help universities prepare for and normalize leadership change. Those who were less enthusiastic about term limits offered sound criticisms. Some participants wondered why an institution would push a good leader out because of some arbitrary end date. Others pointed out times when the demands of a university may not align neatly with the contractual calendar; for example, it would be unwise for a university president to leave in the middle of an ambitious fund-raising campaign.

What I learned from this research has swayed me in the direction of favoring some limitation on the length that any senior leader should hold a position. Perhaps a university might adopt some soft term limits—for instance, a shared understanding that no leader should be expected to serve more than ten years. This prevents an associate dean from getting stuck in a role that no longer feels challenging or a dean from burning themselves out. Leaders are freed from worrying whether they are leaving at the right time (a decision that often produces considerable anxiety). It also helps to ensure that leaders leave with enough energy and ambition to do meaningful faculty work. Such a practice would increase the number of faculty members who have some administrative experience, perhaps, in turn, helping to engender greater trust and shared understanding across the campus. By calling attention to the many ways that former senior leaders add value to their institutions (discussed in greater depth in chapter 5), regularly cycling people through leadership roles provides a university with a deep bench equipped to contribute in other ways, such as serving in midlevel positions (such as department chairs), mentoring colleagues, and becoming public thought leaders.

If we curtail the time-intensive responsibilities assigned to senior leaders, who will do the work? William Bowen, former president of Princeton University, and Eugene Tobin, former president of Hamilton College, have argued that some "vertical modes of decision-making in the academy" might be supplanted by horizontal modes that go beyond current departmental structures.[17] In calling for a cease-fire to the destructive "us-versus-them" rhetoric, they contend that universities should both enable nimble decision-making by administrators and also elevate the voices of all stakeholders (not just tenured faculty). Bowen and Tobin call for broader conversations involving all stakeholders: What superfluous activities can we cease in the name of our core functions? How do we meet our mission and cut our budget? What investments will yield the best outcomes for students? There is no reason to fear that universities will cease to function if we redistribute responsibilities that currently reside in one leader; indeed, we might even strengthen shared governance in the process.

The Role of Governing Boards

The findings from this study suggest that members of governing boards could be doing more to safeguard institutions from the vulnerability, costs, and uncertainty caused by senior leadership turnover. Several participants described experiencing tense, unraveling relationships with their supervisors; in particular, long-serving, otherwise-successful provosts often experienced irreconcilable differences with a new president. I would caution members of governing boards and search committees to be more discerning about candidates' disposition for the office. On the basis of the experiences of several participants in this study, boards should more closely vet candidates for narcissistic tendencies. In a job interview, it can be hard to distinguish charisma and confidence from narcissism; but failing to vet a leader's disposition will almost certainly result in a potentially destructive wave of resignations (e.g., provosts, deans, cabinet members). Appointing a president who is ill equipped to lead people may risk causing greater instability within and across the institution.

142 STEPPING AWAY

COLLECTED WISDOM 17

Advice for Governing Boards That Hire
Senior Leaders

Searching for and selecting a new senior leader—especially a president—is an institutional inflection point. It's hard not to get swept up in the visioning conversations, the prospect of institutional change, the allure of captivating candidates, and the symbolism of it all. Welcoming a new leader reminds all that everything is possible. In these moments, it is critical for members of governing boards and those who are responsible for hiring and evaluating senior academic leaders to remember their role to support leaders and, even more importantly, the *institutions* they are entrusted with sustaining.

Don't Limit Yourself
Drawing on thirty years of service as the president of both Adelphi University and Ramapo College, in *How University Boards Work*, Robert Scott reminds boards that there is more than one set of qualities and experiences that make for a great president. Strong candidates will demonstrate "intellectual curiosity, the ability to communicate clearly and coherently in both writing and speaking, a desire to listen, respect for higher education values and traditions as well as for others, and a commitment to the institution's mission and integrity."* Rather than try to replicate a past leader's style or educational pedigree, boards should frame the selection of a new president as a moment for the institution to reassert its core values in a contemporary context.

Engage the Right Help
Scott endorses engaging a search firm to carry out a national search. Boards might delegate among themselves the task of interviewing prospective firms, but boards should enter this process ready to do their due diligence in checking references, clarifying the services provided, and understanding the methods they use to vet candidates and the firm's commitments to diversity and equity. At the same time, boards might consider whether the firm's value justifies the cost, which may range from $25,000 to more than $200,000.† After investigative journalists determined that search consultants cost Illinois taxpayers more than $6 million over nine years,

---

* Scott, *How University Boards Work*, 99.
† Berman, "This Is How Much Colleges Spend Just Searching for a New President." Berman cites an analysis performed by James Finkelstein determining that the average cost of engaging a search firm to search for a public institution president was $78,796, and costs ranged from $25,000 to $160,000. Sabrowsky, "Presidential Search Costs to Exceed Those of Previous Years." Sabrowsky's reporting determined that the University of Minnesota paid a search firm $224,000 to conduct a presidential search in 2018.

legislators adopted a law prohibiting their use (the law included a provision that a governing board could appeal by providing sufficient justification).*

Institutions should be leery of contracting a firm that sets its fees according to the leader's negotiated salary, a structure that disincentivizes a firm from reducing costs. Regardless of whether an external firm is engaged, the board should take care to appoint a search committee that is sufficiently diverse, prepared, and resourced to carry out an all-consuming, energy-intensive process.

At the Beginning of an Appointment, Already Be Thinking about the End

If the new leader you hire is successful—serving for a decade or longer—there is a good chance that those who were involved in negotiating the leader's initial contract will not be there at its end. As a result, ensure that the "exit" terms are clearly spelled out. This includes what will happen if the leader leaves their post prematurely— whether they'll receive a paid sabbatical (and if so, for how long) and other details (departmental affiliation, teaching expectations, research expectations and support, salary, etc.).

Some boards might be so confident in their hiring judgment to think that contingency plans are unnecessary. But be wary of such hubris. No board expects its new leader to fall short of expectations, to fail, or to resign before their contract ends. Insofar that your primary loyalty is to the institution and not to the individual, spelling out these terms is your duty.

Policy, Precedent, and the Law

Many states, university systems, and even some private institutions have policies that dictate, among other things, the standard length of an administrative term, review procedures, salary levels, and other considerations (e.g., requiring that the leader reside in a campus residence). Before entering a negotiation, boards should be fully versed on all relevant policies. It can also be helpful to understand precedent (rereading the contracts for the last two or three presidents will achieve this).

Don't Give Away the Farm

In attempting to hire the most desirable candidate, some governing boards will do anything to close the deal—offering generous salaries, performance bonuses, deferred compensation packages, discretionary spending accounts, and the like. Such enticements might bring a particularly tough negotiation to an end, but at what cost?

Under the strictest assurances of confidentiality, many senior leaders in this study confessed that their institutions were *overly* generous offering more salary, benefits, or perks than were strictly necessary. CUPA-HR, the leading association for human

---

* Kiley, "Illinois Law Will Restrict Universities' Use of Search Firms."

144 STEPPING AWAY

resources professionals in higher education, recommends a series of structures that can help prevent boards from overdoing it, such as performing comparable salary analyses, developing an executive compensation philosophy, and using the institution's mission as the basis for negotiation.* It is only a matter of time before the compensation details become public knowledge through mandated reporting on annual tax forms. Overpaying a president can diminish the university's coffers while also garnering the wrong kinds of attention in the higher ed press.

Ensure a Smooth Handover
While a new leader will be a magnet for attention, the board should continue to work with the outgoing leader until their term officially ends—and to facilitate in the sharing of information to the incoming leader. Expect a lame duck to tie up any remaining loose ends before departing—completing pending program reviews, bringing policy disputes to resolution, or bringing closure to any personnel disputes. In addition, the board should establish a clear timeline and schedule during which time an outgoing president will remain available for consultation.

* Johnson, Hyatt, and Brantley, "Paying the President."

A governing board's responsibilities do not end with selecting a new leader. With college presidents serving on average for just six and a half years, trustees must take steps to shield institutions from the strain of turnover.[18] By taking responsibility for enacting some of the changes discussed here, such as restructuring leadership positions and shifting the culture to promote more candid discussions of burnout, governing boards will bolster their university's resiliency. But that's not all boards must do—they must use the power of the purse to realign spending and institutional priorities.

COLLECTED WISDOM 18

How Governing Boards Normalize and Prepare for Leadership Change

Not only do governing boards possess responsibility for selecting a senior academic leader, but effective boards support smooth leadership transitions when they leverage their authority appropriately, ask clarifying questions, and keep the focus on the institution's long-term success.* When everyone plays their part, the university is prepared for whatever the future brings.

What Can and Should the Board Do?

In *How University Boards Work*, former Adelphi University president Robert Scott attributes much presidential turnover to the following: "a lack of clarity of expectations, dysfunctional boards, erratic or unethical behavior, political interference, student and faculty protests, and more."† Even the best university board cannot protect a leader or an institution against all risks, but it can certainly do a great service by alleviating a president's stress rather than being the source of it. In public universities, gubernatorially appointed regents might strategize with a president on how best to use their political influence and relationships to support the institution's best interests. In private institutions, board members can call on their networks to provide knowledge and financial investment.

Learn to Read the Signs

The research on senior executives substantiates our tacit understanding: *it's lonely at the top*. It is not always in the best interest of a leader to openly divulge their struggles—for fear that volunteering information about their personal lives, deteriorating health, or a mounting sense of professional dissatisfaction might prompt the governing board (or their subordinates) to lose confidence. Since leaders may understandably withhold such disclosures, members of the governing board must attune themselves to notice what goes unsaid:

- Have you seen physical changes that suggest the leader is burned out or neglecting their health?
- What work energizes the leader? What work exhausts them? What kind of work are they doing now?
- What, if anything, does the leader say about their life after administration?
- How does the leader describe the meaning they derive from their work?

---

* AGB, "Principles of Trusteeship."
† Scott, *How University Boards Work*, 12.

146 STEPPING AWAY

While the president might not confide this kind of information to their governing board, boards can encourage the leader to hire a leadership coach to provide confidential advice and be a strategy partner. Boards can include work-life balance in a leader's annual review and encourage the leader to take accrued leave. Recognizing the toll that leadership can take, boards must always look for the signs that leaders are neglecting their needs and, in turn, neglecting the needs of the institution. Making a hard job feel sustainable and prioritizing holistic well-being will hopefully keep your leader in the game for the long haul.

Normalize Leadership Change

A truly great leader does more than keep the seat warm for their successor. Expanding our definition of leadership achievement to include what the Association of Governing Board (AGB) calls "change-leadership traits" ensures that a leader is safeguarding the institution to weather change. Boards should encourage and evaluate these traits within leaders because institutional capacity and resilience will be critical during a leadership transition. AGB recommends that boards include the following criteria in their evaluation of presidents:

- Does the president understand relevant theories of change and how they apply in an academic setting?
- How adept is the president at engaging the board in upstream discussions of the need for change and the strategies to achieve it?
- Does the leader actively engage the appropriate people throughout the institution and the larger community of stakeholders, if appropriate, in the change process?
- Does the leader display the talent to create or recognize good ideas? Is the leader capable of discarding unproductive, stale, or misplaced strategies?
- Does the president exhibit the ability to change leadership styles and strategic objectives?
- Has the executive demonstrated a capacity to spring back from criticism, failure of a particular tactic or strategy, or the emergence of a new obstacle?
- Has the president shown readiness to select, promote, and sustain competent team members? Is the leader willing and able to make personnel changes when things aren't working?*

Expect Presidents to Infuse Succession Planning into Their Leadership Practice

Keeping the long-term interests of the institution in mind, boards should exercise their influence by holding presidents and chancellors accountable for creating self-sustaining and renewing institutional cultures. Boards should periodically ask senior

---

* MacTaggart, "How Presidential Evaluations Must Change."

leaders to report on how they have invested in the professional development of their direct reports, cabinet members, and other institutional leaders (e.g., deans, department chairs, staff directors). One potential form this might take is a succession planning memorandum.* Not only does such a plan demonstrate to the board that individuals develop new knowledge and skills to navigate the unknown, but it also helps leaders undergo a thoughtful, honest assessment of whether they are providing sufficient guidance, mentorship, and opportunities for growth.

* Scott, *How University Boards Work*, 170–176.

Money: The Elephant in the Room

While I was conducting my research, Lou Anna Simon resigned as president of Michigan State University, following a sex-abuse scandal involving Larry Nassar, a former physician to the Michigan State gymnastics team. In late 2021, the Michigan Court of Appeals ruled that there was insufficient evidence to prove that Simon had knowledge of abuse happening on campus.[19] While the case is most likely to be remembered in the context of the institutional response to the Me Too movement, it brought considerable public attention to the issue of executive compensation in higher education. Before the Nasser scandal, Simon was the country's sixth-highest-paid college president, earning close to $1 million annually. For comparison, a 2017 report by the American Association of University Professors compiled data from more than a thousand institutions and determined that the average salary of a full professor was $102,403, and the average salary for a college president was $334,617.[20] For an even more salient comparison, the *Chronicle of Higher Education* determined that in 2019, the average compensation for public college presidents was $544,136 (inclusive of salary and other perks); nineteen public university presidents earned more than $1 million.[21] The terms of Simon's contract were somewhat unusual in that, upon returning to the faculty, she would continue to receive her full presidential base salary.[22] The fact that Simon would be paid the same upon leaving office—especially in a state facing an anticipated budget deficit—only fueled the public's growing belief that colleges are not doing enough to make higher education affordable.

This case stands out for a few reasons. Simon's resulting faculty salary was not comparable to that of faculty members with similar rank and discipline at Michigan State (or frankly, at any institution). While the demands of a senior leadership position often harm a scholar's productivity, and

148 STEPPING AWAY

post-administrative compensation is often adjusted accordingly to reflect lost opportunity costs, continuing to pay former presidents the same as sitting presidents strikes me as a particularly generous interpretation of "accordingly." Temporarily, let us put aside the questions of whether it is ever appropriate to pay a college president a million dollars (or, for that matter, to pay a NCAA football coach several million dollars) and focus exclusively on the inappropriateness of paying a *former* college president a million dollars a year. While Simon's seven-figure paycheck might be an outlier, an analysis by James Finkelstein and Judith Wilde found that many senior leaders enjoy financially lucrative "platinum parachutes." Examining the contracts of more than one hundred public university presidents, Finkelstein and Wilde determined that if an individual were to receive all or most of their promised benefits and remained employed as a faculty member for a decade, their university might be obligated to pay that individual $4.5 million in base salary and up to another $1 million in fringe benefits.[23]

I turn now to a sensitive topic: executive compensation. Throughout my data collection and analysis, I enacted my role as a careful listener and faithful spokesperson, seeking to bring forward perspectives absent from our shared understanding about how leaders return to the faculty. While some participants made strong arguments in favor of the status quo, more participants shared my view that across US higher education, colleges and universities have a structural problem: many are paying their *former* presidents and provosts too much upon returning to the faculty.

COLLECTED WISDOM 19

Rethinking Post-Administrative Salaries

In *The Cost of Talent: How Executives and Professionals are Paid and How It Affects America*, Derek Bok, the former president of Harvard University, sketches a broad argument that lucrative compensation packages (in business, law, tech, and yes, even higher education) have led the nation to compromise its shared values and drain the talent pools for jobs in K–12 education and the public sector. To counter these trends, he proposed a paradigm shift: "Building an organizational culture that inspires commitment is a markedly different remedy from all those previously described (e.g., raising tax rates, increasing public sector salaries). It does not involve manipulating rewards to align acquisitive instincts with organizational goals. Instead, it seeks to change the attitudes of executives and professionals and cause them to perceive a greater meaning in their jobs. Rather than alter the pay people receive for their work, it tries to change the value of work itself."* While it may be challenging to shift ingrained cultural attitudes equating valuable work with higher levels of monetary compensation, change is possible within colleges and universities. Here are six reasons why colleges must abandon such compensation structures:

- *Overly generous packages send mixed messages.* Former senior leaders who return to the faculty demonstrate that many colleges have already attained the status of what Bok called an "organizational culture that inspires commitment."† Given what we have learned from the stories in this book, college leaders see themselves as faculty members. They identify deeply with their professorial roles, find meaning in their work, and relish the autonomy that academia affords them. This suggests that former leaders are often intrinsically motivated to return to the faculty and not simply to profit.
- *Big paychecks are retirement disincentives.* Generous annual salaries make the prospect of "staying on" the faculty more attractive than retirement. Given that upward of two-thirds of a university's budget may be committed to salary and benefits, continuing to keep two presidents, a few provosts, and half a dozen deans on the books for multiple years is a financial liability. Alternatively, one-time deferred compensation packages with the promise of a more modest faculty salary can demonstrate a board's appreciation while also offering the predictability of a one-time cost.
- *Inflated salaries may create compression issues.* Administrators who return to the faculty with high salaries only exacerbate the earning disparities between faculty members within a department. Other faculty members may request to have their salaries raised to come in line with that of a former administrator.
- *Overly generous offers may not be necessary.* In my research, several former college leaders told me—without much prodding—that their institutions had been *too* generous with them. They probably would have agreed to take less money. Many planned to return to the faculty for the lifestyle and opportunities it afforded them. But when a high number was offered, they simply agreed.
- *Platinum parachutes create challenging dynamics for boards and new leaders.* In a university, high salaries eventually become public knowledge under current IRS reporting requirements. When a board agrees to be generous with an outgoing leader, it commits significant institutional funds for the foreseeable future. Not only will a future leader lose the ability to redirect these funds, despite having had nothing to do with their predecessor's exit negotiations, but the new leader will invariably have to explain why so-and-so continues to earn half a million

---

* Bok, *Cost of Talent*, 294.
† Bok, 192.

150 STEPPING AWAY

dollars while other needs remain underfunded (e.g., mental health resources, scholarships, faculty merit pay).

- *Paying former administrators like current administrators compromises institutional values.* Recognizing that each institution has its own local values, as an industry, we share a commitment to knowledge, educating future citizens, and improving society. To the extent that we invest considerable resources in those who previously led our institutions, we hinder our ability to carry out our core commitments to students and society.

Many participants equated being regarded as a "peer" as the true marker of a successful faculty transition. While many ex-administrators in the study described undertaking thoughtful steps to reestablish their credibility with their faculty peers, the issue of compensation remains a wedge. Most participants prided themselves on having retained their faculty values throughout their administrative appointments—they explained how they used their "faculty lenses" to make decisions and advocated for measures to elevate the interests of students, faculty, staff, and the institution as a whole over personal gain. Participants who saw their career in phases—faculty member, administrator, and faculty member again—expected their salary to rise and fall to reflect shifting professional responsibilities. A small number of participants in this study made the argument that they were justified in receiving this level of compensation, recognizing that it might be double or triple what their similarly situated peers earned. They framed their case by saying that administrative service comes with considerable costs: sacrificing time with family, dampening scholarly productivity, and performing duties that take a measurable toll on physical and mental well-being.

The terms and variability of post-administration faculty compensation differs considerably between public and private institutions. In many but not all public universities, state laws establish so-called faculty retreat rights—including the terms of appointment and compensation scale—for leaders who return to the faculty. These laws might specify how salaries are calculated; for example, returning leaders will be paid nine-twelfths (75 percent) of their administrative salary to reflect the move from an annual contract to an academic-year appointment. One former provost was originally hired with this understanding, only to see the law change during her appointment:

The University System Board was being criticized by the state legislature for not kind of keeping [former administrators who returned to the faculty] under control. . . . Well, how this relates to me is [the System Board] decided they didn't like the retreat packages that we all have—just out of the blue: "Okay, we don't like it." The standard for ages has been you go back with 75 percent [pay]; you just go back to a nine-month contract. You go back to 75 percent of the salary that you had as an administrator. That's the deal we all have. If you can negotiate more, and plenty of people have, more power to you.

When the participant began collecting 75 percent of her administrative salary, it was, in her words, "on the front page of the damn newspaper, basically alleging that [she was] sitting around collecting money for doing nothing." This highlights, in part, how little the general public knows about what it means to return to the faculty.

In contrast to the standardized terms for executive contracts at some public universities, terms are more variable at privates. Many administrators at private universities told me that they were able to negotiate or renegotiate their retreat packages with almost no parameters at different moments during their tenure. Some spoke of enticements to extend their service, such as a provost who was offered a six-figure financial bonus to stay on for at least one year after an unplanned presidential departure. Few private institutions have policies establishing how former administrators who return to the faculty should be paid. One ex-provost at a private university described the favorable terms he negotiated for himself:

I said, "The last two provosts who departed, both of whom went back to the faculty at least for a time, were at the salary level of a distinguished, endowed chair, not at a regular faculty [level]." [The president] gave me that, which also means a reduced teaching load. I asked for a salary equal to our highest paid distinguished/endowed chair, teaching load equal to our distinguished/ endowed chair, which was two to four courses a year instead of the normal six, and this year off with full pay at my provost salary. [The president] gave me that. Then, I have a [dependent] who's in school still [and receives tuition remission]. The president said, "Even if you leave, if you take a presidency somewhere else, we'll let your [dependent] finish up on the tuition plan."

At private institutions, there are few structural barriers in place to prevent an individual from securing such benefits (many at considerable expense to the university).

Although a handful of former leaders defended their reduced teaching loads, higher salaries, or other benefits (e.g., tuition remission, discretionary funding), more participants criticized the practice of using administrative salary as a baseline to determine faculty pay. Within the study, there was a chorus of former leaders who called for this discordant (and expensive) practice come to an end. They struggled to justify how any leader who returns to the faculty warrants being paid the same or nearly the same—on a per-month basis—as they did while serving in their administrative role. Given that many were freed from all or most supervisory duties, that their presence was no longer compulsory at campus events, and that they gained greater control over their time, many thought it only right to be paid far less.

One study participant disclosed, "I'm being paid as much not to be a university president as I was paid to be one." The participant was not boasting, adding, "in all honesty, I still feel queasy about it." Rather than scrutinize problematic terms in individual contracts, I see this as a systemic problem. Compensation is out of step with individual motivations for returning to the faculty. The stories shared in this book provide a strong rationale for rethinking this assumption and adjusting compensation packages in the future. Upon reviewing why leaders return to the faculty and having a more nuanced view of the value they add, governing boards are better informed to rethink compensation. The evidence presented in this study demonstrates that some academic leaders bring innumerable benefits—tangible and intangible—to their institutions. Former leaders supplied a wealth of institutional knowledge, played important roles as mentors and translators, and raised the reputation of their institutions through their extraordinary teaching, service, and scholarship. Yet, the practice of continuing to compensate *former* leaders as if they continued to perform leadership duties raises serious questions of equity, academic values, and financial sustainability. In the day and age of rising tuition costs, soaring student debt, and state divestment from public higher education, continuing to pay former senior leaders as if they were current leaders no longer appears to be economically tenable, politically wise, or morally justifiable. Just as Simon's critics wondered why a former president should continue to draw a seven-figure paycheck while performing a job that equally qualified others do for a fraction of the cost, the findings of this study also highlight the persistent contradictions between the rhetoric and practice of stepping away.

In closing, drawing on the suggestions from study participants, I offer a modest proposal for how boards might more fairly and appropriately compensate senior academic leaders who return to the faculty. Upon returning to the faculty, a senior leader ought to be given one year of paid academic leave at nine-twelfths (75 percent) of their administrator's salary (a leader who was paid $250,000 would receive $187,500); this essentially preserves the status quo. Then, upon resuming full-time faculty duties, the individual should be offered a nine-month salary that represents the average of all full professors in their home department. Market differences prevail, so a president who returns to the Economics Department will probably earn more than one who returns to Modern Languages and Cultures. This proposal already follows a widely accepted practice across the academy: universities routinely peg faculty salaries to disciplinary norms. If the scholarly record of former senior leaders justifies it, they might be awarded a named professorship or an honorary chair with some extra perks, like a reduced teaching load to offset research time or travel funding. It might also be appropriate for a university to award a former senior leader something like one-time "re-start-up" funds to furnish a lab or buy other materials; such funds should be comparable with what new hires receive to launch their career. Otherwise, in general, boards and universities should not entertain additional requests; doing so commits resources that could be better allocated to achieve the institution's mission and perpetuates a practice that many leaders find incongruous with their motivations for returning to the faculty. While some administrators may not be as thrilled about this proposal, I would argue this: to be seen as a faculty member and complete the transition back to the faculty means that it's only fair to get paid like one.

Governing boards have one arrow left in the quiver when it comes to containing the potential cost of post-administrative salaries: make it more attractive for a senior leader to leave. The suggestion came from a study participant, who offered, "I think that there are—there are some real challenges to having former administrators hanging around in faculty offices. There are also some huge upsides, but there are some huge challenges. I don't take as a given that a school would want to make it attractive for a former administrator to rejoin the faculty. I think it would be perfectly reasonable for a school to say, 'We want to give former administrators very comfortable transition packages so that it's attractive for them not to be here.'" This proposal allows a campus to avoid the potential awkwardness of having too many former leaders on the faculty and gives the board the ability to contain personnel costs over time. Some participants who have a deep desire to return to teaching or who are not yet emotionally ready to retire might decline such an offer. But in some cases, this compromise might represent the ultimate win-win (giving institutions reduced financial uncertainty and former leaders an attractive payout).

Concluding Message: New Conceptions of Senior Academic Leaders Who Return to the Faculty

In reflecting about leaving the presidency of a small private college, Chris offered, "It's hardly a stepping down. I'm not troubled too much by the phrase. And I've used it myself. But I think that 'stepping away' captures it better. You know, I've thought of it less as about where I'm leaving than where I'm going." Rather than grieve the loss of power, status, and resources of the presidency, Chris expressed genuine excitement about ending his career doing the things he most loved: teaching students, engaging in important scholarly debates, and having enough flexibility in his schedule to follow his curiosities. Rather than linger on what leaders leave behind, this book strives to adopt this forward-looking view. What is on the other side of leadership?

In the introduction, I cited the veteran provost Rita Palm's description of the growing divide between administrative and faculty cultures: "Before universities became the complex organizations they are today, administrators were still faculty members, they thought like faculty members, and they were accepted by other faculty as colleagues, and they could easily return to full-time faculty status when their administrative stint was complete. After twenty-five years in academic administration, I have come to accept the fact that this ideal state has become quite rare."[24] Palm's assessment reminds us that there was a time in living memory when academic leaders and faculty members more regularly saw eye to eye as equals. But as real and perceived hostilities have increased, Palm implies that our universities have not done enough to prepare senior academic leaders to return to the faculty and that faculties are not well equipped to welcome them back. Higher education's preferred rhetoric remains dominated by terminology that only perpetuates division and polarization by drawing allusions to the "dark side" and "turncoats." The oft-repeated phrase "stepping down" has for too long equated returning to the faculty with the loss of power, status, and prestige. And it turns out that few administrators see it that way.

But there is room for hope. Many participants in this study believed and demonstrated that it was possible to return to the faculty, albeit to return as a different kind of faculty member who saw their institution through a new lens. While they occasionally encountered colleagues who regarded them suspiciously, doubting their motivations for returning to the faculty, the participants profiled in this book largely found returning to the classroom to be invigorating, resuming scholarly projects to be intellectually stimulating, and sharing their experience to be rewarding. My hope is that learning from participants' firsthand accounts provides a multidimensional view of how stepping away can enable a former senior leader to discover unique ways to serve their students and their universities anew. As senior leaders begin to contemplate life after leadership, I hope that they embrace the fulsome possibilities that returning to the faculty might hold. Stepping away from the office of president, provost, or dean is an invitation to step *toward* new challenges and deep fulfillment.

Acknowledgments

This project grew out of a conversation with Michael Fischer, former vice president for student and academic affairs at Trinity University. When Mike told me that he was "stepping down" and "returning to the faculty," my head began to spin with questions about what it might mean for me, my career, my university—but also what it might mean for my mentor, colleague, and friend. Following that conversation, I can remember going back to my office to search for anything written on the topic. Finding just a handful of articles, I decided to begin studying the experiences of people like Mike. More than six years later, these questions still make my head spin. The relationships I subsequently formed with the more than fifty participants in the study made this project fulfilling and rewarding in ways I could never have imagined. To the participants in this study, known here only by pseudonyms, thank you for providing me so much joy, insight, encouragement, and inspiration. I offer special thanks to Mike, who, over the years, has continued to ask me great questions, give helpful advice, and cheer me on from our regular booth at Cappychino's.

In my very first class as a doctoral student at the University of Texas at Austin, my advisor, Patricia Somers, planted seeds about identity, transition, and life-span development that informed the kind of scholar I most wanted to be; her continued support and guidance enabled me to cross the stage as a newly minted doctoriña. The members of my dissertation committee, Beth Bukoski, Jennifer Jellison Holme, and Marilyn Kameen, always pushed me, and their feedback improved my research. At UT, I was fortunate to learn from some of the best teachers I've ever had, including Victor Sáenz, Julie Schell, Mark Gooden, Gregory Vincent, and Edwin Sharpe.

Beyond the Forty Acres, I had the privilege of learning from the methodologist Kathy Charmaz through the pages of her books and during an intensive master class on constructivist grounded theory she taught at the

University of the Incarnate Word in San Antonio in 2017. my NVivo "coach," Stuart Robertson, boosted my confidence and expanded my technical skills immeasurably. Without my broadcasting heroes and heroines—Terry Gross, Diane Rehm, Ira Glass, and Brené Brown—I would not be the interviewer I am today.

This research was generously supported by The University of Texas at Austin through the Pena Scholarship, the Donald I. and Gwen Rippey Endowed Scholarship, the John and Susanne Roueche Endowed Scholarship, a continuing fellowship from the College of Education, and a Dissertation Writing Fellowship from the Graduate School. UT's Department of Educational Leadership and Policy furnished travel grants that enabled me to present at several academic conferences. A Scholar Award from the International Chapter of the P.E.O. Sisterhood further supported the end stages of my project. My former employer, Trinity University, generously provided me with the time to develop this study, a grant to offset research expenses, and a site license for NVivo software. Thank you to all who made considerable investments in me and my learning.

The kindhearted team at Rutgers University Press brought this book into existence. Former editor Lisa Banning approached me about my project early in my research. Kimberly Guinta, editorial director, was forgiving when I missed my deadline (more than once) during the pandemic, and senior editor Peggy Solic helped me over the finish line. Two anonymous readers provided insightful feedback to my proposal, and their feedback helped me reimagine this book as a manual to guide others on their pathway back to the faculty. Additional thanks to the army of interns, gifted copy editor Andrew Katz, the brilliant design team, and the many other hands who helped me complete this book.

My personal and professional networks buoyed me with emotional support throughout my doctoral journey and everything that came after it. My extended Trinity University family cheered me on, propped me up, and fed me during the "blurry years" marked by commuting between San Antonio and Austin. My colleagues in academic affairs—Deneese Jones, Michael Fischer, Mark Brodl, Duane Coltharp, Tim O'Sullivan, David Ribble, Michael Soto, Peggy Sundermeyer, Tammie Dillow, and Sarah Perales—exhibited unwavering kindness and picked up my slack time and time again when I was on a deadline. I finished the manuscript as an American Council on Education Fellow in residence at the University of New Mexico. I'm forever indebted to President Garnett Stokes for letting me learn from her and her wonderful senior team, including Terry Babbitt, Teresa Costantinidis, James Holloway, and Cinnamon Blair. At ACE, my mentor, Sara Jayne Steen, president emerita at Plymouth State University, has given me some of the most generous and gentle feedback I have ever received and delivered it in a way that I could really hear it. Leo Lambert, president emeritus of Elon University, has written such a beautiful foreword that I don't have the words to thank him properly.

A girl couldn't ask for better friends in the late Corinne Pache, Julie Post, Andrew Kania, Tim O'Sullivan, Ana Romo, Tom Jenkins, Pat Norman, Sarah Erickson, Jack Thurston, Nathan Davis, Curtis Swope, Kathryn O'Rourke, Rubén Dupertuis, Claudia Stokes, Stephen Jones, the late Kim Fischer, Mia and Chad Spigel, Becca and Jarrod Atchison, Vicki Aarons, Sussan Siavoshi, Dick Burr, and Lynn Murray-Chandler. Thank you for your literal and metaphorical high-fives, snarky texts, willingness to listen to me gush on about my work, and having the tact to change the subject at the perfect moment. I hadn't anticipated that my time at UT would result in so many lifelong friendships, but I am so glad it did. Thanks for your friendship and all that you continue to teach me: Jason and Cory Grove, Ashley and Hillary Jones, Denise Carr, Laura Struve, Ryan Miller, Justin Samuels, and Ashley Stone. I am particularly grateful for the encouragement of my late classmate Emily Johnson.

My family—especially my mom and my sister, Kristin—remain steadfast cheerleaders of everything I've ever done (even when I haven't deserved it). My father passed away in 2020, and if not for the work ethic he instilled in me, I never would have finished this project. I'm fortunate to be one of those people who really enjoys her in-laws, and my life became richer when I joined the Keating, Marias, and Rogers families.

Final and deepest thanks go to my husband, Patrick Keating, for encouraging me, modeling discipline as a writer and researcher, giving me space when I need space, buying me a really nice desk chair, cleaning the litter box, never looking at the clock when I say that I *only* need five more minutes to finish something, and patiently correcting the same grammatical mistakes for almost twenty years. Patrick, I vow to keep "accepting your changes."

Appendix

Interview Protocols

First Interview

Part One: Characteristics

A. Institutional Characteristics:

Most recent administrative job title: _____

Check each that describes your academic institution:

☐ Public

☐ Private

☐ Religiously Affiliated

☐ Undergraduate only (B.A. Only)

☐ Undergraduate and Master's Programs

☐ Ph.D. Granting Institution

Total # of students: _____

Total # of faculty under your supervision: _____

B. Personal Characteristics:

Gender: _____

Marital Status:_____

Race:_____

Age: _____

Academic Discipline (of terminal degree): _____

Year of your first full-time faculty appointment: _____

Year of your first full-time administrative appointment: _____

Date that you completed your administrative service: (MM/DD/YYYY)

_____

Date that you returned to the faculty / will return: (MM/DD/YYYY)

_____

160 Appendix

What pseudonym (first name only) would you like for me to use for you in this study? _____

Part Two: Interview Questions (60–75 Minutes)

1 Please begin by describing your professional responsibilities as an administrator. What's in your portfolio?
2 Would you begin by sharing with me two of your greatest achievements as an academic leader? How did you accomplish these outcomes?
3 What factors led you to become an administrator in the first place?
4 Could you describe the events that led you to return to the faculty?
   a. Possible probes: Was the decision voluntary? Why not retire?
5 How do you feel about returning to the faculty?
6 Is there anything that happened during your administration—or something you did as an administrator—that you think will effect how you will be received by the faculty?
7 When you announced your intention to step down as an administrator and return to the faculty, what has the reception been?
   a From your administrative peers / the board
   b From the faculty
   c From others (e.g., staff, students, alumni, parents, friends of the university . . .)
8 Let's explore some facets of your future work in greater depth: teaching, research, and service. What are some of your goals, anticipations, or anxieties related to each area?
   a Teaching
   b Research
   c Service (to the university, the profession, the community)
9 If you plan to take a leave/sabbatical, what will you do with your time? Do you plan to spend time on campus during your leave?
   a Probe: If yes, when/why will you come to campus? If no, why not?
10 What about this upcoming change is the greatest source of anxiety for you? Excitement?
11 What does it mean for you to be a faculty member at this stage of your career?
12 What, if any, interactions have you had with the person who will succeed you in your previous role? How do you feel about the new power dynamic of being a faculty member reporting to new leadership?
13 What, if anything, has your institution done so far to support you in your transition from administrator to faculty member? What else, if anything, would help?

14 Can you tell me how you expect the transition from administrator to faculty member will impact your personal relationships? Have your family or friends noticed a change in you?

15 Is there something else you think I should know about your experience to inform my study?

16 Could you recommend any other professional colleagues who might participate in my study (he/she must have been a senior campus leader at a postsecondary institution who has returned to the faculty or is in the process of doing so)?

Second Interview

This protocol was used to interview study participants between six and twelve months after the first interview. Some follow-up questions were tailored to individuals. For example, if in the first interview, a participant had talked about being excited about teaching a new course, I would ask how the class went. I would share the transcript from the first interview with the participant prior to the conversation to jog their memory.

Questions about the Present

1 How are you?

2 What have you been doing since the last time we spoke (about a year ago)?
   a What about your transition has gone according to plan?
   b What has been different than expected (including things that proved to be easier or harder than expected or things that were just *different*)?

3 Have you been back to campus?
   a If yes, how did it go? How did you feel? Can you describe any interactions you have with colleagues or other stakeholders (e.g., administrators, students, alumni, faculty peers)?
   b If no, has that been intentional? When do you think you might go back next?

4 I am curious about what you thought about when reviewing the transcript from our previous conversation.
   a Do you think that our previous conversation accurately captured your thoughts and feelings from a year ago? Is there anything you want to expand upon or correct?
   b Have you noticed any changes since our last conversation? Have you had any new feelings?
   c Speaking today, would you answer any of the previous questions differently than you did one year ago?

5 What, if any, interactions have you had with the person who will succeed you in your previous role? How do you feel about the new power dynamic of being a faculty member reporting to new leadership? (Have you talked to your department chair? How's that dynamic?)

6 [If the participant has yet to resume teaching] As you get closer to returning to full-time teaching, what about this upcoming change is the greatest source of anxiety for you? Source of excitement?

7 What, if anything, has your institution done so far to support you in your transition from administrator to faculty member? What else, if anything, would help or would have helped?

8 With whom—if anyone—have you talked about the experience of returning to the faculty?

9 I want to (re)ask you a question I asked you last time. What might your spouse/friends/family say is different about you now compared to when you served as a campus administrator?

10 What else is on your mind? What haven't we discussed that you think it's important for me to know about your ongoing return to the faculty?

Notes

1. Stepping Away

1 Several scholars and studies of academic leaders have charted the growing frequency of senior leadership changes and analyzed the root causes for trends such as the declining tenure of college presidents. See Bryan J. Cook and Young M. Kim, *The American College President 2012* (Washington, DC: American Council on Education, Center for Policy Analysis, 2012); Jacqueline Elizabeth King and Gigi G. Gomez, *On the Pathway to the Presidency: Characteristics of Higher Education's Senior Leadership* (Washington, DC: American Council on Education, 2008), iii–12; and Patrick H. Sanaghan, Larry Goldstein, and Kathleen D. Gaval, *Presidential Transitions: It's Not Just the Position, It's the Transition* (Lanham, MD: Rowman and Littlefield, 2009).

2 James Martin and James E. Samels, *Presidential Transition in Higher Education: Managing Leadership Change* (Baltimore: Johns Hopkins University Press, 2006).

3 Jonathan S. Gagliardi et al., *American College President Study 2017* (Washington, DC: American Council on Education, 2017); and Robert C. Andringa and Allen P. Splete, *Presidential Transitions in Private Colleges: Six Integrated Phases Essential for Success* (Washington, DC: Council for Christian Colleges and Universities, 2005).

4 Cook and Kim, *American College President 2012*.

5 King and Gomez, *On the Pathway to the Presidency*, 6.

6 Gagliardi et al., *American College Presidents Study 2017*.

7 James Finkelstein and Judith Wilde, "Does Your President Have a Platinum Parachute?," *Inside Higher Ed*, June 1, 2017, https://www.insidehighered.com/advice/2017/06/01/examination-college-presidents-platinum-parachutes-essay.

8 James Finkelstein and Judith Wilde, "Platinum Parachutes Revisited," *Inside Higher Ed*, July 29, 2019, https://www.insidehighered.com/views/2019/07/29/failed-presidencies-shouldnt-be-rewarded-platinum-parachutes-opinion.

9 Emma Whitford, "Retirement Wave Hits Presidents amid Pandemic," *Inside Higher Ed*, October 1, 2020, https://www.insidehighered.com/news/2020/10/01/many-college-presidents-are-leaving-say-pandemic-isnt-driving-them-out.

10 John Ross, "COVID-19 Changes at the Top in Australia," *Inside Higher Ed*, March 19, 2021, https://www.insidehighered.com/news/2021/03/19/australian-universities-face-turnover-top.

11 William A. Henk, Shelley B. Wepner, and Heba S. Ali, "Factors Academic Deans Consider in Deciding Whether to Remain in Their Positions," ACAD, October 25, 2021, https://acad.org/resource/factors-academic-deans-consider-in-deciding-whether-to-remain-in-their-positions/.

12 Kathryn Ecclestone, "Lost and Found in Transition: Educational Implications of Concerns about 'Identity,' 'Agency' and 'Structure,'" in *Researching Transitions in Lifelong Learning*, ed. John Field, Jim Gallacher, and Robert Ingram (Abingdon, UK: Routledge, 2009), 12.

13 Two empirical studies of the experiences of senior academic leaders who return to the faculty include Frederick R. Cyphert and David L. Boggs, "The Transition from Administrator to Professor: Expectations and Experiences," *Review of Higher Education* 9, no. 3 (1986): 325–333; and Gaye Luna and Catherine Medina, "Coming Full Circle: Mid-career Women Leaving Administration and Returning to Faculty," *Advancing Women in Leadership Journal* 21 (2006).

14 Many former administrators have reflected on their careers, offering insights and advice to current and aspiring leaders and the institutions they serve. A few particularly good examples are William G. Bowen, *Lessons Learned: Reflections of a University President* (Princeton, NJ: Princeton University Press, 2013); Robert F. Carbone, *Presidential Passages: Former College Presidents Reflect on the Splendor and Agony of Their Careers* (Washington, DC: American Council on Education, 1981); Peter Tyrell Flawn, *A Primer for University Presidents: Managing the Modern University* (Austin: University of Texas Press, 1990); and Larry A. Nielsen, *Provost: Experiences, Reflections, and Advice from a Former "Number Two" on Campus* (Sterling, VA: Stylus, 2019).

15 Fred Schwarzbach, "Back to the Faculty: Not as Easy as It Sounds," *Chronicle of Higher Education*, October 6, 2019), https://www.chronicle.com/article/back-to-the-faculty-not-as-easy-as-it-sounds/; Paul Sale, "Leaving the Dark Side for the Light: Twelve Strategies for Effective Transition from Academic Administrator to Faculty Member," *Administrative Issues Journal Education Practice and Research* 3, no. 2 (October 2013), article 8; Courtney Leatherman, "Returning to the Faculty Can Be an Ordeal for All," *Chronicle of Higher Education*, April 10, 1991, https://www.chronicle.com/article/returning-to-the-faculty-can-be-an-ordeal-for-all/.

16 Leatherman, "Returning to the Faculty Can Be an Ordeal for All."

17 Ronald G. Ehrenberg, "Being a Quadruple Threat Keeps It Interesting," in *Faculty Career Paths: Multiple Routes to Academic Success and Satisfaction*, American Council on Education/Praeger Series on Higher Education, ed. Gretchen M. Bataille and Betsy E. Brown (Westport, CT: Praeger, 2006), 120.

18 Carol J. Pardun, former director of the University of South Carolina's School of Journalism and Mass Communications, quoted in Audrey Williams June, "Ex-Administrators Reveal the Secret That Eased Their Return to the Faculty," *Chronicle of Higher Education*, August 27, 2018, https://www.chronicle.com/article/ex-administrators-reveal-the-secret-that-eased-their-return-to-the-faculty/.

19 Judith Shapiro, "The Dear Departed: Reflections on Presidential Transitions," *Chronicle of Higher Education*, March 3, 2013, http://www.chronicle.com/article/The-Dear-Departed-Reflections/145027/.

20 Several scholars have charted the expansion of campus administrators, the restructuring of faculty work, and the decline of faculty influence in shared governance. Some books on the subject include Derek Bok, *The Cost of Talent: How Executives and Professionals Are Paid and How It Affects America* (New York: Free Press, 1993); William Gordon Bowen and Eugene M. Tobin, *Locus of Authority: The Evolution of Faculty Roles in the Governance of Higher Education* (Princeton, NJ: Princeton University Press, 2017); Mary Burgan, *What Ever Happened to the Faculty? Drift and Decision in Higher Education* (Baltimore: Johns Hopkins University Press, 2006); and Jack H. Schuster et al., *The American Faculty: The Restructuring of Academic Work and Careers* (Baltimore: John Hopkins University Press, 2008).

21 Janice C. Griffith, "Transition from Faculty to Administrator and Transition Back to the Faculty," *New Directions for Higher Education* 2006, no. 134 (2006): 68.

22 Sheila Slaughter and Larry L. Leslie, *Academic Capitalism: Politics, Policies, and the Entrepreneurial University* (Baltimore: Johns Hopkins University Press, 1999).

23 Numerous scholars have charted the rise of neoliberal practices and the growing conflict between faculty and administration in modern research institutions, including Larry Hubbell, "Understanding Faculty and Administrator Conflict in the University," *International Journal of Education Research* 7, no. 1 (March 2012): 16–28; Adrianna Kezar and Sean Gehrke, "Faculty Composition in Four-Year Institutions: The Role of Pressures, Values, and Organizational Processes in Academic Decision-Making," *Journal of Higher Education* 87, no. 3 (2016): 390–419; and Sheila Slaughter and Gary Rhoades, "State and Markets in Higher Education: Trends in Academic Capitalism," in *American Higher Education in the Twenty-First Century: Social, Political, and Economic Challenges*, ed. Michael N. Bastedo, Philip G. Altbach, and Patricia J. Gumport (Baltimore: Johns Hopkins University Press, 2016), 503–540.

166 Notes

24 Benjamin Ginsberg, *The Fall of the Faculty: the Rise of the All-Administrative University and Why It Matters* (Oxford: Oxford University Press, 2013), 1. 24.

25 James Monks, "Job Turnover among University Presidents in the United States of America," *Journal of Higher Education Policy and Management* 34, no. 2 (2012): 139–152.

26 American Council of Trustees and Alumni, Institute for Effective Governance, *How Much Is Too Much? Controlling Administrative Costs through Effective Oversight* (Washington, DC: American Council of Trustees and Alumni, Institute for Effective Governance, July 2017). ACTA defines administrative costs according to the National Center for Education Statistics (NCES) definition: "including expenses for general administrative services, executive direction and planning, legal and fiscal operations, and public relations/development." National Center for Education Statistics, "2016–17 Survey Materials: Glossary, 2016," 2016, https://surveys.nces.gov/ipeds/Downloads/Forms/IPEDS Glossary.pdf.

27 Bowen, *Lessons Learned*, 143.

28 Sylvia Goodman, "Why U. of Michigan and Cal State Are Changing Their Presidents' Contracts," *Chronicle of Higher Education*, July 15, 2022, https://www.chronicle.com/article/why-u-of-michigan-and-cal-state-are-changing-their-presidents-contracts?cid2=gen_login_refresh&cid=gen_sign_in.

29 Bowen, *Lessons Learned*, 143.

2. Studying Administrative Transitions in the Modern American University

1 Nancy K. Schlossberg, "A Model for Analyzing Human Adaptation to Transition," *Counseling Psychologist* 9, no. 2 (1981): 5.

2 Norma Chick and Afaf Ibrahim Meleis, "Transitions: A Nursing Concern," in *Nursing Research Methodology: Issues and Implementation*, ed. Peggy L. Chinn (Boulder, CO: Aspen, 1986), 239.

3 Herminia Ibarra, "The 3 Phases of Making a Major Life Change," *Harvard Business Review*, August 6, 2021, https://hbr.org/2021/08/the-3-phases-of-making-a-major-life-change.

4 Joseph Berger, Bernard P. Cohen, and Morris Zelditch, "Status Characteristics and Social Interaction," *American Sociological Review* 37, no. 3 (June 1972): 254, 243.

5 Cecilia L. Ridgeway, "Expectation States Theory and Emotion," in *Handbook of the Sociology of Emotions*, ed. Jan E. Stets and Jonathan H. Turner (New York: Springer, 2006), 347–367.

6 Theodore D. Kemper and Randall Collins, "Dimensions of Microinteraction," *American Journal of Sociology* 96, no. 1 (1990): 51.

7 Kathryn M. Moore, *Leaders in Transition: A National Study of Higher Education Administrators* (Washington, DC: American Council on Education, 1982).

8 Michael D. Cohen and James G. March, *Leadership and Ambiguity: The American College President* (Boston: Harvard Business School Press, 1974).

9 Cook and Kim, *American College President 2012*, 20.

10 Scott C. Beardsley, *Higher Calling: The Rise of Nontraditional Leaders in Academia* (Charlottesville: University of Virginia Press, 2017); Gagliardi et al., *American College President Study 2017*; Roger D. Wessel and Marybelle C. Keim, "Career Patterns of Private Four-Year College and University Presidents in the United States," *Journal of Higher Education* 65, no. 2 (1994): 211–225.

11 Gagliardi et al., *American College President Study 2017*.

12 Rita Bornstein, *Legitimacy in the Academic Presidency: From Entrance to Exit* (Westport, CT: Praeger, 2003).

13 Laura McKenna, "Why Are Fewer College Presidents Academics?," *Atlantic*, December 3, 2015.

14 Arthur G. Jago, "How Three Bad Decisions Signaled Doom at Mizzou," *Chronicle of Higher Education*, July 22, 2020, https://www.chronicle.com/article/how-three-bad-decisions-signaled-doom-at-mizzou/.

15 Many sources describe how senior academic leaders come to their positions through nonlinear trajectories. A particularly strong example is Beardsley, *Higher Calling*.

16 Jeffrey Bradfield et al., *Pathways to the University Presidency* (London: Deloitte University Press / Georgia Tech Center for 21st Century Universities, 2017), 3.

17 Of the limited research that has been done on the career trajectories of chief academic officers, two excellent resources include Brent D. Cejda, Cynthia B. McKenney, and Catherine W. Fuller, "Leaving Office: Position Changes of Chief Academic Officers," *Community College Journal of Research and Practice* 25, no. 2 (2001): 137–146; and Herman A. Berliner et al., *Chief Academic Officers and the Future Leadership of American Higher Education* (New York: TIAA-CREF Institute and the American Council on Education, 2009), 1–13.

18 King and Gomez, *On the Pathway to the Presidency*, 6.

19 Gagliardi et al., *American College President Study 2017*.

20 Cook and Kim, *American College President 2012*, 17.

21 Jyotsna Mishra, *Becoming President: Patterns of Professional Mobility of African American University Presidents* (Lanham, MD: University Press of America, 2007).

22 Robbie P. Hertneky, "Composing Our Lives—as Women and as Leaders," *Advances in Developing Human Resources* 14, no. 2 (2012): 140–155.

23 Sylvia Ann Hewlett and Carolyn Buck Luce, "Off-Ramps and On-Ramps: Keeping Talented Women on the Road to Success," *Harvard Business Review*, March 2005.

24 Gagliardi et al., *American College President Study 2017*.

25 Alice H. Eagly and Linda L. Carli, "Women and the Labyrinth of Leadership," *Harvard Business Review*, September 2007, https://hbr.org/2007/09/women-and-the-labyrinth-of-leadership.

26 Marjorie Hass, *A Leadership Guide for Women in Higher Education* (Baltimore: Johns Hopkins University Press, 2021), 5.

27 Hass, 9.

28 Luna and Medina, "Coming Full Circle."

29 Victoria H. Jo, "Voluntary Turnover and Women Administrators in Higher Education," *Higher Education* 56, no. 5 (October 2008): 565–582.

30 Carbone, *Presidential Passages*.

31 Cook and Kim, *American College President 2012*; Gagliardi et al., *American College President Study 2017*; Kerr Clark, *Presidential Discontent: Perspectives on Campus Tensions: Papers Prepared for the Special Committee on Campus Tensions* (Washington, DC: American Council on Education, 1970); Art Padilla and Sujit Ghosh, "Turnover at the Top: The Revolving Door of the Academic Presidency," *Presidency* 3, no. 1 (2000): 30–37; Andringa and Splete, *Presidential Transitions in Private Colleges*.

32 Cohen and March, *Leadership and Ambiguity*.

33 Gagliardi et al., *American College President Study 2017*.

34 Monks, "Job Turnover among University Presidents."

35 Berliner et al., *Chief Academic Officers and the Future Leadership*.

36 James J. Duderstadt, *The View from the Helm: Leading the American University during an Era of Change* (Ann Arbor: University of Michigan Press, 2007).

37 Craig Cameron, "Exiting the Deanship," *Chronicle of Higher Education*, November 10, 2006, https://www.chronicle.com/article/exiting-the-deanship/.

38 Eric Kelderman, "Politics and the Pandemic Are Straining the Role of Campus Leadership," *Chronicle of Higher Education*, October 12, 2021, https://www.chronicle.com/article/politics-and-the-pandemic-are-straining-the-role-of-campus-leadership.

39 James Monks, "Public versus Private University Presidents Pay Levels and Structure," *Economics of Education Review* 26, no. 3 (2007): 338–348.

40 Padilla and Ghosh, "Turnover at the Top"

41 Jeffrey J. Selingo, *What Presidents Think: A 2013 Survey of Four-Year College Presidents* (Washington, DC: Chronicle of Higher Education, 2013), 10.

42 Mimi Wolverton, Walter Gmelch, and Marvin L. Wolverton, "Finding a Better Person-Environment Fit in the Academic Deanship," *Innovative Higher Education* 24, no. 3 (1999): 203–226; Tracy L. Morris and Joseph S. Laipple, "How Prepared Are Academic Administrators? Leadership and Job Satisfaction within US Research Universities," *Journal of Higher Education Policy and Management* 37, no. 2 (2015): 241–251.

43 Katherine A. Tunheim and Gary N. McLean, "Lessons Learned from Former College Presidents of the Evangelical Lutheran Church in America: A Phenomenological Study," *Christian Higher Education* 13, no. 3 (2014): 199–210.

44 Henk, Wepner, and Ali, "Factors Academic Deans Consider."

45 Laurel Archer Copp, "When the Dean Steps Down," *Journal of Professional Nursing* 11, no. 4 (1995): 197–198.

46 Mary Ann Swain, "Reflections on Academic Administration," *New Directions for Higher Education* 2006, no. 134 (2006): 25–36.

47 Bornstein, *Legitimacy in the Academic Presidency*; Mark Mallinger, "Faculty to Administration and Back Again," *Journal of Management Inquiry* 22, no. 1 (2012): 59–67; Milton D. Glick, "Becoming 'One of Them' or 'Moving to the Dark Side,'" *New Directions for Higher Education* 2006, no. 134 (2006): 87–96; Copp, "When the Dean Steps Down"; Carbone, *Presidential Passages*.

48 Duderstadt, *View from the Helm*, 347.

49 See the Center for Retirement Research at Boston College: https://crr.bc.edu/.

50 Manfred F. R. Kets de Vries, "3 Tips for a Smooth Transition into Retirement," *Harvard Business Review*, September 30, 2020, https://hbr.org/2020/09/3-tips -for-a-smooth-transition-into-retirement.

51 John W. Moore and Joanne M. Burrows, *Presidential Succession and Transition: Beginning, Ending, and Beginning Again* (New York: American Association of State Colleges and Universities, 2001), 34.

52 JP Morgan Chase Institute, "Past 65 and Still Working: Big Data Insights on Senior Citizens' Financial Lives," August 2016, https://www.jpmorganchase .com/institute/research/labor-markets/insight-past-65-and-still-working.

53 Flawn, *Primer for University Presidents*, 195.

54 Margaret Heffernan, *Uncharted: How to Navigate the Future* (New York: Simon and Schuster, 2020), xiii.

55 Michael W. Firmin, "Transitioning from Administration to Faculty: Addictions to Break," *Journal of Practical Leadership* 3 (2008): 144, 146.

56 Cyphert and Boggs, "Transition from Administrator to Professor."

57 Luna and Medina, "Coming Full Circle," 6, 8.

58 Cameron, "Exiting the Deanship."

59 George Justice, "Back to the Classroom after 11 Years in Administration," *Chronicle of Higher Education*, September 11, 2018, https://www.chronicle.com/ article/back-to-the-classroom-after-11-years-in-administration/; George Justice, "After Administration: The Search for a Professional Niche," *Chronicle of Higher Education*, December 16, 2020, https://www.chronicle.com/article/ after-administration-the-search-for-a-professional-niche; Mallinger, "Faculty to Administration and Back Again."

60 Nielsen, *Provost*, 288.

61 Griffith, "Transition from Faculty to Administrator," 73.

62 Mallinger, "Faculty to Administration and Back Again," 66.

63 Moore and Burrows, *Presidential Succession and Transition*, 39; Flawn, *Primer for University Presidents*, 197–198.

64 Sanaghan, Goldstein, and Gaval, *Presidential Transitions*, 127.

65 Flawn, *Primer for University Presidents*, 196.

66 Moore and Burrows, *Presidential Succession and Transition*.

67 Jo Cahill et al., "An Exploration of How Programme Leaders in Higher Education Can Be Prepared and Supported to Discharge Their Roles and Responsibilities Effectively," *Educational Research* 57, no. 3 (2015): 272–286.

68 Numerous sources describe the inadequacy of succession planning in colleges and universities; a few of those sources include Andringa and Splete, *Presidential Transitions in Private Colleges*; Robert Birnbaum, "Presidential Succession and Institutional Functioning in Higher Education," *Journal of Higher Education* 60, no. 2 (1989): 123–135; and Cyphert and Boggs, "Transition from Administrator to Professor."

69 Mary Brown Bullock, "Presidential Transitions: Planning the Last Year," *Presidency* 10, no. 2 (2007): 32–35.

70 Judith Wilde and James Finkelstein, "Tenure Is under Attack, So Why Do College Presidents Have Retreat Rights?," *Higher Ed Dive*, April 19, 2022, https://www.highereddive.com/news/tenure-is-under-attack-so-why-do-college-presidents-have-retreat-rights/622098/.

71 Dennie L. Smith, Kayla B. Rollins, and Lana J. Smith, "Back to the Faculty: Transition from University Department Leadership," *Innovative Higher Education* 37, no. 1 (December 2011): 53–63.

72 Griffith, "Transition from Faculty to Administrator," 68.

73 Sanaghan, Goldstein, and Gaval, *Presidential Transitions*.

74 Luna and Medina, "Coming Full Circle."

75 Eugene Arden, "Is There Life after Administration?," *Academe* 83, no. 4 (1997): 30–32.

76 Elliot W. Eisner, foreword to *Theory and Concepts in Qualitative Research: Perspectives from the Field*, ed. David J. Flinder and Geoffrey E. Mills (New York: Teachers College Press, 1993), vii.

77 Ian Dey, *Grounding Grounded Theory: Guidelines for Qualitative Inquiry* (Bingley, UK: Emerald, 2008), 171.

78 Juliet Corbin and Anselm Strauss, *Basics of Qualitative Research: Techniques and Procedures for Developing Grounded Theory* (Thousand Oaks, CA: Sage, 2008).

79 Sharan B. Merriam and Elizabeth J. Tisdell, *Qualitative Research: A Guide to Design and Implementation* (San Francisco: Jossey-Bass, 2016), 131.

80 Kathy Charmaz, *Constructing Grounded Theory: A Practical Guide through Qualitative Analysis* (London: Sage, 2013), 1.

81 Norman K. Denzin and Yvonna S. Lincoln, "Competing Paradigms in Qualitative Research," in *The Landscape of Qualitative Research*, 2nd ed., ed. Norman K. Denzin and Yvonna S. Lincoln (Thousand Oaks, CA: Sage, 1998), 111.

82 Donna M. Mertens, *Research and Evaluation in Education and Psychology: Integrating Diversity with Quantitative, Qualitative, and Mixed Methods*, 3rd ed. (Thousand Oaks, CA: Sage, 2009), 16.

83 Charmaz, *Constructing Grounded Theory*, 29.

84 Charmaz, 239.

85 Margo Ely et al., *Writing Qualitative Research: Living by Words* (New York: Falmer, 1997), 332.

86 Charmaz, *Constructing Grounded Theory*, 240.

87 Risa Palm, "Perspectives from the Dark Side: The Career Transition from Faculty to Administrator," *New Directions for Higher Education* 2006, no. 134 (2006): 65.

88 Lawrence A. Palinkas et al., "Purposeful Sampling for Qualitative Data Collection and Analysis in Mixed Method Implementation Research," *Administration and Policy in Mental Health and Mental Health Services Research* 42, no. 5 (2013): 533–544.

89 Charmaz, *Constructing Grounded Theory*, 53.

90 Ruthellen Josselson, *Interviewing for Qualitative Inquiry: A Relational Approach* (New York: Guilford, 2013).

91 Lewis A. Dexter, *Elite and Specialised Interviewing*, Handbooks for Research in Political Behaviour (Evanston, IL: Northwestern University Press, 1970).

92 Adrianna Kezar, "Transformational Elite Interviews: Principles and Problems," *Qualitative Inquiry* 9, no. 3 (2003): 395-415.

93 John W. Creswell, *Qualitative Inquiry and Research Design: Choosing among Five Approaches* (London: Sage, 2013), 86.

94 Corbin and Strauss, *Basics of Qualitative Research*; Barney G. Glaser and Anselm L. Strauss, *The Discovery of Grounded Theory: Strategies for Qualitative Research* (Oxon, UK: Routledge, 2017).

95 Charmaz, *Constructing Grounded Theory*, 67.

96 Charmaz, 57.

3. First Steps

1 I tried—unsuccessfully—to determine where, when, and why the tradition of returning to the faculty began. The practice was not common among the colonial colleges. In the early 1600s and 1700s, few presidents served longer than five years, most succumbing to illness and dying in office. In an email, the historian John Thelin confirmed that as early as the nineteenth century, college presidents were selected from the faculty and that these presidents

172 Notes

continued to teach seminars while carrying out their administrative duties. Thelin posited that since tenure did not become a common practice until the late nineteenth century, it would be hard to imagine a college president being fired and retreating to the faculty before then. I hope that a reader might be able to help me trace the origins of this practice so that we can better study how it has changed over time.

2 Luna and Medina, "Coming Full Circle."

4. The Messy Middle

1 Brené Brown, "Brené on Day 2," *Unlocking Us with Brené Brown* (podcast), Season 2, Episode 1, September 2, 2020, https://brenebrown.com/podcast/brene-on-day-2/#transcript.

2 Brown.

3 Many scholars and practitioners have written about integrating elements of their former selves with their "new" self (post-administration). A few standout examples include Brian L. Foster, "From Faculty to Administrator: Like Going to a New Planet," *New Directions for Higher Education* 2006, no. 134 (2006): 49–57; Palm, "Perspectives from the Dark Side"; and Griffith, "Transition from Faculty to Administrator."

4 Chick and Meleis, "Transitions," 240.

5. "Working for Myself"

1 Kevin H. Pickus, "Teaching Lessons That a Professor Learned as an Administrator (Opinion)," *Inside Higher Ed*, December 16, 2021. https://www.insidehighered.com/advice/2021/12/16/teaching-lessons-professor-learned-administrator-opinion. Leo Lambert's foreword to this book represents an example of a personal reflection on how he performed his role as president emeritus of Elon University.

2 A few writers making this distinction include Ecclestone, "Lost and Found in Transition"; and David L. Dotlich, James L. Noel, and Norman Walker, *Leadership Passages: The Personal and Professional Transitions That Make or Break a Leader* (San Francisco: Wiley, 2004).

3 Bok, *Cost of Talent*, 166.

6. Reimagining Leaders, Reimagining Leadership

1 American Council of Trustees and Alumni, *How Much Is Too Much?*, 1.

2 Two particularly excellent essays on mission creep and how faculty experience external pressures are Leslie D. Gonzales, "Faculty Sensemaking and Mission

Creep: Interrogating Institutionalized Ways of Knowing and Doing Legitimacy," *Review of Higher Education* 36, no. 2 (2013): 179–209; and KerryAnn O'Meara and Alan Bloomgarden, "The Pursuit of Prestige: The Experience of Institutional Striving from a Faculty Perspective," *Journal of the Professoriate* 4, no. 1 (2011): 41–73.

3 Swain, "Reflections on Academic Administration," 28.

4 Douglas T. Hall, "Unplanned Executive Transitions and the Dance of the Subidentities," *Human Resource Management* 34, no. 1 (1995): 71–92, addresses these issues in the business world. Duderstadt, *View from the Helm*, draws similar conclusions about higher education.

5 Flawn, *Primer for University Presidents*, 203.

6 Adam Grant, "There's a Name for the Blah You're Feeling: It's Called Languishing," *New York Times*, April 19, 2021, https://www.nytimes.com/2021/04/19/well/mind/covid-mental-health-languishing.html.

7 Ibid.

8 Ibid.

9 George D. Parsons and Richard T. Pascale, "Crisis at the Summit," *Harvard Business Review*, March 2007.

10 Gagliardi et al., *American College President Study 2017*.

11 Ellen Wexler, "Why Universities Hire Two Deans to Lead Their Law Schools," *Inside Higher Ed*, April 6, 2016, https://www.insidehighered.com/news/2016/04/06/why-universities-hire-two-deans-lead-their-law-schools.

12 I am grateful for being introduced to these models by Rachel L. Montgomery, a graduate student at Pennsylvania State University, in the roundtable presentation "Unpacking the Perceived Benefits and Drawbacks of Administrative Co-Leadership" at the annual meeting of the Association for the Study of Higher Education (ASHE) held in Tampa, Florida, in November 2017.

13 Colorado College, "Interim Leadership Positions Announced," Colorado College, July 20, 2020, https://www.coloradocollege.edu/newsevents/newsroom/interim-leadership-positions-announced.html#.YeXrihPMKDU.

14 Brenda Gillen, "Q&A with Former Acting Co-Presidents Mike Edmonds & Robert G. Moore," *Colorado College Bulletin*, Summer 2021.

15 Robert A. Gervasi, "Leadership Changes at Mount Union," Mount Union College memo, August 1, 2022 (in author's possession).

16 Kristin G. Esterberg and John Wooding, *Divided Conversations: Identities, Leadership, and Change in Public Higher Education* (Nashville, TN: Vanderbilt University Press, 2013).

17 Bowen and Tobin, *Locus of Authority*, 203.

18 Gagliardi et al., *American College President Study 2017*.

19 Jaclyn Diaz, "Former Michigan State Officials Were Cleared in Nassar Sexual Abuse Investigation," NPR, December 23, 2021, https://www.npr.org/2021/12/

23/1067157520/former-michigan-state-officials-get-convictions-and-charges
-tossed.

20 Colleen Flaherty, "The More Things Change," *Inside Higher Ed*, April 11, 2017, https://www.insidehighered.com/news/2017/04/11/aaup-faculty-salaries -slightly-budgets-are-balanced-backs-adjuncts-and-out-state. Flaherty's reporting references *Visualizing Change*, the American Association of University Professors' annual report on the economic status of the profession for 2016–2017.

21 Dan Bauman and Jacquelyn Elias, "What Presidents Make: 2019 Executive Compensation," *Chronicle of Higher Education*, July 16, 2020, https://www .chronicle.com/article/what-presidents-make.

22 Susan Svrluga, "Most of Her Presidential Salary and Lots of Perks. Michigan State Contract Suggests She Will Be Very Well Paid after Resigning amid Nassar Scandal," *Washington Post*, October 27, 2021, https://www.washingtonpost .com/news/grade-point/wp/2018/01/25/most-of-her-presidential-salary-and -lots-of-perks-michigan-state-contract-suggests-she-will-be-very-well-paid -after-resigning-amid-nassar-scandal/.

23 Finkelstein and Wilde, "Platinum Parachutes Revisited."

24 Palm, "Perspectives from the Dark Side," 65.

Bibliography

AGB. "Principles of Trusteeship." July 14, 2021. https://agb.org/principles-of -trusteeship/.

American Council of Trustees and Alumni, Institute for Effective Governance. *How Much Is Too Much? Controlling Administrative Costs through Effective Oversight.* Washington, DC: American Council of Trustees and Alumni, Institute for Effective Governance, July 2017.

Andringa, Robert C., and Allen P. Splete. *Presidential Transitions in Private Colleges: Six Integrated Phases Essential for Success.* Washington, DC: Council for Christian Colleges and Universities, 2005.

Arden, Eugene. "Is There Life after Administration?" *Academe* 83, no. 4 (1997): 30–32. https://doi.org/10.2307/40251614.

Bauman, Dan. "39 Private-College Leaders Earn More than $1 Million." *Chronicle of Higher Education*, December 4, 2006. https://www.chronicle.com/article/39 -private-college-leaders-earn-more-than-1-million/.

Bauman, Dan, and Jacquelyn Elias. "What Presidents Make: 2019 Executive Compensation." *Chronicle of Higher Education*, July 16, 2020. https://www.chronicle .com/article/what-presidents-make.

Bauman, Dan, Julia Piper, and Brian O'Leary. "Executive Compensation at Public and Private Colleges." *Chronicle of Higher Education*, August 31, 2021. https:// www.chronicle.com/article/executive-compensation-at-public-and-private -colleges/?cid=gen_sign_in#id=table_public_2020.

Beardsley, Scott C. *Higher Calling: The Rise of Nontraditional Leaders in Academia.* Charlottesville: University of Virginia Press, 2017.

Berger, Joseph, Bernard P. Cohen, and Morris Zelditch. "Status Characteristics and Social Interaction." *American Sociological Review* 37, no. 3 (June 1972): 241–255. https://doi.org/10.2307/2093465.

Berliner, Herman A., Joan F. Lorden, Risa Palm, Michel A. Smyer, and Peter Yakoboski. *Chief Academic Officers and the Future Leadership of American Higher*

Education. New York: TIAA-CREF Institute and the American Council on Education, 2009.

Berman, Jillian. "This Is How Much Colleges Spend Just Searching for a New President." MarketWatch, June 21, 2016. https://www.marketwatch.com/story/study-raises-questions-about-the-way-college-presidents-are-hired-2016-06-17.

Birnbaum, Robert. "Presidential Succession and Institutional Functioning in Higher Education." *Journal of Higher Education* 60, no. 2 (1989): 123–135. https://doi.org/10.2307/1982173.

Blumenstyk, Goldie. "Outside Chance for Insiders." *Chronicle of Higher Education*, November 4, 2005. https://www.chronicle.com/article/outside-chance-for-insiders/.

Bok, Derek. *The Cost of Talent: How Executives and Professionals Are Paid and How It Affects America*. New York: Free Press, 1993.

Bornstein, Rita. *Legitimacy in the Academic Presidency: From Entrance to Exit*. Westport, CT: Praeger, 2003.

Bowen, William G. *Lessons Learned: Reflections of a University President*. Princeton, NJ: Princeton University Press, 2013.

Bowen, William G., and Eugene M. Tobin. *Locus of Authority: The Evolution of Faculty Roles in the Governance of Higher Education*. Princeton, NJ: Princeton University Press, 2017.

Bradfield, Jeffrey, Sonny Chheng, Cole Clark, and Jeffrey J. Selingo. *Pathways to the University Presidency*. London: Deloitte University Press / Georgia Tech Center for 21st Century Universities, 2017.

Brodie, Keith H., and Leslie Banner. *Keeping an Open Door: Passages in a University Presidency*. Durham, NC: Duke University Press, 1996.

Brown, Brené. "Brené on Day 2." *Unlocking Us with Brené Brown* (podcast), Season 2, Episode 1, September 2, 2020. https://brenebrown.com/podcast/brene-on-day-2/#transcript.

Bullock, Mary Brown. "Presidential Transitions: Planning the Last Year." *Presidency* 10, no. 2 (2007): 32–35.

Burgan, Mary. *What Ever Happened to the Faculty? Drift and Decision in Higher Education*. Baltimore: Johns Hopkins University Press, 2006.

Cahill, Jo, Jan Bowyer, Catherine Rendell, Angela Hammond, and Sharon Korek. "An Exploration of How Programme Leaders in Higher Education Can Be Prepared and Supported to Discharge Their Roles and Responsibilities Effectively." *Educational Research* 57, no. 3 (2015): 272–286. https://doi.org/10.1080/00131881.2015.1056640.

Cameron, Craig. "Exiting the Deanship." *Chronicle of Higher Education*, November 10, 2006. https://www.chronicle.com/article/exiting-the-deanship/.

Carbone, Robert F. *Presidential Passages: Former College Presidents Reflect on the Splendor and Agony of Their Careers*. Washington, DC: American Council on Education, 1981.

Cejda, Brent D., Cynthia B. McKenney, and Catherine W. Fuller. "Leaving Office: Position Changes of Chief Academic Officers." *Community College Journal of Research and Practice* 25, no. 2 (2001): 137–146. https://doi.org/10.1080/10668920150218515.

Charmaz, Kathy. *Constructing Grounded Theory: A Practical Guide through Qualitative Analysis*. London: Sage, 2013.

Cheng, Shaoming. "Executive Compensation in Public Higher Education: Does Performance Matter?" *Research in Higher Education* 55, no. 6 (2014): 581–600. https://doi.org/10.1007/s11162-014-9328-9.

Chick, Norma, and Afaf Ibrahim Meleis. "Transitions: A Nursing Concern." In *Nursing Research Methodology: Issues and Implementation*, edited by Peggy L. Chinn, 237–257. Boulder, CO: Aspen, 1986.

Clark, Kerr. *Presidential Discontent: Perspectives on Campus Tensions: Papers Prepared for the Special Committee on Campus Tensions*. Washington, DC: American Council on Education, 1970.

Cohen, Michael D., and James G. March. *Leadership and Ambiguity: The American College President*. Boston: Harvard Business School Press, 1974.

Colorado College. "Interim Leadership Positions Announced." July 20, 2020. https://www.coloradocollege.edu/newsevents/newsroom/interim-leadership -positions-announced.html#.YeXrihPMKDU.

Cook, Bryan J., and Young M. Kim. *The American College President 2012*. Washington, DC: American Council on Education, Center for Policy Analysis, 2012.

Copp, Laurel Archer. "When the Dean Steps Down." *Journal of Professional Nursing* 11, no. 4 (1995): 197–198. https://doi.org/10.1016/s8755-7223(95)80016-6.

Corbin, Juliet, and Anselm Strauss. *Basics of Qualitative Research: Techniques and Procedures for Developing Grounded Theory*. Thousand Oaks, CA: Sage, 2008. .

Cotton, Raymond D. "Why Colleges Should Avoid Abrupt Terminations." *Chronicle of Higher Education*, October 27, 2006. http://www.chronicle.com/article/ Why-Colleges-Should-Avoid/46771.

Creswell, John W. *Qualitative Inquiry and Research Design: Choosing among Five Approaches*. London: Sage, 2013.

Cyphert, Frederick R., and David L. Boggs. "The Transition from Administrator to Professor: Expectations and Experiences." *Review of Higher Education* 9, no. 3 (1986): 325–333. https://doi.org/10.1353/rhe.1986.0026.

Denzin, Norman K., and Yvonna S. Lincoln. "Competing Paradigms in Qualitative Research." In *The Landscape of Qualitative Research*, 2nd ed., edited by Norman K. Denzin and Yvonna S. Lincoln, 105–117. Thousand Oaks, CA: Sage, 1998.

Dexter, Lewis A. *Elite and Specialised Interviewing*. Handbooks for Research in Political Behaviour. Evanston, IL: Northwestern University Press, 1970.

Dey, Ian. *Grounding Grounded Theory: Guidelines for Qualitative Inquiry*. Bingley, UK: Emerald, 2008.

Diaz, Jaclyn. "Former Michigan State Officials Were Cleared in Nassar Sexual Abuse Investigation." NPR, December 23, 2021. https://www.npr.org/2021/12/23/1067157520/former-michigan-state-officials-get-convictions-and-charges-tossed.

Dotlich, David L., James L. Noel, and Norman Walker. *Leadership Passages: The Personal and Professional Transitions That Make or Break a Leader*. San Francisco: Wiley, 2004.

Duderstadt, James J. *The View from the Helm: Leading the American University during an Era of Change*. Ann Arbor: University of Michigan Press, 2007.

Eagly, Alice H., and Linda L. Carli. "Women and the Labyrinth of Leadership." *Harvard Business Review*, September 2007. https://hbr.org/2007/09/women-and-the-labyrinth-of-leadership.

Ecclestone, Kathryn. "Lost and Found in Transition: Educational Implications of Concerns about 'Identity,' 'Agency' and 'Structure.'" Essay. In *Researching Transitions in Lifelong Learning*, edited by John Field, Jim Gallacher, and Robert Ingram, 9–27. Abingdon, UK: Routledge, 2009.

Ehrenberg, Ronald G. "Being a Quadruple Threat Keeps It Interesting." In *Faculty Career Paths: Multiple Routes to Academic Success and Satisfaction*, American Council on Education / Praeger Series on Higher Education, edited by Gretchen M. Bataille and Betsy E. Brown, 119–122. Westport, CT: Praeger, 2006.

Ehrenberg, Ronald G., John Jesse Cheslock, and Julia Epifantseva. "Paying Our Presidents: What Do Trustees Value?" *Review of Higher Education* 25, no. 1 (2001): 15–37. https://doi.org/10.1353/rhe.2001.0014.

Eisner, Elliot W. Foreword to *Theory and Concepts in Qualitative Research: Perspectives from the Field*, edited by David J. Flinders and Geoffrey E. Mills, vii–x. New York: Teachers College Press, 1993.

Ely, Margo, Margaret Anzul, Maryann Downing, and Ruth Vinz. *Writing Qualitative Research: Living by Words*. New York: Falmer, 1997.

Esterberg, Kristin G., and John Wooding. *Divided Conversations: Identities, Leadership, and Change in Public Higher Education*. Nashville, TN: Vanderbilt University Press, 2013.

Finkelstein, James, and Judith Wilde. "Does Your President Have a Platinum Parachute?" *Inside Higher Ed*, June 1, 2017. https://www.insidehighered.com/advice/2017/06/01/examination-college-presidents-platinum-parachutes-essay.

———. "Platinum Parachutes Revisited." *Inside Higher Ed*, July 29, 2019. https://

www.insidehighered.com/views/2019/07/29/failed-presidencies-shouldnt-be
-rewarded-platinum-parachutes-opinion.

Firmin, Michael W. "Transitioning from Administration to Faculty: Addictions to Break." *Journal of Practical Leadership* 3 (2008): 144–148.

Flaherty, Colleen. "The More Things Change." *Inside Higher Ed*, April 11, 2017. https://www.insidehighered.com/news/2017/04/11/aaup-faculty-salaries -slightly-budgets-are-balanced-backs-adjuncts-and-out-state.

Flawn, Peter Tyrell. *A Primer for University Presidents: Managing the Modern University*. Austin: University of Texas Press, 1990.

Foster, Brian L. "From Faculty to Administrator: Like Going to a New Planet." *New Directions for Higher Education* 2006, no. 134 (2006): 49–57. https://doi .org/10.1002/he.216.

Gagliardi, Jonathan S., Lorelle S. Espinosa, Jonathan M. Turk, and Morgan Taylor. *American College President Study 2017*. Washington, DC: American Council on Education, 2017.

Gay, Ross. *The Book of Delights*. Chapel Hill, NC: Algonquin Books of Chapel Hill, 2019.

Gervasi, Robert A. "Leadership Changes at Mount Union." Mount Union College memo, August 1, 2022. In author's possession.

Gillen, Brenda. "Q&A with Former Acting Co-Presidents Mike Edmonds & Robert G. Moore." *Colorado College Bulletin*, Summer 2021.

Ginsberg, Benjamin. *The Fall of the Faculty: The Rise of the All-Administrative University and Why It Matters*. Oxford: Oxford University Press, 2013.

Glaser, Barney G., and Anselm L. Strauss. *The Discovery of Grounded Theory: Strategies for Qualitative Research*. Oxon, UK: Routledge, 2017.

Glick, Milton D. "Becoming 'One of Them' or 'Moving to the Dark Side.'" *New Directions for Higher Education* 2006, no. 134 (2006): 87–96. https://doi.org/10 .1002/he.220.

Gonzales, Leslie D. "Faculty Sensemaking and Mission Creep: Interrogating Institutionalized Ways of Knowing and Doing Legitimacy." *Review of Higher Education* 36, no. 2 (2013): 179–209. https://doi.org/10.1353/rhe.2013.0000.

Goodman, Sylvia. "Why U. of Michigan and Cal State Are Changing Their Presidents' Contracts." *Chronicle of Higher Education*, July 15, 2022. https://www .chronicle.com/article/why-u-of-michigan-and-cal-state-are-changing-their -presidents-contracts?cid2=gen_login_refresh&cid=gen_sign_in.

Grant, Adam. "There's a Name for the Blah You're Feeling: It's Called Languishing." *New York Times*, April 19, 2021. https://www.nytimes.com/2021/04/19/ well/mind/covid-mental-health-languishing.html.

Griffith, Janice C. "Transition from Faculty to Administrator and Transition Back to the Faculty." *New Directions for Higher Education* 2006, no. 134 (2006): 67–77. https://doi.org/10.1002/he.218.

Hall, Douglas T. "Unplanned Executive Transitions and the Dance of the Subidentities." *Human Resource Management* 34, no. 1 (1995): 71–92. https://doi.org/10.1002/hrm.3930340106.

Hass, Marjorie. *A Leadership Guide for Women in Higher Education.* Baltimore: Johns Hopkins University Press, 2021.

Heffernan, Margaret. *Uncharted: How to Navigate the Future.* New York: Simon and Schuster, 2020.

Henk, William A., Shelley B. Wepner, and Heba S. Ali. "Factors Academic Deans Consider in Deciding Whether to Remain in Their Positions." ACAD, October 25, 2021. https://acad.org/resource/factors-academic-deans-consider-in-deciding-whether-to-remain-in-their-positions/.

Hertneky, Robbie P. "Composing Our Lives—as Women and as Leaders." *Advances in Developing Human Resources* 14, no. 2 (2012): 140–155. https://doi.org/10.1177/1523422311436303.

Hewlett, Sylvia Ann, and Carolyn Buck Luce. "Off-Ramps and On-Ramps: Keeping Talented Women on the Road to Success." *Harvard Business Review*, March 2005.

Hubbell, Larry. "Understanding Faculty and Administrator Conflict in the University." *International Journal of Education Research* 7, no. 1 (March 2012): 16–28.

Ibarra, Herminia. "The 3 Phases of Making a Major Life Change." *Harvard Business Review*, August 6, 2021. https://hbr.org/2021/08/the-3-phases-of-making-a-major-life-change.

Jago, Arthur G. "How Three Bad Decisions Signaled Doom at Mizzou." *Chronicle of Higher Education*, July 22, 2020. https://www.chronicle.com/article/how-three-bad-decisions-signaled-doom-at-mizzou/.

Jo, Victoria H. "Voluntary Turnover and Women Administrators in Higher Education." *Higher Education* 56, no. 5 (2008): 565–582. https://doi.org/10.1007/s10734-008-9111-y.

Johnson, Joe, Tom Hyatt, and Andy Brantley. "Paying the President: Best Practices in Executive Compensation." *Higher Education Workplace* 7, no. 1 (Spring 2015): 26–30. https://www.cupahr.org/hew/files/HEWorkplace-Vol7No1-Paying-the-President.pdf.

Jordan, Jennifer, and Michael Sorrell. "Why Reverse Mentoring Works and How to Do It Right." *Harvard Business Review*, October 3, 2019. https://hbr.org/2019/10/why-reverse-mentoring-works-and-how-to-do-it-right.

Josselson, Ruthellen. *Interviewing for Qualitative Inquiry: A Relational Approach.* New York: Guilford, 2013.

JP Morgan Chase Institute. "Past 65 and Still Working: Big Data Insights on Senior Citizens' Financial Lives." August 2016. https://www.jpmorganchase.com/institute/research/labor-markets/insight-past-65-and-still-working.

June, Audrey Williams. "Ex-Administrators Reveal the Secret That Eased Their Return to the Faculty." *Chronicle of Higher Education*, August 27, 2018. https://www.chronicle.com/article/ex-administrators-reveal-the-secret-that-eased-their-return-to-the-faculty/.

Justice, George. "After Administration: The Search for a Professional Niche." *Chronicle of Higher Education*, December 16, 2020. https://www.chronicle.com/article/after-administration-the-search-for-a-professional-niche.

———. "Back to the Classroom after 11 Years in Administration." *Chronicle of Higher Education*, September 11, 2018. https://www.chronicle.com/article/back-to-the-classroom-after-11-years-in-administration/.

———. "I Was a Dean, Now I'm Not." *Chronicle of Higher Education*, March 25, 2018. https://www.chronicle.com/article/i-was-a-dean-and-now-im-not/.

Kelderman, Eric. "Politics and the Pandemic Are Straining the Role of Campus Leadership." *Chronicle of Higher Education*, October 12, 2021. https://www.chronicle.com/article/politics-and-the-pandemic-are-straining-the-role-of-campus-leadership.

Kemper, Theodore D., and Randall Collins. "Dimensions of Microinteraction." *American Journal of Sociology* 96, no. 1 (1990): 32–68. https://doi.org/10.1086/229492.

Kets de Vries, Manfred F. R. "3 Tips for a Smooth Transition into Retirement." *Harvard Business Review*, September 30, 2020. https://hbr.org/2020/09/3-tips-for-a-smooth-transition-into-retirement.

Kezar, Adrianna. "Transformational Elite Interviews: Principles and Problems." *Qualitative Inquiry* 9, no. 3 (2003): 395–415. https://doi.org/10.1177/1077800403009003005.

Kezar, Adrianna, and Sean Gehrke. "Faculty Composition in Four-Year Institutions: The Role of Pressures, Values, and Organizational Processes in Academic Decision-Making." *Journal of Higher Education* 87, no. 3 (2016): 390–419. https://doi.org/10.1353/jhe.2016.0013.

Kiley, Kevin. "Illinois Law Will Restrict Universities Use of Search Firms." *Inside Higher Ed*, July 20, 2012. https://www.insidehighered.com/news/2012/07/20/illinois-law-will-restrict-universities-use-search-firms.

King, Jacqueline Elizabeth, and Gigi G. Gomez. *On the Pathway to the Presidency: Characteristics of Higher Education's Senior Leadership*. Washington, DC: American Council on Education, 2008.

Lakoff, George, and Mark Johnson. "Conceptual Metaphor in Everyday Language." *Journal of Philosophy* 77, no. 8 (1980): 453–486. https://doi.org/10.2307/2025464.

Leatherman, Courtney. "Returning to the Faculty Can Be an Ordeal for All." *Chronicle of Higher Education*, April 10, 1991. https://www.chronicle.com/article/returning-to-the-faculty-can-be-an-ordeal-for-all/.

Luna, Gaye, and Catherine Medina. "Coming Full Circle: Mid-career Women Leaving Administration and Returning to Faculty." *Advancing Women in Leadership Journal* 21 (2006). https://doi.org/10.21423/awlj-v21.a273.

MacTaggart, Terrence. "How Presidential Evaluations Must Change." *Trusteeship* 20, no. 1 (2012). https://agb.org/trusteeship-article/how-presidential-evaluations-must-change/.

Mallinger, Mark. "Faculty to Administration and Back Again." *Journal of Management Inquiry* 22, no. 1 (2012): 59–67. https://doi.org/10.1177/1056492612461950.

Martin, James, and James E. Samels. *Presidential Transition in Higher Education: Managing Leadership Change.* Baltimore: Johns Hopkins University Press, 2006.

McGee, Jon. *Breakpoint: The Changing Marketplace for Higher Education.* Baltimore: Johns Hopkins University Press, 2015.

McKenna, Laura. "Why Are Fewer College Presidents Academics?" *Atlantic*, December 3, 2015.

Merriam, Sharan B., and Elizabeth J. Tisdell. *Qualitative Research: A Guide to Design and Implementation.* San Francisco: Jossey-Bass, 2016.

Mertens, Donna M. *Research and Evaluation in Education and Psychology: Integrating Diversity with Quantitative, Qualitative, and Mixed Methods.* 3rd ed. Thousand Oaks, CA: Sage, 2009.

Mishra, Jyotsna. *Becoming President: Patterns of Professional Mobility of African American University Presidents.* Lanham, MD: University Press of America, 2007.

Monks, James. "Job Turnover among University Presidents in the United States of America." *Journal of Higher Education Policy and Management* 34, no. 2 (2012): 139–152. https://doi.org/10.1080/1360080x.2012.662739.

———. "Public versus Private University Presidents Pay Levels and Structure." *Economics of Education Review* 26, no. 3 (2007): 338–348. https://doi.org/10.1016/j.econedurev.2005.11.003.

Montgomery, Rachel L. "Unpacking the Perceived Benefits and Drawbacks of Administrative Co-Leadership." Paper presented at the Association of the Study of Higher Education (ASHE) annual meeting, Tampa, FL, November 10, 2017.

Moore, John W., and Joanne M. Burrows. *Presidential Succession and Transition: Beginning, Ending, and Beginning Again.* New York: American Association of State Colleges and Universities, 2001.

Moore, Kathryn M. *Leaders in Transition: A National Study of Higher Education Administrators.* Washington, DC: American Council on Education, 1982.

Morris, Tracy L., and Joseph S. Laipple. "How Prepared Are Academic Administrators? Leadership and Job Satisfaction within US Research Universities." *Journal of Higher Education Policy and Management* 37, no. 2 (2015): 241–251. https://doi.org/10.1080/1360080x.2015.1019125.

National Center for Education Statistics. "2016–17 Survey Materials: Glossary, 2016." 2016. https://surveys.nces.gov/ipeds/Downloads/Forms/IPEDSGlossary.pdf.

Nielsen, Larry A. *Provost: Experiences, Reflections, and Advice from a Former "Number Two" on Campus.* Sterling, VA: Stylus, 2019.

Northrup, Kate. "Want to Be More Productive? Try Doing Less." *Harvard Business Review*, June 29, 2020. https://hbr.org/2020/05/want-to-be-more-productive-try-doing-less.

O'Meara, KerryAnn, and Alan Bloomgarden. "The Pursuit of Prestige: The Experience of Institutional Striving from a Faculty Perspective." *Journal of the Professoriate* 4, no. 1 (2011): 41–73.

Padilla, Art, and Sujit Ghosh. "Turnover at the Top: The Revolving Door of the Academic Presidency." *Presidency* 3, no. 1 (2000): 30–37.

Palinkas, Lawrence A., Sarah M. Horwitz, Carla A. Green, Jennifer P. Wisdom, Naihua Duan, and Kimberly Hoagwood. "Purposeful Sampling for Qualitative Data Collection and Analysis in Mixed Method Implementation Research." *Administration and Policy in Mental Health and Mental Health Services Research* 42, no. 5 (2013): 533–544. https://doi.org/10.1007/s10488-013-0528-y.

Palm, Risa. "Perspectives from the Dark Side: The Career Transition from Faculty to Administrator." *New Directions for Higher Education* 2006, no. 134 (2006): 59–65. https://doi.org/10.1002/he.217.

Parsons, George D., and Richard T. Pascale. "Crisis at the Summit." *Harvard Business Review*, March 2007.

Pickus, Kevin H. "Teaching Lessons That a Professor Learned as an Administrator (Opinion)." *Inside Higher Ed*, December 16, 2021. https://www.insidehighered.com/advice/2021/12/16/teaching-lessons-professor-learned-administrator-opinion.

Ridgeway, Cecilia L. "Expectation States Theory and Emotion." In *Handbook of the Sociology of Emotions*, edited by Jan E. Stets and Jonathan H. Turner, 347–367. New York: Springer, 2006.

Ross, John. "COVID-19 Changes at the Top in Australia." *Inside Higher Ed*, March 19, 2021. https://www.insidehighered.com/news/2021/03/19/australian-universities-face-turnover-top.

Sabrowsky, Helen. "Presidential Search Costs to Exceed Those of Previous Years." *Minnesota Daily*, September 13, 2018. https://mndaily.com/190826/news/adcost/.

Sale, Paul. "Leaving the Dark Side for the Light: Twelve Strategies for Effective Transition from Academic Administrator to Faculty Member." *Administrative Issues Journal Education Practice and Research* 3, no. 2 (October 2013): article 8. https://doi.org/10.5929/2013.3.2.5.

Sanaghan, Patrick H., Larry Goldstein, and Kathleen D. Gaval. *Presidential Transitions: It's Not Just the Position, It's the Transition*. Lanham, MD: Rowman and Littlefield, 2009.

Santos, Laurie. "Coronavirus Bonus, Episode 5: Help Others to Help Yourself." *The Happiness Lab* (podcast), March 30, 2020. https://www.happinesslab.fm/coronavirus-bonus-episodes/episode-5-help-others-to-help-yourself.

———. "Season 3, Episode 6: The Kindness of Strangers." *The Happiness Lab* (podcast), September 19, 2021. https://www.happinesslab.fm/season-3/episode-6-the-kindness-of-strangers.

Schlossberg, Nancy K. "A Model for Analyzing Human Adaptation to Transition." *Counseling Psychologist* 9, no. 2 (1981): 2–18. https://doi.org/10.1177/001100008100900202.

Schuster, Jack H., Martin J. Finkelstein, Jesus Francisco Galaz-Fontes, and Mandy Liu. *The American Faculty: The Restructuring of Academic Work and Careers*. Baltimore: John Hopkins University Press, 2008.

Schwarzbach, Fred. "Back to the Faculty: Not as Easy as It Sounds." *Chronicle of Higher Education*, October 6, 2019. https://www.chronicle.com/article/back-to-the-faculty-not-as-easy-as-it-sounds/.

Scott, Robert A. *How University Boards Work: A Guide for Trustees, Officers, and Leaders in Higher Education*. Baltimore: Johns Hopkins University Press, 2018.

Selingo, Jeffrey J. *What President's Think: A 2013 Survey of Four-Year College Presidents*. Washington, DC: Chronicle of Higher Education, 2013.

Shapiro, Judith. "The Dear Departed: Reflections on Presidential Transitions." *Chronicle of Higher Education*, March 3, 2013. http://www.chronicle.com/article/The-Dear-Departed-Reflections/145027/.

Shriberg, Art. "From Deaning to Teaching: A Senior Administrator Returns to the Faculty." *Academe* 80, no. 4 (1994): 37–38. https://doi.org/10.2307/40250641.

Slaughter, Sheila, and Larry L. Leslie. *Academic Capitalism: Politics, Policies, and the Entrepreneurial University*. Baltimore: Johns Hopkins University Press, 1999.

Slaughter, Sheila, and Gary Rhoades. "State and Markets in Higher Education: Trends in Academic Capitalism." In *American Higher Education in the Twenty-First Century: Social, Political, and Economic Challenges*, edited by Michael N. Bastedo, Philip G. Altbach, and Patricia J. Gumport, 503–540. Baltimore: Johns Hopkins University Press, 2016.

Smith, Dennie L., Kayla B. Rollins, and Lana J. Smith. "Back to the Faculty: Transition from University Department Leadership." *Innovative Higher Education* 37, no. 1 (2011): 53–63. https://doi.org/10.1007/s10755-011-9186-8.

Svrluga, Susan. "Most of Her Presidential Salary and Lots of Perks. Michigan State Contract Suggests She Will Be Very Well Paid after Resigning amid Nassar Scandal." *Washington Post*, October 27, 2021. https://www.washingtonpost.com/news/grade-point/wp/2018/01/25/most-of-her-presidential-salary-and

-lots-of-perks-michigan-state-contract-suggests-she-will-be-very-well-paid
-after-resigning-amid-nassar-scandal/.

Swain, Mary Ann. "Reflections on Academic Administration." *New Directions for Higher Education* 2006, no. 134 (2006): 25–36. https://doi.org/10.1002/he.214.

Tunheim, Katherine A., and Gary N. McLean. "Lessons Learned from Former College Presidents of the Evangelical Lutheran Church in America: A Phenomenological Study." *Christian Higher Education* 13, no. 3 (2014): 199–210. https://doi.org/10.1080/15363759.2014.904654.

Wessel, Roger D., and Marybelle C. Keim. "Career Patterns of Private Four-Year College and University Presidents in the United States." *Journal of Higher Education* 65, no. 2 (1994): 211–225. https://doi.org/10.2307/2943925.

Wexler, Ellen. "Why Universities Hire Two Deans to Lead Their Law Schools." *Inside Higher Ed*, April 6, 2016. https://www.insidehighered.com/news/2016/04/06/why-universities-hire-two-deans-lead-their-law-schools.

Whitford, Emma. "Retirement Wave Hits Presidents amid Pandemic." *Inside Higher Ed*, October 1, 2020. https://www.insidehighered.com/news/2020/10/01/many-college-presidents-are-leaving-say-pandemic-isnt-driving-them-out.

Wilde, Judith, and James Finkelstein. "Tenure Is under Attack, So Why Do College Presidents Have Retreat Rights?" *Higher Ed Dive*, April 19, 2022. https://www.highereddive.com/news/tenure-is-under-attack-so-why-do-college-presidents-have-retreat-rights/622098/.

Wolverton, Mimi, Walter Gmelch, and Marvin L. Wolverton. "Finding a Better Person-Environment Fit in the Academic Deanship." *Innovative Higher Education* 24, no. 3 (1999): 203–226. https://doi.org/10.1023/b:ihie.0000047411.49250.c6.

Wooden, Ontario. "Privatization and Federal Funding for Higher Education." In *Privatization and Public Universities*, edited by Douglas M. Priest and John Edward St. John, 38–63. Bloomington: Indiana University Press, 2006.

Index

academic capitalism, 6, 165n20, 165n23, 172n2

adding value, 7–10, 14, 100, 102–17, 120, 140–41, 152

American College Presidency Study, 1–2, 22–23, 163n1

American Council on Education (ACE), 1–2, 5, 39, 129

Association of Governing Boards (AGB), 5, 39, 146

autonomy, negotiating, 7–10, 14, 100, 118–20, 124–25

boundaries, setting, xv, 65, 74, 110–11

burnout, 11, 74, 126, 133–37, 144–46; and languishing, 134–35; preventing, 137–41; and summit syndrome, 137

Charmaz, Kathy, 36–38, 39, 47–48. *See also* Constructivist grounded theory; research methodology

clothing and dressing differently, 9, 89–90, 93

constructivist grounded theory, 13, 36–38; and data collection and analysis 43–45. *See also* Research methodology

COVID-19 pandemic, xvi, 3, 19, 26, 69, 134, 139, 164n9, 168n38

executive contracts, 2, 5, 15, 35, 72, 102–3, 115, 124–25, 129–31, 137, 138, 143, 148, 151–52, 166n28

expectation states theory, 22–23

family, impact of stepping away on, 77, 87–89, 90–91

future, imagining parallel, 7–10, 13, 50–60

governing boards, guidance, 5, 14, 34–35, 117, 141–47, 152–53

groundwork to return to the faculty, 53, 66, 81–82, 139–40

"hanging back," 34, 96–97, 102–3, 111–13, 127

hiring presidents from outside of academia, 23, 101

identities, shifting, 61–62, 66–67, 104, 112–13, 125–26, 140, 173n4; and roles at home, 87–88

involuntary job change, 41, 48, 53, 54, 56, 60–61, 79, 120, 123

joys of returning to the faculty, 4, 32, 54, 76–77, 100, 102–3, 108, 120–22, 137, 140–41, 149–50, 154

leadership trajectories in academia, 2, 22–24, 49, 150, 167n17; and gender, 24, 30–31

mentoring others, 89, 103, 107–9, 110–11, 113, 124, 135, 141, 146–47. *See also* reverse mentoring

microprocess, 7, 9, 50, 70

onboarding a successor, 110, 116, 132

participant characteristics, 39–43
planning to manage a transition, inadequacy of, 29–30, 100, 120–21
post-tenure review, 121–22
preparing for leadership turnover, 29–30; and organizational preparation, 34–35, 128–29, 130–31, 136, 141–47
psychological demands of role change, 24, 30–31, 35, 82, 118–20, 124–25

reacquainting with faculty role, 7–10, 14, 92–97
reasons leaders leave their roles, 10–12, 26–28; burnout, 60–61; financial hardship, 27; interpersonal tensions 43, 51, 141; job satisfaction, 24–25; partisan divides, 25
reintegrating into an academic department, 65, 67, 71–72, 86, 92–93, 105, 108–9, 114–15, 120–22, 129, 131, 132–33
reinventing the self, 7–10, 14, 81–90, 99, 137, 172n3
research, resuming, 53, 58, 73–76, 85, 87, 100, 103, 106–7, 121–22
research methodology, 36–43; and anonymity, 43, 46; and data collection and analysis, 43, 46–48; and recruiting efforts, 38–39. See also constructivist grounded theory
restructuring leadership roles, 129–30, 137–41; and co-administrative models, 138–39, 173n12
retirement, 15–16, 29, 53–53, 124–26; and disincentives, 148–49
retreat rights for administrators, 15, 35, 143–44, 150–52

reverse mentoring, 95. See also mentoring others
role and status confusion, 7–10, 13–14, 47, 60–68; and gender and race, 63–64, 93–94

sabbatical, 35, 74–77, 108, 118, 120, 130, 138, 139–40
salaries: administrators, 2, 27, 143–44; faculty, 6, 174n20; former administrators, 35, 102–3, 147–54; in private and public institutions, 150–52
Schlossberg, Nancy, 17–19, 126
service, resuming, 71–72, 99, 102, 105–7, 115, 120
social interaction theory, 21
Stepping Away Model, 7–10, 13–14, 48–49
stigma associated with becoming an administrator, 3, 63, 82, 140, 154
succession planning, 34, 116, 136, 139–41, 146–47

teaching, resuming, 9, 25, 30, 51, 54, 59, 75, 77, 85, 94–96, 98, 105, 108–9, 112, 118, 120–22, 129
tenure of leaders, declining, 26, 144, 168n31
term limits for administrators, 140–41
terms for career transition, xvi, 4, 25–26, 47, 140, 153–54; and conceptual metaphors 25
time, experiencing and using differently, 7–10, 14, 47, 72–79, 98, 118, 120, 129–30
transition theory, 17–20, 126

work-life balance, 76–77, 106–7, 137–39, 145–46; and gender, 24, 31
workplace transitions, 19–20, 21–22

About the Author

LISA JASINSKI, PhD, is a scholar-practitioner of higher education who explores dimensions of academic leadership, pedagogical innovation, and strategic initiatives. For more than fifteen years, she has supported senior academic leaders, including three vice presidents for academic affairs at Trinity University in San Antonio, Texas, and one president at the University of Texas at San Antonio. She served as an American Council on Education Fellow in residence in the President's Office at the University of New Mexico and represented the United States as a Fulbright Specialist to Finland.

Available titles in the American Campus series:

Vicki L. Baker, Laura Gail Lunsford, and Meghan J. Pifer, *Developing Faculty in Liberal Arts Colleges: Aligning Individual Needs and Organizational Goals*

Derrick R. Brooms, Jelisa Clark, and Matthew Smith, *Empowering Men of Color on Campus: Building Student Community in Higher Education*

W. Carson Byrd, *Poison in the Ivy: Race Relations and the Reproduction of Inequality on Elite College Campuses*

Nolan L. Cabrera, *White Guys on Campus: Racism, White Immunity, and the Myth of "Post-Racial" Higher Education*

Adrianne Musu Davis, *Black and Smart: How Black High-Achieving Women Experience College*

Sherry L. Deckman, *Black Space: Negotiating Race, Diversity, and Belonging in the Ivory Tower*

Jillian M. Duquaine-Watson, *Mothering by Degrees: Single Mothers and the Pursuit of Postsecondary Education*

Scott Frickel, Mathieu Albert, and Barbara Prainsack, eds., *Investigating Interdisciplinary Collaboration: Theory and Practice across Disciplines*

Kirsten Hextrum, *Special Admission: How College Sports Recruitment Favors White Suburban Athletes*

Gordon Hutner and Feisal G. Mohamed, eds., *A New Deal for the Humanities: Liberal Arts and the Future of Public Higher Education*

Lisa Jasinski, *Stepping Away: Returning to the Faculty after Senior Academic Leadership*

Adrianna Kezar and Daniel Maxey, eds., *Envisioning the Faculty for the Twenty-First Century: Moving to a Mission-Oriented and Learner-Centered Model*

Ryan King-White, ed., *Sport and the Neoliberal University: Profit, Politics, and Pedagogy*

Yang Va Lor, *Unequal Choices: How Social Class Shapes Where High-Achieving Students Apply to College*

Dana M. Malone, *From Single to Serious: Relationships, Gender, and Sexuality on American Evangelical Campuses*

Z Nicolazzo, Alden Jones, and Sy Simms, *Digital Me: Trans Students Exploring Future Possible Selves Online*

Nathanael J. Okpych, *Climbing a Broken Ladder: Contributors of College Success for Youth in Foster Care*

A. Fiona Pearson, *Back in School: How Student Parents Are Transforming College and Family*

Barrett J. Taylor and Brendan Cantwell, *Unequal Higher Education: Wealth, Status, and Student Opportunity*

James M. Thomas, *Diversity Regimes: Why Talk Is Not Enough to Fix Racial Inequality at Universities*